Contemporary Philosophy of Social Science

Contemporary Philosophy

Each volume in this benchmark series provides a clear, comprehensive, and up-to-date introduction to the main philosophical topics of contemporary debate. Written by leading philosophers, the series volumes provide an ideal basis for university students and others who want an engaging and acccessible account of the subject. While acting as an introduction, each volume offers and defends a distinct position in its own right.

Brian Fay: *Contemporary Philosophy of Social Science*
A Multicultural Approach

Contemporary Philosophy of Social Science

A *Multicultural Approach*

Brian Fay

H
61
.F355
1996

The right of Brian Fay to be identified as author of this work has been asserted in accordance
with the Copyright, Designs and Patents Act 1988.

First published 1996

2 4 6 8 10 9 7 5 3 1

Blackwell Publishers Ltd
108 Cowley Road
Oxford OX4 1JF
UK

Blackwell Publishers Inc
238 Main Street
Cambridge, Massachusetts 02142,
USA

Library of Congress Cataloging-in-Publication Data

Fay, Brian.
Contemporary philosophy of social science: a multicultural
approach/Brian Fay.
p. cm.—(Contemporary philosophy; 1)
Includes bibliographical references and index.
ISBN 1–55786–537–X (cloth: alk. paper).—ISBN 1–55786–538–8 (pbk.: alk. paper)
1. Social sciences—Philosophy. 2. Multiculturalism. I. Title. II. Series: Contemporary
philosophy (Cambridge, Mass.); 1. H61F355 1996
300'.1—dc20
95–42638
CIP

British Library Cataloging in Publication Data

A CIP catalogue record for this book is available from the British Library.

Typeset in 10 on 12 pt Garamond 3
by Best-set Typesetter, Ltd., Hong Kong
Printed in Great Britain by Hartnolls Ltd, Bodmin, Cornwall

This book is printed on acid-free paper

To all my students in CSS 273

Contents

Contents

Acknowledgments

My thoughts about the material of this book have developed in large part through teaching the "Junior Colloquium" (CSS 273) in the College of Social Studies (CSS) at Wesleyan University for almost twenty years. Those in the fall, 1994 class read a version of some of the book's chapters and helped me to see their weaknesses; particular thanks go to them. But students in all the classes have challenged and educated me. Hence the dedication of the book to them.

Several colleagues and friends at Wesleyan – Don Moon (Government Department), Joe Rouse (Philosophy Department), Victor Gourevitch (Philosophy Department), Linc Keiser (Anthropology Department), Lydia Goehr (now at Columbia University's Philosophy Department), and Barry Gruenberg (late of Wesleyan's Sociology Department) – have enriched my understanding in near continuous dialogue over many years. I have been blessed to have such lively and intelligent intellectual and personal companions. Marc Perlman (once of Wesleyan's Department of Ethnomusicology, now of Brown University's) read the last chapter of the book and made many helpful suggestions; indeed, my thinking about multiculturalism has been deeply shaped by his ideas about it. Charlie Scruggs of the English Department at the University of Arizona has also instructed me by his incisive observations over many years and by his sense of the way intellectual issues grow out of and enlighten ordinary experience. Lastly, my fellow editors at *History and Theory* – Dick Vann, Dick Buel, Rick Elphick, Phil Pomper, and Ann-Louise Shapiro – have provided me with an education during our bi-weekly editorial meetings. My thanks to all of these comrades for what they have given me. Also, my apologies for any embarrassments my writing may cause them.

Special thanks to Joe Rouse who read the entire manuscript with his usual deep understanding, and who made numerous critical suggestions that have improved the book. Particularly important was his urging that I write what became section 10.4. This section reflects what he has taught me about objectivity.

Don Moon, as with everything I have written, also read the entire draft and made extensive insightful comments on it. My work is more of a collaboration with him than anything else, a collaboration for which I am profoundly grateful. In fact the book takes off from an essay jointly authored with him, "What Would An Adequate Philosophy of Social Science Look Like?" I am indebted to the editors of *Philosophy of Social Science* for permission to utilize material from this essay.

I also am grateful to the editors of the *Journal for the Theory of Social Behaviour* for allowing me to use material from two essays, "Practical Reasoning, Rationality, and the Explanation of Intentional Action," and "*Critical* Realism?"; and to the Regents of the State University of New York for giving me permission to rework material from my essay, "General Laws and Explaining Human Behavior," which appeared in *Changing Social Science*, edited by Daniel Sabia and Jerald Wallulis.

The comments of an anonymous reader provided by Blackwell helped me to sharpen and focus the book. To him or her I am most indebted.

Finally, Steve Smith at Blackwell encouraged me to undertake this project, gave it definition with his suggestion to organize the material around the topic of multiculturalism, and helped improve it with his criticisms and observations. But most especially he has been so supportive throughout that I cannot thank him enough. In short, he has been a marvelous editor.

Introduction: A Multicultural Approach to the Philosophy of Social Science

This book approaches the philosophy of social science in a new way, one centered on the experience of sharing a world in which people differ significantly from one another. This approach is best called "multicultural" because it is multiculturalism that draws attention to the opportunities and dangers of a world of differences. A multicultural philosophy of social science poses new questions and employs new concepts to address issues inherent in the study of human beings; it also puts older questions and concepts in the philosophy of social science in a new light.

Why the need for a new philosophy of social science? Throughout much of its history the basic question in the philosophy of social science has been: is social science scientific, or can it be? Social scientists have historically sought to claim the mantle of science and have modeled their studies on the natural sciences. Consequently the philosophy of social science has traditionally consisted in assessments of social science's success in this regard, of the ways social science is like and unlike natural science. However, although this approach has yielded important insights into the study of human beings, it no longer grips philosophers or practitioners of social science. Some new approach more in touch with current intellectual and cultural concerns is required.

The question of the scientific standing of social inquiry has run out of steam in part because for many natural science no longer induces the kind of reverence it once did. Implicit in much previous philosophizing about social inquiry was the presupposition that natural science is the benchmark against which all cognitive endeavors must be measured. But in the current intellectual climate natural science has lost this privileged position. The reasons for this are complex: they include the abuses of Big Science by governments and industry in such areas as nuclear weaponry; the dangers of technology inspired by the natural sciences, dangers which

1

portend ecological disasters; widespread awareness of alternative forms of knowing; and the somewhat uninspiring picture that the sciences paint of humans existing in a cold and indifferent universe. But philosophically the demise of science as the paradigm of intellectual activity is tied to the death of positivism and the concomitant emergence of perspectivism.

We will explore positivism and perspectivism in more detail in upcoming chapters, since one of the main purposes of the book is to examine and put to rest concerns raised by perspectivism. At this point suffice it to say that, in opposition to positivism which conceives science as the method *par excellence* for seeing Reality directly, perspectivism asserts that every epistemic endeavor – including science – takes place from a point of view defined by its own intellectual and political commitments and interests. According to perspectivism we cannot see "directly" into anything, least of all Reality. All seeing is seeing from a particular perspective. Even in the natural sciences the influence of theoretical and cultural points of view now seems unquestionable.

For many, perspectivism has only been a midpoint on the journey from positivism to relativism. Since every act of cognition necessarily occurs within a particular perspective, relativism claims that no rational basis exists for judging one perspective better than any other. For example, most modern Euro-Americans may rate western medicine superior to voodoo as a way of dealing with disease. But this is done not on the basis of some neutral criteria of assessment. Criteria used to assess beliefs and actions are themselves dependent on a larger perspective; thus in valorizing western medicine all that is being said is that it fits better than voodoo with Euro-American conceptions and presuppositions (which isn't surprising since it was itself framed in terms of them!). From another, less scientific perspective, voodoo may be preferable.

On a relativist view, science is just one of a number of possible perspectives, no worse but certainly no better than any other. True, science is the preferred approach in the "West" where it has gained hegemony and in the process silenced many alternatives. But this just shows that those in the West value the sorts of achievements made possible by science (in particular, the technical control of nature). But this doesn't prove that science is inherently superior as a way of knowing.

Relativism undermines the traditional pre-eminent standing of science by subverting its claims to specialness. It also topples faith in science in another way. Relativism engenders a keen appreciation for the role political power plays in shaping what we think and do – including the frameworks we inhabit. (Here the names of Gramsci (1971) and Foucault (1977 and 1981) figure prominently.) This is not accidental. Since changes from one framework to another cannot be rationally justified, they must be brought about and enforced by extra-rational means. Thus, a positivist might think that scientists are in power simply because their ideas are true (or appear to be so), or because they employ a method most likely to arrive at truth. However, since we know that assessments of truth-value must occur within a given perspective, the question becomes why one perspective rather than another predominates; and since perspectives cannot be shown true or better without invoking criteria of assessment themselves located within a perspective, causes other than satisfying some criteria of assessment must be at work. This is a reason why many recent studies of science concentrate on the extra-rational mechanisms by which scientific orthodoxy is enforced. Thus to relativists the "hegemony" of science (to use Gramsci's well-worn term) shows not its intellectual primacy but instead the power of certain groups to dominate intellectual and political institutions.

The upshot of this concentration on power is an inevitable debunking of science. In extreme relativism, little or no difference remains between science and propaganda; but even in moderate relativism basic epistemic commitments, including those of science, are necessarily non-rational. But this renders the endeavor to ascertain whether social inquiry is or can be like the natural sciences – an endeavor which presupposes that the natural sciences are the paragons of rational activity – pointless.

In this way relativism has radically undermined confidence that natural science can produce a truthful picture of the physical world, much less serve as the model for reliable knowledge of the human world. Indeed, relativism has called notions like truth and reliable knowledge into doubt. As a result, preoccupation with the issue of relativism has replaced concern with the scientific character of the human sciences.

To its adherents relativism is a Good Thing (at least from the modern Euro-American perspective!). In the first place it provides a way of speaking about others who are different from us and thereby sensitizes us to these differences. Since we all look at and live in the world from within our own particular framework, others must experience Reality differently from the way we do. In this way relativism is meant to guard against ethnocentrism (the view that everyone is just like us). In the second place, because we have no independent basis for criticizing the way others think or act, our attitude should be one of tolerance and appreciation rather than the judgmentalism that has so often marred human thought and practice. In this way relativism is meant to guard against chauvinism.

In this way relativism encourages multiculturalism. The term "multiculturalism" has become something of a trendy buzzword. This is unfortunate because multiculturalism refers to something crucial in the contemporary world: that people importantly different from one another are in contact with, and must deal with, each other. All multiculturalists focus on understanding and living with cultural and social difference; but beyond this rather anemic commitment the nature of multiculturalism is a hotly debated topic. The most prevalent version is what might be called "the celebration of difference"; on this view differences among various groups of people should be highlighted and honored.

Multiculturalism so conceived poses profound problems for the study of human beings. Let me explain how. According to the construal of multiculturalism which celebrates cultural and social difference, each society or culture is a single unit separated from other units by boundaries that define it in part by distinguishing it from others. Moreover, individuals are reflections of the cultural and social units to which they belong. Personal identity is determined by the cultural and social units into which its members have been enculturated and socialized.

Because they are different, these cultural and social units often conflict with one another; indeed, some of them will inevitably attempt to undermine or dominate the others. Strong units attempt to overwhelm weaker ones, and in the end seek to make the weaker units just like them. In so far as they succeed they thereby annihilate the differences between the groups. The natural impetus in a world of differences is thus toward the obliteration of these differences.

Multiculturalism construed as the celebration of difference is a response to this natural impetus. It insists on cultural and social integrity and on esteeming this integrity in others. It urges each group to find and nurture its own center and at the same time to recognize and support the efforts of those in different units to do likewise. Each of us lives within a framework we share with a limited number of others and which differs from the frameworks of others. On this view our job is to realize and celebrate this fact, to applaud the mosaic of colors and shapes which comprise human life on this planet.

But multiculturalism so conceived poses an epistemic problem: *if others live within their own framework and we live within ours, how can we understand them?* We think and act in terms of our own framework and they in theirs, so that we are forced to consider them in terms other than their own. In so far as their terms differ fundamentally from ours, it appears that we are thus bound to misunderstand them. A multicultural world which stresses ethnic, gender, racial, religious, class, and cultural differences – where people are keen to discover and protect their own particularities – leads to a fragmentation of social knowledge. Ultimately it appears to say that only those of one kind can know others of that kind. Only women can understand other women; only African-Americans can know African-Americans.

4

Put succinctly, multiculturalism appears to say that it takes one to know one.

But this means that social inquiry is severely compromised. For if only women can write about women or judge what is written about them (and the same is true for Catholics, the Azande, homosexuals, and . . .), the idea of an open community of scholars engaged in dialogue in terms of public evidence is utterly vitiated.

Both multiculturalism understood as the celebration of difference and the relativism behind it raise fundamental challenges to the quest to understand others. This is deeply disturbing not least for multiculturalism and relativism themselves. The power of these ideas depends on the ability to understand the ways people differ. But if their implications are that such understanding is impossible, then they seem to lead to their own demise. On reflection multiculturalism and relativism appear to be self-defeating.

Given the appeal of multiculturalism and relativism in contemporary intellectual and political life, and given the problems they raise regarding the possibility of understanding others, the basic question of philosophy of social science today ought not to be whether social inquiry is scientific; rather, it ought to be whether understanding others – particularly others who are different – is possible, and if so, what such understanding involves. This is precisely the central question of this book.

By framing the central question of the philosophy of social science in this way certain old topics in the field – such as the relation between reasons and causes; the nature of meaning; the character of interpretation and its relation to causal explanation; the role of social scientific laws; the possibility of objectivity – assume a new urgency. But more importantly, new questions and new ways to deal with them come to the fore. In particular, questions about what it means to know someone else (chapter 1); about "the" self and its relation to others (chapter 2); about the nature of human culture and society (chapter 3); about relativism itself (chapter 4); about rationality and intelligibility (chapter 5); about the complexities of cross-cultural understanding (chapters 6 and 7); and about the role of the past in understanding the present (chapters 8 and 9) move to center stage in investigations concerning social inquiry. These questions often are not found in treatises in the philosophy of social science, or are often relegated to peripheral roles. A prime contention of this book is that today they must be central to the discipline.

The organization of the book attempts to capture our situation of living in a multicultural world under the sway of relativism. Each chapter title poses a question which is intended to arise out of typical multicultural experiences and which raises an important philosophical problem. For example, chapter 1 asks, "Do you have to be one to know one?" This question emerges out of typical multicultural experiences of difference: if I and those of my group live and think in our own distinctive way, how can I or we ever "really know" those in other groups who live and think in their own distinctively different ways? Perhaps only those in my group can really know what it's like to be us; perhaps, then, one has to be one to know one? Another example is the question of chapter 3: "Does our culture or society make us what we are?" This question too arises out of simple reflection on multicultural experience: if I am different from others because I belong to different groups from theirs, then is my identity essentially a function of my group membership? I hope it will be clear that the questions which focus the discussions in all the other chapters of the book also derive from multicultural experience. These questions set the agenda for a multicultural philosophy of social science in the way questions regarding the scientific status of social science set the agenda for earlier philosophies of social science. At least in the first instance, it is the questions it asks which makes a philosophy of social science multicultural.

Having commenced with a question, each chapter then proceeds to present a doctrine (an "ism") which answers the chapter's question. Each doctrine is meant to capture contemporary multicultural intuitions. Thus, in chapter 1 the doctrine of solipsism—that only I (and perhaps others like me) can know me—is meant to express the sense that only people of similar experience and background can "really know" one another, a sense encouraged by the multicultural experience of difference. Or again, the doctrine of holism—that individuals are solely a function of their place in a social group or a broad system of meaning—is intended to voice the idea that I am who and what I am by virtue of the groups into which I have been socialized or enculturated, an idea reinforced by my appreciation of the ways I differ from others who are members of different groups. A multicultural philosophy of social science is distinctively multicultural because of the doctrines it considers.

(Please note that many of the "isms" which are examined have become common parlance in social science and the philosophy of social science. But being so has meant that they have many different meanings to many different people; sometimes what I mean by a doctrine is not the same as what some other writer means by it. Consequently I explicitly define the doctrines so that they have a particular meaning in this text; also I sometimes refer to other meanings which they might have, and to other books in which these other meanings can be found. In my definitions I have tried to distill what I take to be the central core of a doctrine, leaving its more sophisticated variations and subtle shadings for other works which have different purposes from those of this book. Sometimes this might lead proponents of a doctrine to say that it has been caricatured; but the risk of this charge is outweighed by the gain in clarity my method produces.)

Having begun with a question and a doctrine which answers this question both of which arise out of multicultural experience, each chapter than explores both what is wrong and what is right about its particular doctrine. In general, analysis shows that the "isms" aren't so much false as one-sided, that a fuller view needs to take into account both the "ism" and its criticisms, and that when this is done the presuppositions lying behind the chapter titles' questions are problematic. The upshot is to undermine these questions and the intuitions which support them.

In all of this the book argues that relativism in its strong forms, and multiculturalism understood as the celebration of difference, are mistaken though not entirely wrong. That is, something is centrally correct about both relativism and multiculturalism so understood but these doctrines as normally conceived are limited and one-sided; consequently they need to be re-thought. Part of the work of this book, therefore, is a re-definition of both relativism and multiculturalism.

Prevailing conceptions of relativism and multiculturalism emphasize difference, cultural integrity, and resistance to cultural domination; they think in rigidly dualistic categories of "self" vs. "other"; of "us" vs. "them"; of "sameness" vs. "difference"; of "assimilation" vs. "separatism"; and of "insider" vs. "outsider." The book subverts these conceptions and their attendant dualisms. In place of difference it emphasizes interchange; in place of integrity it emphasizes openness and interaction; in place of resistance it emphasizes learning. Throughout it replaces a dualistic mode of thought with a dialectical one. (Of course, how this is accomplished will be explained in the body of the text.) Besides entertaining certain questions and analyzing certain doctrines, then, a philosophy of social science is multicultural in that it underwrites a (dialectical) mode of thinking more apt for multicultural living than alternative ways of thinking.

In earlier intellectual and political climates a bright beacon by which social science ought to orient itself was clearly visible. Today, however, we live in a period which questions the very idea of science in particular and knowledge in general. Ours is a time of skepticism: skepticism about truth, objectivity, knowledge, and even the possibility of understanding those different from ourselves. Such skepticism is healthy; but taken to extremes it can degenerate into cynicism: that what passes for knowledge is merely the imposed views of the politically strong and the historically victorious ("History is simply the story told by the winners"). With this view social inquiry as a possible source of knowledge and wisdom vanishes.

Skepticism has consequences even more dangerous than the death of social inquiry. It leads to doubt about the possibility of rational analyses and solutions to pressing social problems. This doubt in turn encourages either social and political quietism, social withdrawal, self-absorption, and despair, or bellicose insistence on the worth of one's own perspective and culture. Not for nothing have critics of multiculturalism and relativism argued that these philosophical positions inevitably lead to "californization" (in which, to the world's cruelties, passive narcissists can only murmur, "Whatever"), or to "balkanization" (in which armed camps confront each other in mutual incomprehension and antagonism).

Underneath its technical analyses, this book is meant to provide a more adequate vision for a multicultural world. For though it hopes to do justice to relativism and multiculturalism understood as the celebration of difference, it also seeks to show how these views as normally conceived are self-defeating and debilitating. In their place it proposes a new conception of social science in the context of a new conception of multiculturalism—a conception it calls "interactionism" (chapter 11).

The issues raised by examining the nature of social inquiry from within the context of multiculturalism are thus profound, wide-ranging, and relevant to some of the most pressing problems of our time. The primary purpose of this book is to deepen and enliven the conversation about the nature of social inquiry. But beyond this its intention is to provide a view better suited to the exigencies of a multicultural world.

1

Do You Have To Be One To Know One?

1.1 Solipsism

We've all made or heard statements like the following: "You can't know what it was like because you weren't there"; "I had no idea what you were feeling until I had the same feeling myself"; "Only another woman can know what it's like for a woman to walk alone down a strange street at night"; and "I'll never *really* know what it was like to be a knight during the Crusades." These statements – and countless others like them – contain the germ of a thesis which many today think a truism and which many others trumpet as a great discovery that will liberate us from the narrow belief that everyone is just like us. This thesis consists of the claim that in order to understand another person or group one must be (or be like) this person or a member of this group. (Sometimes the thesis includes the term "truly", as in "in order to *truly* understand another one must be this other".) Thus, to (truly) understand women, one must be a woman; or to (truly) understand Catholics, one must be a Catholic oneself. I call this the thesis that "You have to be one to know one." (Its technical name is *insider epistemology*: to know other insiders one has to be an insider oneself.)

This thesis is an instance of a more general philosophical position called *solipsism* (literally "one-self-ism"). Solipsism is the theory that one can be aware of nothing but one's own experiences, states, and acts. If "one" is defined narrowly to mean a single individual person, then the thesis that "You have to be one to know one" becomes the claim that only you can know yourself. If "one" is conceived more broadly to mean those in a particular group, then the thesis "You have to be one to know one" transmutes into the assertion that only those of a certain group can understand members of this group.

9

We need to examine this solipsistic thesis in both its narrower and broader forms at the very outset because if it were true it would completely undermine the scientific study of human beings, making the term "social science" an oxymoron. The reason for this is twofold. First, science requires that all phenomena be in principle available for inspection and analysis to all investigators; but if only those who are alike can understand each other, then a barrier would exist for those investigators who are not like those being studied. Second, since you could understand only those who are like you, you couldn't even understand the findings of investigators who were unlike you. On both accounts there could be no genuine sharing of knowledge among people of different sorts. We all would be epistemically trapped in our own little homogeneous worlds, mysteries to each other – a condition fundamentally anathema to science.

If the thesis that "You have to be one to know one" were true it would radically affect everything else I want to discuss in the rest of this book; this is why I turn to it first. Besides, it raises extremely interesting questions of special relevance to our multicultural world, and so is an interesting place to commence in any case.

Begin by reflecting on what makes you distinctively you. For instance, what makes you fundamentally different from a door or a virus or a tomato plant? Your answer to this question might begin by noting that none of these things can think or feel or imagine; none of them is aware of its surroundings, or has attitudes toward them. In short, none of them has mental experience. What distinguishes you from them is that you have a mind and are conscious. Indeed, the capacity for consciousness is basic to who and what you are.

An odd thing about consciousness is that you are the only one who actually has your consciousness; only you experience what you feel or see what you see. You may tell others what you feel or see (or believe or desire), but you have to use words to describe your mental states, and how do you know that you mean the same thing as others when they use the same words? You may say that you see a red ball, but how do you know that others see the same thing as you when they say that they see red? There appears to be no way to tell because they cannot have your perceptual color experience nor you theirs. Moreover, they cannot observe your thoughts and feelings, nor you theirs. Mental phenomena are invisible; they take place "inside" where no one else can go. Philosophers have described all of this by saying that each person has privileged access to his or her own mental states and processes.

Both these observations – that your mental life is fundamental to who you are, and that you have privileged access to your own mental life – seem commonplace and uncontroversial. However, if consciousness is fundamental to what a person is, and if only that person has genuine access to this consciousness, then it seems to follow that only that person can know him or herself (assuming that to know someone one must know that person's states of consciousness – a plausible assumption given that states of consciousness are fundamental to the identity of persons). This is a rather startling conclusion, making as I have said any notion of a science of human beings completely impossible. So from rather innocuous premises a conclusion follows quite naturally to the effect that social science is a fraud.

Consider a less radical version of this doctrine, one more sociological than psychological. My experience has been deeply shaped by the fact that I am male, a (former) Catholic, American, and middle class. Because of these characteristics I look at the world in a certain way, and people treat me in a particular manner. My Catholic upbringing, for example, gave me a view of myself as fallen and as needing to be redeemed by something other than myself or the natural world; it made me think that certain desires and behaviors are bad, and led me to (try to) repress them; even my body was shaped by certain typical Catholic disciplines (kneeling, for instance). Even when in later life I reacted against this upbringing, I was still reacting against my particular Catholic heritage, and in this way this heritage continues to shape me; it will do so until I die.

It seems obviously true that I am in part who and what I am in strong measure because of the groups to which I belong (to which in many cases I had no choice but to belong). If I had been born and raised in New Guinea then I would be quite other than what I am: I would not only describe the world differently, I would experience it differently. I would be a different person who would be living in a different world from the one I now inhabit. Generalizing, everyone's identity is importantly a function of the social and cultural world in which they live.

This means that in a world of social and cultural diversity people are really quite different from one another. Indeed, where these social differences are profound, people must be radically different from one another. A female Pakistani Muslim living in the slums of Lahore has very little in common with an upper-class Protestant white male living in St. John's Wood in London. Their worlds are so different, and have shaped them in such different ways, that it seems clear that what is true about one may well not be true about the other.

If one marries this doctrine of the social identity of people with the doctrine that one has to have a certain experience in order to know this experience, the results for social science are devastating. If one's identity is a function of one's social group, and if only people of like identity can have a certain experience, and if one has to have an experience in order to know

11

it, then only people who are members of a specific class or group can know the experiences of the members of this class or group. Only African-Americans can really know what it is like to be an African-American, and so only African-Americans can tell what it is to be an African-American. Similarly for other groups: the working class can only be studied fruitfully by those who are themselves members of the working class; only English historians can write a good history of England; only women can describe and explain the actions, feelings, and relations of women. Every group must be its own social scientist.

The idea that every group must be its own social scientist has particular appeal in a world such as ours which is acutely aware of the differences among types of people along ethnic, religious, gender, national, and class lines. Scientific and historical accounts are often used to justify or criticize particular political and social arrangements, and are therefore often weapons in ideological struggles of those attempting to establish their own particular identity and to validate the worth of their own culture and society. Moreover, such accounts have often embodied slanted, prejudiced descriptions of particular groups or types of people; countless histories and anthropologies have run roughshod over those aspects of peoples' lives which make them distinct, ridiculing these aspects or ignoring them. Consequently, groups may want to have only their own members explaining who they are, believing that only their own kind can truly understand their experiences, feelings, and actions.

The doctrines I have been discussing – that only one who has a certain experience can know this experience, and that every group must be its own scientist – are versions of the thesis that "You have to be one to know one." This solipsistic thesis presently has great currency. In part this derives from the multicultural nature of contemporary social and political life in which differences among groups are stressed (indeed, strenuously insisted upon). But it also derives from certain beliefs about experience and knowledge which seem intuitively unproblematic. The question is, however, whether this thesis is true. I shall try to show in the rest of this chapter in what very limited ways it is and in what more important ways it is not.

1.2   Knowing and Sharing Experiences

For the moment let's assume that the thesis is true, that in fact you have to be one to know one. Then to what are we committed?

In order to understand this thesis, a more precise definition of "know" must be given. "Know" might mean "be able to identify" (as in "I know that they are members of Parliament"); alternately, "know" might mean

12

"be able to describe and explain" (as in "I know why Italian governments are so unstable"); or "know" might mean "to have the same experiences as" (as in "I know what it's like to give birth to a child, as I too am a mother"). The conception of "know" which most clearly fits the thesis that "You have to be one to know one" is obviously the third of these senses of "know": if I know another only when I have the same experiences as this other then it seems naturally to follow that in order to know another I must be identical with this other. Assume for the moment, therefore, that "know" means "to have the same experiences as" (later this definition of "know" will be called into question, especially as it pertains to the social sciences).

A little reflection will show that if "know" is parsed as "to have the same experiences as" then ultimately the most that you can know is yourself. Here's why. The nature of an experience is in part a function of the nature of the person having that experience. The experience of visiting Auschwitz, for instance, is likely to be quite different for a Jew from what it is for a gentile; indeed, it is likely to be different for a Jew whose parents died in this death camp from a Jew who had no relatives harmed in the Holocaust. Experiences are in part constituted by what might be called the interpretive assumptions a person brings to a particular situation; that is, they are shaped by the expectations, memories, beliefs, desires, and cultural prejudices which go to make them up. When a small woman walks down a darkened city street it is a different experience from that of a heavyweight male boxer who walks down the same street. It follows that, since your experiences will necessarily be different from my and everyone else's experiences, and since by stipulation we are assuming that "know" means "to have the same experiences as," therefore you cannot know anyone else but yourself.

Couldn't this conclusion be avoided by your becoming someone else and therefore having their experiences? In *Black Like Me* John Howard Griffin (1961) describes how he put on blackface and travelled as a black man through the American South in the late 1950s. Whites treated him as if he were black, insisting that he use the "colored" drinking fountains, ride in the back of the bus, and keep his eyes cast downward to show proper deference. Griffin did this because he thought that only by becoming black in the eyes of others and thus having the experiences of black people could he know what it was to be a black person in segregated America. Wasn't this a way of having the experiences of others and so a way of coming to know them?

Without in any way demeaning Griffin's efforts, the answer to this question is surely in the negative. For no matter how realistic Griffin appeared to be black he was not black and so could not have the experiences of blacks in the South. For one thing, Griffin knew that at any moment he

13

could simply wash his blackface off and resume being white. For another, his entire upbringing was in the white world and his sense of himself derived from it. At most Griffin knew himself to be a white person pretending to be black, a pretence he could abandon at any time. (Imagine him being stopped on an isolated road by a bunch of rednecks intent on "baiting the nigger." The truly black person is stuck with his blackness, but Griffin could – if things got rough – simply reveal his identity ("I'm just an actor practicing a role for a film . . ."). The knowledge of this ability fundamentally changes the experience of being racially harassed.) Pretending to be x, and knowing that one is pretending to be x, is utterly different from being x.

Assuming that you cannot literally become another, couldn't you be sufficiently *like* others to have the same experiences as they do? Maybe you are not a tennis player and so cannot experience directly what it is like to play at Wimbledon. But perhaps you are a boxer; couldn't you thereby have a sufficiently similar experience of competing face-to-face against another in a sports match to know indirectly what it is like to play at Wimbledon? But the problem is that you are more than just a boxer; you may also be a white male; a former Catholic; a Californian born of Irish and Alsatian parents one of whom was extremely violent; tall; middle class; graduate-schooled in the United Kingdom; and so on. All these factors will color what you see and feel, including your sense of athletic competition; your experience of Wimbledon may be quite different from mine or any one else's. Literally countless personal characteristics shape your experience; the more these are taken into account the smaller the pool of potential like-experiencers. Ultimately the pool will be so precisely refined that only one member will be left of the class of which you are: namely, you. Only you possess all the relevant details which make your experiences what they are, so ultimately only you can have your experiences. So if "know" means "have the same experiences as," then only you can know yourself.

But the situation is even more restrictive than this. You are what you are only at a particular time (call it t). The moment t passes you are different from what you were at t (in part because of your experiences at t). At a certain time in my life my wife and I had a child. This experience fundamentally transformed me: I was attached to this small creature and this small creature to me in a way that gave me a connection to future generations (and past generations) which I never had before. It also made me vulnerable in a way I found very upsetting: at any moment something I could not control could injure this creature I loved so much. These changes are permanent in me in that they will not disappear when my child grows up and becomes an independent adult: she will always be my offspring, and my sense of myself will always reflect this fact. Prior to her birth I experienced the world in a way deeply different from the way I experience it now. The same sorts of transformative experiences have undoubtedly happened in your life.

What you experience at time t you can only experience at that particular time and not at some later time (call it t + 1). Your experiences at t + 1 are quite different from those at t just because you are different at these two times. Thus, I experienced my relationships with my parents quite differently at the age of thirty from what I did at the age of ten. Indeed, at the age of thirty I simply could not have the experience of my parents which I had when I was ten (in part because I had the experiences I did at that age, and in part because of all the other experiences I had since then). As Thomas Wolfe said, "You can't go home again."

Could this difficulty be overcome simply by remembering what you experienced in the past and in this way re-experiencing it? No. How you remember an experience which occurred in the past is importantly affected by the experiences you have had since then. Remembering the past is a function of where you are in the present. Think of how you remembered your school days when you had just graduated and compare it with memories you have of them now. How you imagined them then and how you imagine them now undoubtedly are different because your sense of significance has been altered as a result of all you have experienced in the meantime. (Just the other day I read an entry in my journal recorded ten years ago which described a memory of an event in my childhood; I was struck by how much my current memory of the same event differs in crucial ways from the recorded one.) Memory involves interpretation, interpretation involves rendering the significant and meaningful, and such rendering is in part determined by your current understandings and interests. Thus, memory cannot be a way to gain direct access to past experiences. (We will pursue the notion of interpretation more fully in chapters 6, 7, and 9.)

But all this implies that if "know" means "to have the same experiences as" then, since you cannot have the experiences at t + 1 that you had at t, and you can't rely on your memory at t + 1 to duplicate what you experienced at t, at t + 1 you cannot know even yourself at t!

If the thesis that "You have to be one to know one" is true then the only one who can know you is you yourself, and all that you can know is yourself at this very moment. You cannot know yourself as you were in the past, even the immediate past. But this conclusion is very troubling: it is tantamount to saying that no one, not even you, can know you (given that you are an entity which extends beyond this present instant). The thesis that "You have to be one to know one" implodes: it presents itself as an

15

account of what it means to know someone but it ends with the conclusion that such knowledge is impossible. Something is wrong.

Perhaps we defined "know" too strictly. Instead of "to have the *same* experiences as," perhaps it should be defined as "to have the same *sorts* of experiences as." If defined in this way perhaps others (including yourself at a later time) who are sufficiently similar to you could know what it is like to be you and so could know you. This might occur if through empathy another sufficiently close to you could feel the same kind of feelings as you do, and so could grasp your experiences.

But what does "sufficiently close" mean here? A black female slave who loses her daughter to sickness may very well understand a similar loss experienced by a white slaveowner even though in virtually all other respects they are not close to one another. Here people who are very different from one another seem to be able to have experiences which are similar.

But doesn't this example show only that "one" needs to be defined in terms of having the same kind of experience (so that both the black slave and the white slaveowner are "one" in the sense that both have experienced the death of a child)? But at what level of generality is "kind of experience" to be specified? In important respects the death of the child of the two parents must be shaped by their different social situations and the different prospects of their respective children; but if these factors are to be ignored in order to focus on the similarities of their experiences, then there must be some basis on which to make this decision.

This basis cannot simply be: if objectively the two events are the same, then assume that the experiences are roughly the same. People experience the same events in different ways: an indifferent mother may not experience the death of an unwanted child in the same way a loving mother will. Moreover, quite similar experiences may occur even though they are provoked by objectively quite different circumstances. Perhaps the grief I experience when my child moves away from home to live far away is not unlike the grief you felt when your child died, even though objectively the situations are not the same (recall the remarks of the father in the story of the Prodigal Son who had run away but who returns: ". . . this brother of yours was dead and has come back to life" [Luke 11:32]). The issue is the similarity of experiences but no one-to-one correlation exists between objective circumstance and inner experience. So the basis for determining whether two experiences are sufficiently similar such that one person can understand another cannot be objective circumstance.

Perhaps one might respond: the *experiencers* must be like one another in the relevant respects. But what constitutes the relevant respects? It certainly cannot be having the same basic sort of experience, for this would be

16

utterly circular. This impasse is quite general: the whole point of the thesis that "You have to be one to know one" is that another cannot know what your experiences are unless he or she is like you in the relevant respects. So to define these respects on the basis of having similarity of experience is completely unhelpful.

This leaves us in the following position: people who are quite different from one another and who live in quite different situations may well have experiences sufficiently similar such that one can understand the other. The basis for deciding whether this is the case is not whether they are objectively from the same group or class, nor whether they are objectively in the same circumstances, but whether their experiences themselves strongly resemble each other. This can only be determined by a detailed description and examination of their experiences. But note: this kind of examination can go forward only on the assumption that people who are *unalike* can have similar experiences.

Such an assumption undermines at least one version of insider epistemology. By allowing that others objectively quite unlike you might still have experiences enough like yours to allow them to know what you are experiencing is to admit that others quite unlike you may understand at least part of you. In other words, others do *not* even have to be like you – let alone be you – to know you. But if to be one is defined as having a particular experience, and if knowing a particular experience consists in having it, then doesn't this support that version of insider epistemology which claims that to know someone you must have the same experiences as that person?

The answer to this question is yes, assuming that "know" is parsed as "to have the same sorts of experiences as." But is this the best way to construe "know"? Does knowing an experience consist simply in having it? To these questions we must now turn.

1.3 Knowing and Being

The thesis that "You have to be one to know one" posits a strong connection between being one and knowing one. In the first place, the thesis explicitly claims that being one is a *necessary* condition for knowing one: it says that only if you are one can you know one. Moreover, it suggests (although it does not imply) that being one is *sufficient* for knowing one: if to know one is to have the same experiences as one, and if to be one is precisely to have the experiences of one, then it seems that simply by being one you thereby know one. But as reflection will now show, being one is neither a sufficient nor a necessary condition for knowing one. This reflection will also introduce a different and more appropriate conception of the concept "know" than we have been employing up till now.

Start with the claim that being one is sufficient for knowing one. Consider the situation of being a member of the Catholic Church. Assume that you attend church every Sunday as you have since childhood; you do so because it seems "right" to do so. Assume that you positively respond to the music in the services, but that your mind wanders during sermons and biblical readings. Assume that the liturgy is still being said in Latin, so that most of it is utterly incomprehensible to you. Confession is of course in English, but perhaps you go only twice a year, and your sins aren't very interesting or troubling to you. Now, in what sense do you know what it means to be a Catholic?

In one sense you may *not* know what it means even though you practice being one: you may not know much about Catholicism, its history, its dogmas, the meaning of its practices, the values of its symbols. If asked to describe the Mass to a non-Catholic you may be halting, unsure of what follows what, rather unclear about the meaning of the Offertory or the Agnus Dei. You also may not know what other members of your church think or believe or feel about the church. You may not know what is characteristic or unique or essential to Catholicism.

But to this you might respond that there is one evident way in which you know what it means to be a Catholic: you experience being a Catholic while you are at Mass. But what does this experience actually mean? Indeed, what actually is the experience that you have? Attending Mass seems "right," but beyond that you may not be able to say very much: not be able to say in what sense it is right, or what "right" means in this context. You have certain fairly vague feelings, and you are aware that you have them, but you may not be able to identify, or describe, or explain these feelings. Perhaps they are connected to your childhood and your parents; perhaps they have only to do with habit; perhaps they indicate a spiritual longing about which you are ignorant or only dimly aware. *You have the feelings you do, but it does not follow that you thereby know what these feelings are.*

But isn't just having an experience *ipso facto* to know that experience? At first it may seem odd to answer this question in the negative, but further examination of certain characteristic experiences supports this answer. Consider the question, "What do I feel at this moment?" I often ask this of myself. I do so because though I am experiencing a certain feeling this isn't sufficient in itself for me thereby to know the nature of this feeling. The legitimacy of the question shows the gap between "have the experiences of" and "know the experiences of": though I'm feeling something, I don't therefore know what I'm feeling. I'm quite certain that you have found

18

yourself in exactly the same situation of not knowing what you feel or think.

This can be generalized by saying that the mind does not have an unmediated knowledge of itself. Every experience is like a sign whose meaning must be derived from seeing how it is connected to other experiences and the situations in which they are located. My daughter returned last week from a two-week trip to England; today she said to me, "I wish I were still in England." When I inquired further about her feelings it became clear that she did not know what they actually were: did she miss England itself? her cousins? the continual round of activity? visiting new places? being with young adults who made a fuss over her? some of the above? all of the above? She couldn't sort out the experience of . . . what? Knowledge of what we are experiencing always involves an interpretation of these experiences. In this self-knowledge is like other forms of knowledge: it is a discursive state in the sense that it involves being able to say something about its objects.

Consider the distinction between active and reactive responses. This is one of the most important distinctions in our lives. (Spinoza made this distinction a cornerstone of his *Ethics*.) You are active when what you do or say stems from your own inner needs and beliefs; you are reactive when you act or choose on the basis of how you think others want you to act or choose. In being active your actions are generated from within; in being reactive they are a response to something outside you. Activity is necessary for freedom and maturity: only when you are active are you self-determining and do you act as you are (instead of how others want you to be), are you an independent agent rather than a passive puppet. But even though this distinction is crucial it is extremely difficult to draw in the particular events which comprise our lives. You decide to take a new job; what is the character of this decision? Is it from your own inner sense that you need a change, that you want employment more challenging and rewarding? Or is it from your sense that others think you ought to be employed in a more "important" position? Is your move a matter of pleasing yourself or pleasing others? It is extremely difficult to say (as I am sure you will discover if you ask about the nature of some important decision in your own life). Perhaps the decision is an admixture, but even if it is not you cannot feel very confident in your assessment of your motives: to discover the nature of complex mental states requires subtle interpretation and a deep sense of the ways we often mislead ourselves to make ourselves look better. Our lives are littered with cases of having certain intentions, desires, and beliefs but being unable to know precisely what they are.

Being one thus is not a sufficient condition for knowing one. You can be a member of a certain group or be a certain type of person and not know

19

much if anything about this group or this type. More vividly, you can have your own experiences and not know what they are. You are yourself and yet this is not enough to insure that you will know yourself. This might be put somewhat dramatically by saying that just because you are you it does not follow that you know yourself.

If being one isn't sufficient for knowing one, is it necessary? Certain experiences – childbirth, orgasm, surfing a wave, and falling in love come to mind – suggest that it is. How can you know the experience of orgasm, for instance, without actually having had it? Descriptions, portrayals, poems, and discussions all fail to do the trick: they might tell you what orgasm is *like*, but only in a metaphorical and analogical way. Can a blind person who has never experienced sight know what it is to see? Imagine a sense other than the ones you currently possess, and pretend that an alien is trying to describe it to you; how could the alien succeed? Or try to describe the sounds of a bluejay to someone who has no sense of hearing. In all these cases it appears that to know experiences you must have actually had them.

Of course a great deal rides on how "know" is defined. If "know" simply means "to have the same experiences as", then obviously having the experience of x is necessary for knowing x: it's true by definition. In this case one could not "really know" what an orgasm is without having actually experienced one.

But what actually is the experience of having an orgasm – or seeing, or surfing, or falling in love? This question points to the inappropriateness of defining "know" as "to have the same experiences as." Knowing an experience requires more than simply having it; knowing implies being able to identify, describe, and explain. The classical Greeks thought spectatorship superior to participation in athletics precisely because athletes couldn't get sufficient distance from a competition to know its character. The truth of this Greek insight is revealed in the modern failure to draw a proper distinction between doing and knowing. We moderns assume that if someone is able to perform a task well he or she will know what is involved in this task and so will be well qualified to be a media commentator about it. We also assume that only if one is adept at an activity can one know this activity. Thus we assume that only great footballers can be television commentators on football games. Unfortunately, neither of these assumptions is true: many former footballers are terrible commentators because they haven't digested the experience of playing, haven't figured out what is essential or special about it, haven't reflected on its role or meaning, and in the end can't *say* much about it. Knowing football has to do with being able to speak about rather than being able to perform it. Put another way:

footballers may know *how* to play football but may not know *that* football is such and such an activity.

Of course sometimes knowing how can be an aid in knowing that, but not always. Moreover, sometimes *not* being one can facilitate knowing another. All of us have had the experience in which others – sometimes friends, sometimes enemies – know us better than we know ourselves. Often these others are not even like us; indeed, their differences from us often assist in helping them see what we are thinking or feeling. Consider de Tocqueville's *Democracy in America*. No other book gets to the heart of being an American more deeply; many Americans who read it experience a shock of recognition as it not only points out characteristic patterns of behavior, ways of relating, and modes of feeling, but also explains why these are as they are. Yet de Tocqueville was not only not an American but was an aristocratic Frenchman who thought of himself as quite different from Americans and who was out of sympathy with many of the characteristics he observed in them and thought essential to their identity as Americans.

In some instances great social science is like great art: it takes intensely inchoate experiences or relations and renders them clear by giving them a lucid form. Think of the *Protestant Ethic and the Spirit of Capitalism*. In it Weber uncovered and disentangled the nexus of feeling, belief, and action which served to motivate proto-capitalist behavior – a nexus which was opaque to those who experienced it. Weber was undoubtedly clearer about the inner lives of certain sixteenth-century Protestants than they were themselves. Arguably it was precisely because of his distance from the sixteenth century that Weber could accomplish this.

How can others, especially others quite different from us, know us better than we know ourselves? At least four reasons suggest themselves. First, we are often too enmeshed in the flow of our own activity and feeling to grasp what this flow is all about. Precisely because doing or being and knowing are different, and because knowing requires a certain distance from being or doing, being immersed in a certain way of living or acting may prevent one from knowing what one is.

Second, the activities and feelings which make up our lives are often confused and therefore confusing. About many things we feel ambivalent, both desiring or valuing them and, at the very same time, spurning and disvaluing them. Also, our motives are often mixed, indeed sometimes contradictory. We want to accomplish many goals with the same act but not all of them are compatible. Moreover, our feelings and desires are often muddled because complex, rich, and overlapping. Because of these endemic features of human experience we often cannot sort ourselves out. We

21

find it difficult to read ourselves. Others, not so caught up in these ambivalences, admixtures, and confusions can sometimes see through the complexities of our experiences in ways we cannot.

Third, often others can more readily grasp connections between our feelings and experiences on the one hand and external situations and prior events on the other. They can more easily detect causal patterns, influences, and effects because they have a wider view than we who often only see what is immediately in front of us.

Last, and most insidiously, is self-deception. Sometimes we hide ourselves from ourselves out of fear, guilt, or self-protection. In a way extremely difficult to disentangle we actually make ourselves opaque to ourselves, preventing ourselves from knowing what we are really feeling or doing. One doesn't have to be a Freudian to grasp the extensive role which self-deception plays in our lives. It is often others, including professionals trained in this area, who can help break us out of this tunnel of self-induced ignorance.

Given that others may know us when we do not know ourselves, it follows that being one isn't a necessary condition for knowing one. But if being one is neither a necessary nor, as I showed above, a sufficient condition of knowing one, then the deep assumption of the thesis "You have to be one to know one" is mistaken: no strict connection exists between being and knowing. This should not be too surprising once you think about it. Knowing a mental state or process (or anything else, for that matter) involves reflection about this state or process, a stepping back from it to grasp what it is. In much of our lives this second-order thinking goes hand in hand with first-order experiences. But not always: sometimes we have an experience but we are unclear as to its meaning. We may not even know what the experience is. At these times the difference between being and knowing makes itself evident.

Once the difference between being (or experiencing) and knowing reveals itself, the definition of "know" as "to have the same experiences as" appears deeply inadequate. This definition makes sense only if one presupposes that having an experience is at the same time to know this experience. But knowing involves some sort of reflective element which merely having an experience does not require. An adequate definition of "know" has to include this reflective element as one of its essential features.

Consider a simple mental event like perception. For instance, a friend drives my car past me on the road and I say, "There goes my car!" What constitutes my knowing that was my car? The obvious answer is that I saw it. But note that seeing is not just a case of having some pure visual stimulation; it involves a mental act of *recognition*. That is, a successful act of seeing my car requires more than certain light rays hitting my eyes; it

22

demands an act of identification in which an object is distinguished and is recognized as mine. (I may not have expected my car to pass by me this way, and so though I may have visually observed the car I may not have recognized it as mine. Alternatively, I may think that a particular car is mine when in fact it is not. In neither case can I justifiably say "I am seeing my car" precisely because the relevant judgment has not properly occurred.)

Suppose you are walking hand in hand with your lover. You have had a wonderful day together, and are presently bathed in the pleasurable sense of your lover's presence. You might very well say (perhaps to yourself) "I know I am loved." Is this a case of just having an experience, and this experience being sufficient for knowledge? The answer is no: the judgment that you are loved involves a great deal of interpretation on your part, of at least two types: first, you must interpret the glorious but vague feeling as one of being loved; second, this interpretation itself rests on another, that your lover does indeed love you. Once again, mental experience of the sort requisite to warrant the verb "know" involves a cognitive component consisting of an interpretive judgment.

This cognitive component is more evident in other cases of knowing. Consider the claim "I know Hitler." What could be meant by this? I could be claiming that I can recognize Hitler (here "know" would mean "be able to identify"). I could be saying that I can recite many facts about Hitler's life (here "know" would mean "be well informed about"). I could mean that I can identify the sort of person Hitler was (here "know" would mean "be able to classify and describe"). Or I could be asserting that I know what made Hitler tick, what motivated him or concerned him (here "know" would mean "be able to explain"). In all these cases (and there are surely more) claims to know someone involve being able to determine features of his or her mental and behavioral life and to grasp their significance.

With any of these senses of "know" it is obvious that you do *not* have to be one to know one. You don't have to be Hitler, or even to be like Hitler, to be able to identify, classify, describe, or explain Hitler, his actions, his relations, or his emotions. On the basis of his classic book *Hitler: A Study in Tyranny*, Alan Bullock could plausibly claim to know Hitler. Bullock reveals a remarkable range of facts about Hitler, both external (his early years and political intrigues) and internal (his strategic thinking and his desires). Bullock's book also offers credible explanations for why Hitler believed and acted as he did. In none of this would Bullock's claims to knowledge imply or rest on the assertion that he had himself had similar (sorts of) experiences as Hitler.

That knowledge does not require or consist in sharing similar experiences can be seen in the debates over the merits of Bullock's interpretations, debates which have raged ever since the publication of Bullock's book. Bullock interpreted Hitler as more or less in the mold of *realpolitik* – power-driven, cynical, scheming, opportunistic; others (notably H. R. Trevor-Roper (1951)) picture Hitler as a true believer – possessed, demonic, committed to a vision of history as to a religion. The point here is not which of these two (or other) approaches is correct, but of what correctness consists. The claim to know Hitler is *not* a claim to have experienced what Hitler experienced, but rather to be able to make sense of his experiences. The question is not who has more empathetically experienced the world like Hitler, but who can more adequately describe, identify, and explain Hitler's feelings, thoughts, actions, and relations.

Most telling is that the historians in this dispute have probably all known Hitler better than Hitler knew himself. Hitler was a person at the mercy of violent, undigested emotions that erupted over him like hot lava. He knew how to exploit these rages to his own advantage, but he never showed any sense that he understood these inner explosions, that he grasped what they were all about. Indeed, a lot of evidence suggests that Hitler wanted his inner life to be a mystery to himself, that he thought of this mystery as a source of power with which he did not want to tamper. As a consequence Hitler was willfully self-ignorant; he was filled with all sorts of exceedingly complex, grotesque emotions which he hid from himself, and about which he knew little.

Thus, even though Hitler obviously had all the experiences of Hitler, he did not thereby know himself, nor did his having his experiences in itself qualify him as possibly knowing himself. Being Hitler was insufficient for knowing Hitler. Moreover, it wasn't necessary either; indeed, it is probably a downright impediment for doing so. Hitler was systematically unclear to himself and this unclarity was a fundamental ingredient of his personality. Thus, being Hitler, far from being necessary in order to know him, would be an obstacle to knowing him. In this and similar cases *not* being one is required in order to know one.

1.4 Knowing and Meaning

When we want to know someone or some group, what is it we want? I hope it is clear that we do not necessarily want to *be* others, or to have identical or even similar experiences to them. Subjective psychological identification is neither a necessary nor a sufficient condition for knowledge of others. Indeed, in some cases this sort of identification can be a hindrance. Psychological experience is not what we are after, but rather an understanding of this experience. By "understanding" I mean a *sense* of it, a grasp of what it

24

means. *It is not feeling but meaning* which we must have to be said to know someone (even ourselves).

The thesis that "You must be one to know one" mistakenly equates understanding with empathy or psychological closeness or transcultural identification. But we understand others not when we become them (something we cannot do in any case), but only when we are able to translate what they are experiencing or doing into terms which *render them intelligible*. When Freud wished to understand the nightmares of the Rat Man, it was not necessary that Freud have these nightmares himself. Moreover, even if he had managed to have dreamt them through some sort of empathetic identification this would not have been sufficient: the Rat Man himself didn't understand his dreams even though he obviously had experienced them. Freud understood the Rat Man when he was able to interpret the meaning of the Rat Man's dreams, was able to grasp their symbolic content by fitting them into the context of the Rat Man's psychic and social economy.

To know someone else or even ourselves requires not the ability to psychologically unite with them or ourselves at an earlier time but the ability to *interpret the meaning* of the various states, relations, and processes which comprise their or our lives. We will take up what is involved in such interpretation in chapters 6 and 7 but even at this preliminary point it ought to be obvious that interpretation is not psychological identification but exegetical translation in which an entity's or event's meaning is uncovered and rendered comprehensible.

(In this book devoted to explicating the knowledge relevant to the social sciences we will focus on discursive forms of interpretation – those cases in which one is able *to say* in words what the meaning of a person's or group's experiences, relations, and activities is. But note other forms of knowing which are interpretive but not discursive. For instance, the knowledge a dancer possesses of a certain emotion, or the knowledge good portrait painters have of their subjects are also ways of knowing which involve interpreting meaning and translating it into intelligible forms (in this case into movement or lines on a paper) even though these forms are not linguistic.)

The interpretation of meaning is rather like the process of trying to decipher a difficult poem rather than trying to achieve some sort of inner mental union with its author (which may or may not help in such deciphering). To know T. S. Eliot's *Four Quartets* does not require that we become T. S. Eliot (if only imaginatively) – an expatriate American, a poet, a white male, an Anglican, someone who actually believed that "Love is the unfamiliar Name/ Behind the hands that wove/ The intolerable shirt of flame/ Which human power cannot remove." Indeed, even if we could do this it would not guarantee understanding this poem, anymore than it guaranteed that Eliot himself understood his own poem. Poets themselves can be mystified about what they have written, and can be enlightened by others who see meanings closed to the authors themselves. (Of course, sometimes poets are able to interpret their poems very insightfully, just as sometimes agents themselves know best what they are doing. Being an insider or an outsider is not the key element here, but whether one has the requisite openness, sensitivity, and acuity to grasp the significance of activities, experiences, and their expression in literary or other texts.)

In interpreting the meaning of experiences, actions, or their products must interpreters be like those being interpreted? Not if likeness is construed in any very definite way. Hitler's biographers needn't be Hitlerian to write illuminating biographies of him; anthropologists who study the Ilongot needn't be headhunters themselves; nor must studies of women in politics be confined to female political scientists. The ability to make sense of others' behavior and its results sometimes is enhanced by similarity between interpreter and interpreted, but sometimes it is not.

This does not mean that interpreters and interpreted can be radically alien to each other. As we shall see in chapter 5, the interpretation of meaning does require a likeness understood in a very general and abstract way between interpreters and interpreted. To grasp the meaning of an action interpreters must assume that its agent is like the interpreter in being able to have experiences, to think rationally, to feel, to intend, and so forth. Put succinctly, both interpreters and interpreted must be persons. (Wittgenstein wrote: "If a lion could talk we couldn't understand him" (1968, p. 223). By this he meant that differences between our form of life and that of lions is so great that we could make no sense of lions' utterances – indeed, we would be unable even to claim that the noises they emitted were in fact utterances as opposed to mere expressions of biological urgency.)

That interpreters and interpreted must both be persons – and in this sense must both be "one" – is an innocuous point because the "one" here is so abstractly characterized. All those which insider epistemologists wish to separate – men and women, blacks and whites, colonizers and colonized, religious and nonreligious – are all "one" in the general sense of being persons characterized by certain basic capacities. That for you to understand others requires that both you and them be persons, and in this – but only this – sense be "one," is no comfort for insider epistemology.

Insider epistemology claims that knowing others is equivalent to having their experiences, and assumes on this basis that only those alike in all relevant respects can know one another. But once it is clear that knowing others is being able to interpret the meaning of their acts, then psychological identification becomes otiose. Moreover, the only kind of similarity required for the interpretation of meaning is the harmless one that interpreters and interpreted share certain basic capacities and dispositions common to persons as such. Interpreters may be quite unlike those interpreted in all manner of important respects and still be able to grasp the sense of what they do.

1.5   Summing Up

Do you have to be one to know one? If "know" is defined as "having the same experiences as," and the deep differences in people's experiences are insisted upon, then an affirmative answer to this question is initially quite plausible. Only people very like me appear capable of having my characteristic experiences, and so only people like me can understand me. The same is true for you. Thus the doctrine of insider epistemology: you have to be one to know one.

But consider the case of the middle-class journalist reporting on the life of poor southern sharecroppers. Or that of a respectable, sane professor depicting the lives of mental patients institutionalized in asylums. Or a middle-aged anthropologist revealing the joys and pains of old age. Or that of a twentieth-century Frenchman detailing the experience of children in the Middle Ages. In these cases the subjective experience of those being portrayed is so deeply different from those picturing them that trying to capture it seems a Holy Grail doomed forever to be elusive.

And yet James Agee did write *Let Us Now Praise Famous Men* in which he disclosed the texture of the lives of poor southern sharecroppers in the 1930s with a sensitivity and power that cannot be denied. Erving Goffman did the same for institutionalized mental patients in *Asylums*, as did Barbara Meyerhoff for old people attending a day-care center in *Number Our Days*, and Phillippe Ariès for medieval childhood in *Centuries of Childhood*. These are all classic works in which the lived experience of others is revealed in its density and complexity, in its ambiguity and ambivalence, in its emotionality as well as its rationality. How could such books have been written if "You have to be one to know one"?

The answer to this lies in distinguishing knowing from being. I may *be* myself but this doesn't mean that I therefore *know* myself. Knowing an experience doesn't just mean having it: it means being able to say what it is (in some broad sense which includes both discursive and non-discursive expressions). *Knowledge consists not in the experience itself but in grasping the sense of this experience.* For this reason knowledge is not psychic identification but interpretive understanding: knowing ourselves and others is an instance of

27

decoding, clarifying, and explicating rather than an instance of psychic union.

Precisely because knowing is grasping meaning rather than merely experiencing, being one is neither necessary nor sufficient for knowing one. Not sufficient because you can be one and still not know what the life of one is all about; not necessary because you can sometimes grasp the meaning of an experience even if you haven't had it yourself and even if you are quite different from those having it. Indeed, sometimes it is easier for those not "one" to grasp this meaning because they have the requisite distance from the experience to appreciate its significance.

Still, though you needn't actually be one to know one, you surely must be sensitive to them to know what their lives are all about. People are experiencing beings whose activities and relations are deeply affected by their thoughts and feelings. Social scientists simply cannot understand the actions and relations of people unless they can appreciate the nature of these mental events and states, and they cannot do this unless they are sensitive to their lived character. Often by interacting with others or having experiences broadly similar to theirs this sensitivity can be heightened. Historians immerse themselves in their historical sources, anthropologists do extensive field work, psychologists listen to their patients by the hour as ways of gaining insight into the experience of their subjects.

Sensitivity heightened by shared experience is often an important step in understanding the lives of others: this is the truth contained in the thesis that "You have to be one to know one." But genuine understanding goes beyond sensitivity. To know others – indeed to know oneself – is to be able to make sense of their experience. For this one needs, in addition to sensitivity, the ability to decipher the meaning of their experiences. For this you needn't be them or be very much like them (except in the innocuous sense of being able to have experiences and to think and feel in ways persons do).

Further Reading

The philosopher who stands behind my arguments in this chapter is Wittgenstein (1968 and 1980). The commentary by Pitkin (1972) offers an interesting elaboration of Wittgenstein's thought in this regard. Ricoeur (1992) also provides a deep but difficult meditation on the questions of this chapter.

For "insider epistemology" as central to current debates and thinking in history, see Novick

(1988), chapter 14. Novick also offers an excellent discussion of the philosophical background for insider epistemology in chapters 15 and 16 of this work.

Insider epistemology is buttressed by the doctrine of *verstehen* , which holds that knowledge in the social sciences either consists in or depends upon empathic understanding. For classic statements of this doctrine see Dilthey (in Rickman (ed.), 1976, part III) and Weber (1949 (1905)). See also Collingwood (1946, section 5.4). For a discussion of Dilthey's views, see Hodges (1969). For Weber's rather complex ideas about *verstehen*, see Runciman (1972). A good collection of classical and contemporary essays is Truzzi (1974). An excellent overall discussion of *verstehen* can be found in Outhwaite (1975).

For a discussion of understanding others with special reference to questions of ethnocentrism, see Taylor (1981), Geertz (1983), and Hoy (1991). The literature about the rationality of the practices of foreigners is also relevant in this regard; see the classic collections of essays in Wilson (1979) and Hollis and Lukes (1986), and the survey by Ulin (1984). Rosaldo (1989) discusses understanding the Ilongot headhunters in the context of multiculturalism, postmodernism, and anthropology. For a good collection of essays on the topic of understanding other persons, see Mischel (1974).

For a discussion of self-knowledge and its difference from mere experience, see Shoemaker (1963) and the essays by Gergen, Hamyln, Toulman, and Harré in Mischel (1977). The position developed in this chapter is directed against the Cartesian idea of clear and distinct ideas in which the meaning of (some of) our mental states is immediately apparent. Ruth Garrett Millikan calls this "meaning rationalism"; she discusses this and criticizes it in Millikan (1984). This topic is related in interesting ways to the internalism and externalism debate in the philosophy of mind ("are meanings in the head?"); on this see Putnam (1975), Burge (1979 and 1986), and Kripke (1971). Dennett (1991) offers an ingenious account of self-monitoring and self-representation which does not entail meaning rationalism.

For self-deception, see the classic by Fingarette (1969).

2

Do We Need Others To Be Ourselves?

2.1   Atomism

One of the sources of the thesis that "You have to be one to know one" is the belief that you are indeed "one." Each of us appears to be fundamentally both different and separate from others, a self-contained sphere which has its own identity and integrity. From this notion it is not a big jump to the idea that only by being inside this sphere can one understand life within it.

The thesis that the basic units of social life are self-contained, essentially independent, separated entities I shall call *atomism*. According to atomism each of us experiences our own unique states of consciousness to which we have privileged access. Consequently, a wall of privacy ultimately divides each of us from one another. Moreover, each of us is a unique person who contains within ourselves the power to direct our actions on the basis of our beliefs and desires. Thus each human being is a self distinct from other selves. No matter how empathetic I am, only you have your pains; no matter how much I worry about you or advise you or accompany you, only you can live your life. Ultimately even though you and I may interact or communicate with one another, I am me and you are you (or, in the immortal words of Popeye, "I yam what I yam and that's all that I yam"). This commonplace is the kernel of atomism.

From this kernel atomism has developed into an important program in the social sciences. Atomists, insisting on the idea that individuals are self-directing agents, focus on the properties and activities of individuals (including their desires, motives, and choices) to explain human behavior. As Karl Popper put it:

All social phenomena, and especially the functioning of all social institutions, should always be understood as resulting from the decisions, actions, attitudes, etc. of human individuals . . . we should never be satisfied with an explanation in terms of so-called "collectives". . . (Popper, 1948, ii, p. 98)

For atomists society is ultimately the composite of the individuals who constitute it. For this reason they believe social wholes are reducible to, and explainable in terms of, the activity of the individuals who comprise them. As Frederich von Hayek put it:

There is no other way toward an understanding of social phenomena but through our understanding of individual actions directed toward other people and guided by their expected behavior. (von Hayek, 1949, p. 6)

Certain approaches in the social sciences – among them rational choice theories in sociology and political science, and neo-classical approaches in economics – embody this kind of what has been called *methodological individualism* ("methodological" individualism because it proposes a method for social explanation, namely, it accounts for social phenomena ultimately in terms of individual acts and choices). When methodological individualists employ terms which refer to social wholes they do so with the understanding that such wholes are themselves reducible to the activities and states of individuals.

Beneath these methodological claims about the nature of social scientific explanation lies a deeper commitment to the fundamental singularity of individuals. Put briefly, individuals are thought ultimately to be what they are independently of their relations to others. This is the claim of *ontological atomism*. In the words of Hobbes, the father of atomism:

The causes of the social compound reside in men as if but even now sprung out of the earth and suddenly, like mushrooms, come to full maturity, without all kinds of engagement with each other. (Hobbes, 1839, ii, p. 109)

According to ontological atomism basic human needs, capacities, and motivations arise in each individual without regard to any specific feature of social groups or social interactions. Though of course we all interact with others, each of us is claimed to be fundamentally what we are independently of these interactions. Thus, for example, Hobbes thought that all human behavior derived from the operation of a basic set of appetites and aversions which each possessed regardless of his or her social setting, and he thought that the abilities peculiar to us as human beings – the ability to speak, for instance – did not require interaction with others. Or, to cite another version of ontological atomism, Freud claimed that libido is an instinctual force in each individual which is utterly undifferentiated, only later to be channeled into particular social outlets. The fundamental psychic impulses accrue to each individual as an individual, and social relations are to be explained in terms of them and not vice versa. Thus the various phases of childhood development are programmed into children by virtue of their inherent psychic dispositions (though of course the particular forms these phases assume will depend on each child's particular social setting).

Atomism as an approach is reinforced by a general ideology and by particular social conditions in the modern world. The liberal ideology of the Enlightenment held out the ideal of a society of free and equal individuals. According to this ideal we are each what we are as individuals, not as members of this or that group; consequently liberalism argues that our laws and other institutions should be arranged on the basis of the rights and responsibilities of individuals as individuals. Enlightenment liberalism both helped to cause, and in turn is sustained by, the social experiences of those living in modern societies marked by great social mobility, capitalist markets, democratic political practices, individual rights, and value pluralism. All these contribute to the idea that the fundamental unit of social life is the individual and that the individual is a separate and particular entity.

Liberal ideology and the social experiences characteristic of modern societies support the idea that individuals are radically distinct from others who are only externally related to them. If we use the terms "self" and "other" to denominate the individual on the one hand, and those distinct from the individual on the other, we can portray the atomist account of the relation between self and other in the way set out in figure 2.1.

Figure 2.1

On this view, selves are ultimately radically distinct and separate from others.

2.2 "The" Self

Atomism asserts that each of us is a separate individual constituted by our own unique states of consciousness to which we have privileged access and by capacities and needs which we possess independently of others. It pictures the self as a monad, a hard integral entity radically different, and

32

ultimately cut off, from others. But are we all essentially locked within our own selves? Is there a fundamental chasm between me and you, between self and other?

In order to answer this question we need first to examine the notion of "self," only then turning directly to the relation of self and other. When most of us think of our self we picture it as a subject of consciousness ("my self is that which has my experiences such as my perceptions and my desires"), as that which persists through time ("I am today the same person who lived on Serrania Street forty years ago"), and as the source of our activity ("That didn't just happen; I did it"). Understood in this way the self seems to be a single, coherent, persistent entity which as the perduring subject of our consciousness and behavior is the core of our being. The self seems rather like a psychological atom.

However, certain features of our experience call this atomist picture into question. Consider ironic humor directed against yourself. Humor often involves pointing out that which is absurd or ludicrous in some situation. Irony involves a contradiction between the way things seem and the way they are; it plays off the discrepancy between appearance and reality. Ironic humor thus consists in showing something in an outlandish light so that what it appears to be is revealed to be at odds with what it is. (An example: in the midst of some particularly inefficient committee meeting at the University of Southern California a participant might say: "How many Southern Californians does it take to change a light bulb? Five. One to replace the bulb and four to share the experience.")

Ironic humor is an instance of the more general phenomenon of self-distance in which you critically reflect on yourself and your relations from the perspective of someone other than yourself. Some societies encourage this self-distance more than others. Pluralist liberal societies encourage critical self-reflection in which taken-for-granted ideas and ways of living are subject to scrutiny; they even institutionalize such scrutiny in newspapers, universities, theaters, and so on. Other societies (often more isolated, more authoritarian, more hierarchical, and more settled) do not promote such scrutiny — indeed, sometimes positively discourage it. But even in them critical reflection goes on: every society must rationalize its ways of doing things and must amend them to meet new situations; such rationalization and amendment create a space for critique and reassessment. Even in the most totalitarian societies *samizdat* is to be found, and some of the most mordant ironic humor ever conceived was produced in the Soviet Union.

Ironic humor requires a certain critical distance from the object of its humor. This means that when you are the object of such humor as well as its subject you must have a certain detachment from yourself. Unless you

33

are in some sense an "other" to yourself, ironic humor directed toward yourself is not possible. But how can you be an other to yourself unless there is some sense in which your self is not identical with you?

To answer this question, consider the ways this separateness from yourself manifests itself. Sometimes it does so when you realize that your particular arrangements, relations, or dispositions are a function of particular circumstances and not the result of the way things have to be. What seemed natural or obvious or general you now experience as conventional or peculiar or local. (People don't *have* to drive on the right side of the road, no matter how ordained by nature it feels. Reflect on the American who rents a car in Britain and who insists on driving on the right side because "the British drive on the wrong side of the road.") This realization may lead to another: because many of the things which you take to be essential suddenly are revealed as contingent on particular circumstances you may come to see that they might be different. Many of the things we take for granted do not have to be the way they are for us to be what we are. We might very well drive on the left or get divorced or vote conservative or move to Australia and still be who we are.

The recognition of this can have a liberating effect. It opens up the possibility that one could be different from what one is. What seemed unchangeable, given, or essential now appears as alterable. A degree of possibility is interjected into what was thought to be entirely actual. You don't *have* to be married; you don't *have* to stay in your present job; you don't *have* to vote for the candidate supported by your family – these and similar thoughts express the sense that you could be different from what you currently are. What was given suddenly becomes a potential candidate for choice. (Of course, this does not always happen. Sometimes realizing the contingency of things causes one to feel frozen in terror because one suddenly feels no firm ground on which to stand.)

A characteristic feature of selves is that they contain within themselves an element of potentiality. Selves are not objects which simply are what they actually are in the ways trees or ants are; selves are selves in part because they have the capacity to become other than what they are. They can stand outside themselves, assess what they see, and within limits choose to accept or alter or abandon what they perceive. But this means that in an important sense a self can be other to itself.

How can this be? How is it possible that something part of itself can be other to itself? The answer is that selfhood involves self-consciousness. Self-consciousness is one of the keys which makes you a different sort of entity from a lamp or a protein. To be self-conscious is to be aware of oneself as an entity capable of being other than it is. To grasp what this means

34

consider a creature which is both intelligent and curious but which lacks self-consciousness.

Picture an imaginary bird which believes that objects which are shaped like humans *are* humans, and so avoids a field in which a humanoid scarecrow is placed. Further, assume our fictitious bird also believes that humans can hurt it only when they are in close proximity so that it feels no compunction about flying within ten feet of them. Now suppose two events occur: first, a human fifty feet away throws a rock and clips our bird's wing, an event the bird perceives from start to finish; second, our bird notices that the scarecrow never alters its position. If our bird is intelligent then it will alter its beliefs on the basis of the information it gleans from these events: it will come to realize that the power of humans is not confined to close proximity, and that not all objects shaped like humans are in fact humans. Our bird is intelligent because intelligence is the disposition to alter one's beliefs and subsequent behavior on the basis of new information.

But our bird may still be passive toward its situation, waiting for it to reveal new information. A curious creature overcomes this sort of passivity. Our bird would be curious as well as intelligent if it were to eat a variety of seeds in the garden to ascertain whether any besides its usual fare were edible. Curiosity is the disposition to seek out information about one's environment in order to achieve a broader and better supported account of one's world.

But even though our bird is both intelligent and curious it needn't be aware that it is itself a being in the world, nor know or have an opinion of what sort of creature it is. It need not experience itself as an entity which perdures through time, nor grasp that it is the source of its own bodily movements, nor be able to characterize itself in any way. In other words, it need not have *second-order* beliefs and perceptions, that is, beliefs and perceptions about its other beliefs and perceptions of the world and the capacities these involve. Call forming second-order beliefs "reflection," and the disposition to be aware of and to assess one's own perceptions, desires, and beliefs "reflectiveness." A self-conscious creature is not only intelligent and curious about its world but is also reflective about itself and its powers: it is self-aware.

A self-conscious creature is one which is itself the object of its own reflections and assessments. It knows that it forms certain beliefs or desires certain things, and scrutinizes its own perceptions, wants, and opinions and the bases on which these are formed. (Indeed, a reflective creature might well evaluate its second-order beliefs and desires on the basis of some third-order ones: it might demand, for instance, that its ideals be justifiable in some way. It might even have fourth-order beliefs and desires about its third-order ones: it might propose a novel conception of what justifiability consists. Third and fourth order reasoning is in part what philosophy is.)

Understood in terms of self-reflectiveness, self-consciousness is clearly a matter of degree. It may vary from a vague sense of oneself as the center of one's movements to a fully articulated and justified realization of oneself as an agent operative in the world. But the important point is that *by their very nature self-conscious beings cannot be unitary, integral entities.* The self contains within itself an essential element of alienation: its own consciousness of (and therefore distance from) itself. (Also, consciousness of this self-consciousness, and consciousness of this consciousness, etc. The levels of self-differentiation are in theory infinite, though in practice psychological limits restrict them.) Each level introduces a complexity and potential divisiveness within each person. For example, my second-order desire to be gregarious may conflict with my first-order disposition to moroseness. In this case I am at odds with myself: a part of myself isn't integrated with another part; indeed, from the perspective of one part the other part appears alien and unwanted.

But, a respondent might reply, aren't certain elements part of one's "true self" and other elements not? Isn't this "true self" a simple, unified thing? Contemplate the experience of acting differently in different settings (for example, being congenial at work but disagreeable at home). Sometimes these differences are so pronounced that we are bothered by them. This sense of bother is in part the thought that in certain settings we are not being honest, not expressing or feeling what we "really are." Pretence is a frequent occurrence; any acceptable theory of the self has to account for it. But how else to make sense of it except in terms of the commonsense picture which portrays the self as at bottom a fixed, settled entity to which we can be true?

But consider an alternative reading of the fact that we are different in different settings. Perhaps there isn't a "true self" at all; instead maybe the self is rather a way of being which is created anew in the very process of interacting with others and with one's environment. Quantum mechanics provides an analogy. Sub-atomic particles are not hard entities which have an independent existence; rather, they materialize in the process of interaction with other entities. Like sub-atomic particles the self might best be conceived as a probability field which limits the range of possible responses but which "collapses" into discrete feeling and action only when prompted by circumstance. On this account, that we are different in different settings is to be expected; it is not in itself something to bemoan or feel guilty about. (Perhaps the bother we feel about inconsistency depends on a particular picture of the self the abandonment of which would undermine this bother.)

An obvious problem with this view is that it appears to make the self a mere composite rather than a unity. A person who acted in wildly different ways in different settings could not be said to have a self at all. Indeed, a self seems to be a single thing which underlies all the various acts and states of a person. When you say "I did that yesterday and I will do it tomorrow" you seem committed to the view that the I which is the agent responsible for these acts is one and the same entity.

The nature of the unity of the self is an extremely complex topic, but a brief consideration of it might lessen the force of this problem. When we first think of unity we invariably think of it in terms of various elements being part of an underlying object. Unity here derives from the fact that the changes are all alterations of some base entity. For example, sometimes my coffee pot is full of coffee, sometimes not; sometimes it is hot, sometimes cold. But these are all states of one and the same coffee pot, and it is this fact which gives these changes a certain unity. If the self were like the coffee pot it would be an entity which underwent changes (the changes would be its states of consciousness), but these changes would all be changes of an underlying thing (the self). The coffee pot and the self would both be instances of *substantial unity*: changes would be alterations of an underlying substance (a particular entity) and would be unified accordingly.

But not all unities are of this type. Consider a baseball game which consists of nine innings of play. What gives a baseball game its unity is not that its innings are of some underlying entity (the game), but rather that they stand in a particular relation to one another. Here the game isn't an entity which undergoes changes: it simply *is* these changes organized in a particular way. The baseball game is an instance of *relational unity*: the elements comprise a unity because they stand in a certain relation to each other. Unity is not always a matter of some underlying substratum of which various changes are states; it can also occur when parts relate to one another in the proper way.

The relevance of this to the question of the unity of the self is this: perhaps the self is not unified substantially but relationally. That is, perhaps the self is not a thing which undergoes various state changes, but instead just *is* various states of consciousness related in a certain manner. In this case, the self would be more like a verb (an organized temporal flow of mental states) and less like a noun (a particular thing). We often unreflectively presume a substantive conception of unity and so naturally assume that states of consciousness can only be unified if they are states of some underlying substratum (the self). But they can also comprise a unity if they stand in a certain relation to one another. In this case no underlying thing is required for unity; indeed, in this case the self would just be certain states of mind properly related. The self would then be like a baseball game and unlike a coffee pot, unified but not therefore an independent thing.

What kind of relation of mental states might the self be? Consider the use of the pronoun "I." At first it might seem that when we make remarks like "I believe that" we refer to a pre-existing object (the I or the self). The pronoun "I" seems to refer in these locutions to an independent thing, just as the pronoun "you" refers to the person to whom you are speaking, and "it" refers to the object – say, your coffee pot – to which you are pointing. The linguistic practice of first-person utterance seems to require a notion of the self as a substantial unity.

Seeing that this need not be the case might weaken the grip of the substantivist picture of the self. As I said, our intuitive understanding of the mechanics of I-utterances is that they require a pre-existing self which refers back to itself when it uses first-person pronouns (so when I say, "I went to the store" the "I" refers to a thing, the self of the speaker). The problem with this way of construing the matter is that it provides no way for the I to know that it is referring to itself when it makes an I-utterance. The I cannot know it is referring to itself unless it is reflexively self-aware that it refers to itself, and how can it know this? Perhaps, you might respond, the I knows that "I" refers to a pre-existing entity because it observes itself making utterances and so thereby refers to itself. But how does the pre-existing I know that it produced the I-utterance? It cannot be that the I observes itself making it, for how could the I know that it is the I which it is observing?

The general problem is this. When a speaker refers to an independent object like a coffee pot with the pronoun "it," or addresses a person via the pronoun "you," the referents of the respective pronouns are independent of the speaker. But first-person pronouns cannot work in the same way as these pronouns precisely because with them the referrer and the referent are one and the same.

An alternative reading of how I-utterances work suggests itself, one which does not require the existence of a pre-existing self. (This reading is derived from the work of Robert Nozick (1981, chapter 2)). Suppose there is no pre-existing I which does anything; rather suppose that the I comes into being in the very act of reflexively self-referring. To see how this could be so, assume that separate acts A . . . N are performed by an agent without this agent acknowledging that she performed them. Then assume that this agent performs a speech act O which unites A . . . N under the category "I performed these," and which in the very same act self-referentially includes

O within this same category. By O the agent would thus acknowledge both that A . . . N are acts she performed as well as that this acknowledgment is something she also does. Nozick's thesis is that the I is created in and through the act O, that the self is created by means of the activity of reflexively self-referring. If Nozick is correct, and the I comes into being in the very act of reflexively self-referring, then I-utterances can be explained without invoking a prior existing subject.

This examination of how I-utterances work suggests an account of the self as that which emerges in the very act of reflexive self-reference. Or, more accurately, the self is continually being created and recreated in interaction with others as the agent reflexively employs self-referring utterances and first person pronouns. This suggests that selfhood is an achievement made possible only by developing the skill of reflexively self-referring. (Our self-referring practices typically extend further than explicit uses of first-person expressions; a full account of such practices would have to explain implicit self-referential expressions as well as explicit ones.) On this account, the self is not a given thing which has experiences; it is the activity of owning certain experiences. As such, the self would then not be a fixed entity with definite boundaries but a process whose nature was fluid and changeable depending on the sorts of self-referrings undertaken. All this might be summarized by saying the self is not a noun but a verb.

These ideas are speculative. I mention them to suggest an alternative way of considering the self which does justice not only to the unity of our selves but also to the way they are fragmented and fluid. We are much truer to our experience of ourselves if we think of them not as hard, integral entities but as force fields which materialize in the self-reflexive act of self-referring occasioned by interaction with others. The self should be conceived as an ongoing activity of self-creation rather than a pre-existing container of experience. Better to think of it as a multifaceted, internally conflicted field of potential energy which becomes actualized in interaction with others than as a fixed, solid substantial thing. Conceived in this way the notion of "the" self as an integral thing is revealed to be a myth.

2.3 Self and Others

Given the self's fluidity, internal tension, and sensitivity to outside stimuli it should not be surprising that the self is essentially permeable. Indeed, so permeable is it that not only are you not separate from others but rather others are part of you.

This might at first sound strange. Am I not me, and you you? Of course we can interact with each other, but aren't I essentially separate from you? After all, isn't your self-consciousness *your* awareness of *your* self? But a little reflection reveals that many of the ideas and attitudes which comprise what you are derive from others. From your culture you receive the concepts on the basis of which you not only describe yourself and the ideals to which you compare yourself; these concepts are also the basis on which you acquired your identity. Indeed – though this is more difficult to show – your indebtedness to others is even greater than this: you acquired from them not merely the *contents* of your psyche but also the *capacities* distinctive of your selfhood. In these two ways the self is essentially social. Let me show how by examining each of them in turn.

Many of our most common and characteristic intentions are possible only because of the presence of others. Consider the following expressions of intention: "I intend to marry Ann in the spring"; "I intend to deposit my salary in my savings account"; "I intend to vote for the conservative candidate at the next election"; "I intend to enroll in university after a year of travel." The mundane intentions these statements express – to marry, to deposit, to vote, to enroll – presuppose certain social practices. Without the institution of marriage I *cannot* have the intention to marry Ann; without a banking system I *cannot* form the intention to augment my savings account. The same is true for the intentions to vote, enroll in school, ordain priests, pass a law, and so on. Indeed, even the more basic intention to promise to do something – an intention which underlies all contractual and legal relationships – isn't possible without others. When I say "I promise to do x by such and such a time" I thereby commit myself only because of a socially recognized form of personal commitment. In forming our most characteristic intentions and performing our most typical actions other persons are absolutely crucial.

The involvement of others is crucial in other ways. Consider self-development. Becoming a person is in part the process of acquiring a set of norms and ideals which define one's role in a pattern of social relations. For example, the process of becoming a student is in part the process of learning a set of expectations of appropriate behavior, a code of conduct which defines what a student is permitted to do and not do. Most times this code will be internalized in the sense that students will make it their own – will willingly abide by it, and will judge themselves or others negatively when they fail to act in the requisite manner. But even if a student is sociopathic, in the sense that he or she does not internalize these or other norms and ideals, this student will be required to act as if he or she had adopted them. Behavior, feelings, and relations are shaped by certain socially recognized principles such that persons conceive of themselves as bearers of rights and responsibilities within a system of ongoing relationships.

Most intentions are not mere private mental states existing in the mind of an individual. Most intentions are constituted out of social practices — rules, roles, institutions, laws, conventions. Without these social practices most of our intentions could not have been formed. These intentions are therefore inherently social, and beings which characteristically form them are themselves therefore inherently social.

Not only are the contents of our minds constituted out of materials from others, but many of our most characteristic experiences derive from interaction with others. Consider the experience of feeling ashamed. Shame involves embarrassment or fear of being seen by others for behaving or feeling in inappropriate ways. Even if you are not actually caught, you can still feel shame: you might anticipate how you would feel if others were to catch you in the act of performing some deed or having some thoughts which you didn't want them to know you had. In the case of shame your personal experience is a direct function of others' actual or imagined behavior. (Even more complex forms of shame which do not directly depend on the actual or imagined reactions of others are nevertheless social. Thus we might feel shame because we hold an ideal of excellence to which we have failed to live up. But such ideals are themselves internalizations of the standards of our group or modifications of these standards. Even "internal" shame is thus still social.)

Shame involves essential reference to others. In this shame is not unique; love, jealousy, deceit, and condescension all require the real or imagined reactions of others. In these and innumerable other cases states of the self are necessarily related to the perceived states of others. Here self and other are intimately interconnected, not two separate spheres merely colliding with each other. Others provide the raw material out of which experiences like shame or jealousy are fashioned; without them these experiences could not exist.

But the self is interdependent with others in a deeper way than merely their providing the materials for certain typical human experiences. Others are necessary not only for the *content* of our psychic lives but for our ability to be self-conscious creatures. Others are essential for the self to become a self because only through others can a self develop the *capacities* necessary for it to be a self.

This point was made most tellingly by Jean-Paul Sartre. In *Being and Nothingness* Sartre argued that we achieve consciousness of our self only when we become conscious of other conscious beings who are conscious of us. Imagine a creature which is conscious of various objects in the world: a tree, a path, a patch of shadow, a leaf fluttering in the breeze. Assume further that this creature has no experience of any other conscious beings. In this case, our creature would have no basis on which to become aware of itself as another being in the world (and therefore it would not be a self). Such a creature's perceptions would be the means by which objects were detected but it would not experience itself as an object in its world; and, because to be a self implies in part an awareness of oneself as an agent in the world, it would therefore not have a self.

An analogy drawn from Wittgenstein's *Tractatus* might help here. An eye looking out at the world will not see itself; nothing in the visual field will tell the eye that the field is being seen by an eye. From its own viewpoint the eye is not an object in the world. The only way the eye could experience itself as an entity in the world is if the eye could see itself looking at itself (for example, if it could look at itself in a pool of water). The same is true of consciousness: without the experience of being an object there is no basis on which you can be aware of yourself as a self. Needed is something analogous to the eye seeing itself reflected in a pool. This is precisely where another consciousness comes in. For if I become aware that another consciousness is conscious of me, I suddenly become aware that I am an object for it, and I therefore simultaneously become aware of myself as an object for myself. In becoming aware of another's awareness of me I learn that for him or her I am another I; it is through learning this that I discover that I am indeed an I and in this way come to be an I.

Following Sartre in what he calls "the glance," consider the interplay of eyes when a baby first looks at and recognizes its mother as looking and recognizing it. Hardly a more powerful moment exists in the baby's (and the mother's) life. The experience of being seen by its mother and being aware that it is being seen is the moment when self-consciousness begins: instead of being fused with its mother, being incorporated within her, the baby becomes differentiated from her as her gaze at the baby occasions in the baby a sense that it is different from its mother. Thus in this act the baby begins to become its own entity capable of relating to its mother as another entity with which it can either join or oppose; here its selfhood commences.

At its inception self-consciousness is therefore essentially social. You become aware of yourself as a consciousness only through your becoming conscious of another's consciousness of you. That is, only when you become aware of yourself as an object to another do you become aware of yourself as a self. Your being is *your* being (that is, a being for you) only in so far as it is a being for another. In this way, your being is necessarily tied up with my being: *the being of one's self and the being of an other are interrelated.*

The importance of being recognized by others is not confined to the period when self-consciousness emerges. Being recognized by and recognizing others remain throughout life a prime factor shaping the sort of person one is. No one captured this more deeply than Hegel in his discussion in *The Phenomenology of Spirit* of what he called the need for recognition. Hegel thought this was a need not only peculiar to self-conscious beings but distinctive of them. In the first place self-conscious beings characteristically want to be recognized as persons – that is, as conscious entities which are centers of agency – and not just as mere objects in the world of interest only because of their use. In the second place they also want to be recognized as persons of a certain sort, to be thought of as having a particular identity and particular worth. A self-conscious being needs assurance both that it exists and that it is of value. But this assurance logically requires that others acknowledge who and what they are: you cannot assure yourself that you are a person precisely because it is doubts about your personhood which are at issue. You need others to recognize you as a person to insure yourself that you are a person. This need is therefore essentially social because it is a demand for behavior on the part of others and because it is only others who can satisfy it. In so far as this need is distinctive of self-conscious beings they are therefore essentially social in nature.

By being an object to another I not only become aware of myself as a conscious being; I also thereby become aware that there is a potential difference between what others see and what I myself feel or experience. Others see my outside, as it were, but do not necessarily see my inside. Coming to learn this transforms the entire structure of my experience. For now the possibility exists of a disjunction between what I appear to be and what I am. On the basis of this possible disjunction certain characteristic human experiences – playacting, pretending, and lying to name a few – are possible. But of course – and here the phenomenon of shame becomes relevant again – the possible disjunction in any particular case between one's appearance and one's reality is often something one wishes to keep hidden. As an adolescent you may appear as if you are a non-sexual being even though you are beset with lustful thoughts. Moreover, you may not want me to learn this about you and so you may exaggerate your innocence and naivete to make me think that you have no sexuality. But if you were to learn that I had discovered your innermost feelings (say that you learned that I had read your diary), then suddenly you would feel a double shame: I will now know that you have sexual desires and feelings about which you are ashamed, and I will have caught you out pretending not to have them.

The possibility of shame depends on the possible disjunction between appearance and reality; this possible disjunction in turn depends on the sense of oneself as having both an inside and an outside; and this sense in turn depends on being aware of oneself as an object to another. In short, shame necessarily involves others not only in the sense discussed earlier that it is in terms of them that one is embarrassed but in the deeper sense that it is only through them that one can acquire the capacities in terms of which shame is possible.

All this is nicely captured in the story of Adam and Eve in the Garden of Eden. The story shows how directly shame connects to self-consciousness. When Adam and Eve eat the fruit of the tree of the knowledge of good and evil "then the eyes of both were opened, and they knew they were naked and they were ashamed; they sewed fig leaves together and made loincloths for themselves" (Genesis 3:7). Why were they ashamed of their nakedness? Perhaps because they recognized their vulnerability; perhaps because they didn't like the way their bodies looked; perhaps because they became aware of themselves as sexual objects in the sense of being desired by another and they feared as well as delighted in this new-found power. But whatever the nature of their shame, it was at the center of Adam and Eve's coming into self-consciousness ("the eyes of both were opened and they knew they were naked"). Why? Precisely because self-consciousness involves becoming aware that one is an object for another self-conscious creature.

Perhaps the most dramatic instance of the role the recognition of others plays in shaping our personal identity occurs in cases of dynamic interaction. In these cases what occurs in one person is in large measure dependent on the continuing recognition of others, and the person's recognition of this continuing recognition. Consider a case of flirtation (I take this example from Thomas Nagel (1979, p. 44ff.)). You sit at a bar facing a bank of mirrors which enables you to observe other patrons sitting at tables behind you. Suppose that you suddenly notice someone (later you learn this person's name is Y) for whom you feel sexual desire but who is unaware of you or your interest. Suppose that Y then notices you in another mirror though you are not aware of this, and that Y also feels sexual desire for you. Perhaps this causes Y to become flushed, and you observing this flush become even more attracted to Y. At this point your arousal is essentially solitary because neither you nor Y realize that both of you are attracted to each other.

But imagine that suddenly you notice where Y is looking and realize that Y is looking at you with desire. This will not only change your sense of Y but your sense of yourself as well: now you are aware of yourself as the object of Y's desire. This awareness that you are desired will introduce another dimension to your arousal: your desire for Y is increased by your knowledge that Y desires you. But the dynamic need not stop here: Y may now become aware that you desire her (or him) and this may cause in Y the same changes it caused in you, making Y desire you all the more. But this puts you in a position to become aware of Y's awareness and to be further aroused by this new awareness: you sense that Y senses that you sense Y and this introduces yet another round of arousal in you. This new level may in turn be sensed by Y and cause the same sort of increase in arousal in Y. Further, at some point either you or Y may decide to signal to each other that you are aware of what is going on, and this signalling may introduce yet another level in your ongoing exchange. This sort of iteration can continue, but the point ought to be obvious: flirtation is an extremely complicated interaction in which your various mental states are deeply affected by Y's actual and imagined changing mental states (and vice versa), most especially your mutual recognition of each other.

The interactional nature of identity formation exhibited in the case of flirtation has a particular relevance in anthropology and psychology in which ethnographers or other "participant-observers" interact with their subjects. For a long time anthropologists claimed that they were mere observers of the lives of their subjects. Of course they admitted that ethnographers pick and choose from the behavior they observe that which they think most significant or revealing; ethnographic reports were said to be perspectival. This is certainly the case, but it does not sufficiently capture the ways ethnographers are themselves involved in their ethnographies. For the presence of the ethnographer and the recognition of this presence on the part of the subjects are crucial elements in the way these subjects themselves act. Ethnographers are not mere passive or neutral recorders of behavior occurring independently of them; rather, this behavior is deeply affected by the process of each looking at each other looking at each other. This might be put by saying that the relation between ethnographers and their subjects is not merely perspectival but is *positional*: the behavior of each depends in part on their respective positions relative to each other, and to each's recognition of these positions.

Here again an analogy from physics is helpful. According to the Heisenberg Uncertainty Principle an observer cannot measure both the momentum and the position of subatomic particles because in the very act of measuring them the physicist interferes with them. The relation between physicists and their particles is not that between mere observer and observed; in these cases it is rather like that of ethnographers to their subjects, namely, positional: the behavior of the particles and the physicists depends on their mutual interaction and their relative positions with respect to one another. In like manner, the behavior of ethnographic subjects itself is in part precipitated out of the interaction between these subjects and the anthropologists studying them. (Ethnographic subjects are not unique in this; they are merely particular instances of the general fact that all behaviors of persons result from their interactions with others and their recognition of these interactions.)

To have an identity is in part to be related to others in particular ways and to understand that one is so related. To be a person is among other things to be able to be aware of others' responses to you and to be aware of this awareness, to be able to respond to them on the basis of this awareness, to monitor yours and others' response to your response, to be aware of your monitoring, etc. in an ever-evolving cycle of awareness – response – self-awareness. This sort of awareness and response deeply affects everything about us, our desires, fears, hopes, and motivations. In this way our identities derive from the relations we come to form with others.

This is so even in cases in which you reject others' ways of being or you break off relationships with them. In the first place, when you reject others that which might have been unself-conscious and unproblematical for you necessarily now becomes conscious and explicit. "This is the way *we* do things," you intone, or "We are not like *them*"; these and cognate expressions declare the sense that what was unself-conscious in your life has now become a matter of self-conscious definition. In the second place, even when you reject that which you now deem to be an "other" this other is still present as an object over and against which you define who you are. You may militantly reject your father and what he represents but in the very act of rejecting him he remains a part of you by being that which serves as a touchstone in terms of which you conceive yourself. Or notice how national liberation movements need the oppressor in order to form themselves and to keep themselves in existence. Or that post-colonials require the metropolitan to be post-colonial: even when the metropolitan is rejected it continues to provide the focal point around which the energies of the post-colonials are organized. Post-colonials are post-colonials precisely because of their (negative) relation to the metropolitan center.

That self and other are dynamically interrelated even in opposition should not be surprising. Every determination involves negation in which elements essential to an entity are separated from those which are not. To be a certain kind presupposes you are different from other kinds. As a result identity formation in persons is in part a process of self-differentiation which requires an other against which they distinguish themselves. There can be no self without the difference provided by others. In this ironic way selves need others even in their insistence on their difference from them.

46

These are some of the ways humans are essentially social. One of their most distinctive capacities (that of self-awareness) requires the presence of and interaction with others; they act on the basis of roles and rules which they glean only from others; and one of their most characteristic needs — the need for recognition — arises out of their relations to others. This means that as persons we are necessarily connected to others. Each separate self does not construct its own private, individual world nor live in one; rather, each self is a self only because it is part of a community of other selves that builds up a public, social world which uses a common system of symbols and which underwrites an ongoing pattern of interaction whereby these selves recognize and respond to one another. *The self is an essentially social entity*.

But once this is clear the whole idea of "being one" in the sense of being a separate, self-individuated atom is undermined. Each of us is not a closed and bounded entity. Instead we are complex, dynamic compounds emergent from our interactions with others. Selves are the active traces which have been precipitated out of their relations with other selves.

2.4 Summing Up

If the deep assumption of atomism (that selves are encapsulated entities) is incorrect, the relation of self and other needs to be conceived in terms quite different from those of two independent entities confronting one another. Recall that atomism pictured the relationship between self and other this way:

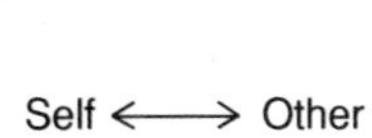

Figure 2.2

But if the self is essentially social, then the following is a better depiction of the relationship between self and other:

Self ⟷ Other

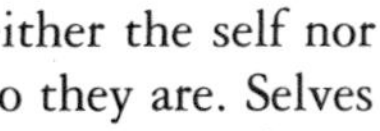

Figure 2.3

Notice that in figure 2.3 neither the self nor the other is enclosed; their interaction is integral to who they are. Selves are not mere others to each other; they mutually help to define each other such that without others

47

selves cannot have the capacity to be selves or the material to be the particular selves they are.

The standard dichotomy of Self vs. Other is too simple. It suggests that the self is a hard, integrated entity and that others are similarly hard and integrated, mere outsiders who confront us as something to be encountered and dealt with, but not as something inherent in what we are. But selves are not simple unities, and others are an integral part of them. Porous selves open and responding to other porous selves – Self and Other dialectically interacting – is a more accurate picture than that provided by atomism.

This is not to deny that atomism contains a kernel of truth, namely, its insistence on the importance of human agency. Atomism maintains that individuals are not mere puppets or other passive objects pushed around by social forces which act independently of them. Instead it distinguishes persons from mere things, persons who as self-conscious and self-directing are centers of activity which respond to their environment but which are not determined by it. Atomism also correctly asserts that social entities like a particular state or family are what they are as a result of the activities of their members. These truths of atomism will only become clear after we examine its opposite – holism – in the next chapter. Only then will the strengths of atomism be as apparent as its weaknesses. (In this way chapters 2 and 3 compose a unit.)

Do we need others to be ourselves? Yes – though, as we shall see in the next chapter, we also need ourselves to be ourselves.

Further Reading

For a discussion of the self as essentially dialogical, in addition to Sartre (1956) and Nozick (1981) mentioned in the text, see Williams (1973), Taylor (1985a,b; 1989; and 1991), and Aboulafia (1986). Behind this approach lies Hegel (1977 (1807)), the first and most important philosopher to conceive self-identity as essentially involving others. For an excellent collection of essays discussing the ideas developed in this chapter, see Mischel (1977). For an account of personhood in terms of first- and second-order beliefs and desires, see Frankfurt (1971). The most developed and sophisticated account of the processual view of selfhood is that of Parfit (1984).

Post-structuralist thought has been most concerned to undermine the idea of a unified, substantial self. On this see Lacan (1977) and Foucault (1978). For a serious critical analysis of leading poststructuralists, see Best and Kellner (1991). Soper (1986) also offers a clear guide through this literature – no mean feat.

Throughout this chapter I have tried to avoid Cartesian assumptions of mind (that it is private, inner, subjective) as opposed to physical entities which are public, outer, and objective. The dualism of mental = private and physical = outer is very common in western European philosophy, but it poses grave conundrums which I think are insoluble. A different strategy – one pursued by Wittgenstein (1968 and 1992), Heidegger (1962), and Dewey (1925) – refuses to buy into this dichotomy; it reconceives the mind (and its cognates like "experience," "perception," "feeling", etc.) in what might be called field terms which pictures the mind as essentially interactive within a field. See in this regard Hark (1994), Johnston (1993), and Vesey (1991).

For a vivid discussion of the way self and other are within each other, see Bhabha (1994). Barta (1994) shows how the notion of "western civilization" is defined over and against the myth of the wild man (satyrs, Caliban, etc.).

On shame, see Williams (1993) for a brilliant historical and philosophical analysis of this phenomenon.

For atomism and methodological individualism, see Part VI of Martin and McIntyre (1994), and Homans (1967).

3

Does Our Culture or Society Make Us What We Are?

3.1 Holism

An idea frequently heard today is that those of one group are fundamentally different from members of other groups. Blacks are supposed to be essentially unlike whites, or men basically dissimilar to women, or those from "non-western cultures" radically different from those in "western cultures." This idea is obviously germane to the question of understanding others. If you are fundamentally different from those in other groups, how can you acquire the information necessary to describe and explain what they do?

The idea of fundamental group difference derives in part from a position at the opposite end of the spectrum from atomism, namely, holism. As I shall use the term, *holism* is the doctrine that properties of individuals are solely a function of their place in society or some broad system of meaning; specifically, it is the doctrine that people's identities are determined by their group membership because identity is produced by social and cultural forces. Holism claims that you are essentially a vehicle by which society and culture express themselves.

Just as atomism underlies a particular form of explanation in the social sciences (methodological individualism), so also does holism, namely, *methodological holism*. Methodological holists insist that social phenomena be studied at their own autonomous macroscopic level of analysis. Moreover, they claim that theories which explain social phenomena are not reducible to theories about the individuals which perform them. The reason is straightforward: individuals are what they are because of the social whole to which they belong; the result is that the individual can only be understood by placing him or her in a social context, not the other way around. It follows that social wholes, not their individual human members, must be the bedrock of any adequate social scientific theory. Methodological holism thus offers a guide for theory construction in the social sciences: look to social wholes for bottom-line explanations.

A crucial figure in the development of holism was Emile Durkheim. Durkheim claimed that society is a reality irreducible to individual psychology and behavior, and that explanations of even the most individualistic appearing acts were a function of impersonal laws and forces characterizing social wholes. His methodological treatise, *The Rules of the Sociological Method* (1938 (1895)), is a classic statement of holism. But it was his astonishing study *Suicide* (1951 (1897)) in which he sought to demonstrate holism's explanatory power. In this work he argued that this most individual of acts was indeed a social fact, that society set the conditions in terms of which suicide occurred. He claimed that individual psychology was incapable of explaining the pattern of various suicide rates, and ultimately was incapable of explaining the forces which led individuals to suicide.

A more modern version of holism is structuralism. *Structuralism* began as an approach to language which claimed that language is a system of signs whose meaning and order do not derive from social life or the creative intentions of individual speakers but solely from the relations of signs to other elements in the system. Each system is marked by an inherent logic which relates the elements to one another, and the job of structural linguistics is to uncover this logic. This basic approach was broadened to become a theory of society. As such, structuralism asserts that conscious agents do not create the system of meaning in which they live; rather as social subjects they are created by this system and live within it. To understand individual behavior, therefore, social scientists must attend to the inner logic which orders the various elements which comprise the social system as a whole.

Lévi-Strauss is the most important thinker in this regard. He analyzed kinship, ceremonies, myths, cooking, marriage, and totems as autonomous systems composed of elementary units whose meaning derived from their patterns of difference, particularly bi-polar opposition. Another forceful extension of structural linguistics to human history was effected by Michel Foucault in his book *The Archaeology of Knowledge*. According to this work history is a sequence of periods constituted by different systems of discourse. Each system possesses its own inner logic, and dominant discourse systems created collective identities by excluding other systems. Historical change is not produced by agents — indeed, agents are only bearers of a system of discourse and are created by it. Rather change is like a geological shift in which one discourse system gives way to another. Thus Foucault argued that social scientists should become archaeologists of linguistic structures encrusted in social institutions.

In later works Foucault rethought the nature of social inquiry but he never totally abandoned his structuralist roots. For example in *The History of Sexuality* he continued to speak of the "construction of the subject," and to urge that:

> We should try to discover how it is that subjects are gradually, progressively, really and materially constituted through a multiplicity of organisms, forces, energies, materials, desires, thoughts, etc. (Foucault, 1981, p. 97)

Foucault analyzed the process by which subjects are created by the physical, social, and discursive space in which they live. Of particular interest is the way new forms of personal existence are brought into being by the labels which are applied to people, their actions and relations. For example, Foucault argued that when the categories "perversion," "homosexuality," and "multiple personality" emerged in the nineteenth century (as a subtle form of medicalized social control) perverts, homosexuals, and multiple personalities came into being. In general, a kind of person is created when the kind itself comes into existence.

Holism has a special appeal in the social sciences for two reasons taken together. In the first place science by its very nature focuses not on individuals but on members of a class. Biologists don't speak about a particular beaver but about beavers in general (indeed, they may generalize even more abstractly in this connection to talk of rodents or animals or organisms). Similarly, economists don't attend to particular purchasers but to buyers and sellers impersonally and in the aggregate; political scientists focus on voters, legislators, and bureaucrats considered as types of people or kinds of roles. (To employ some useful philosophical jargon, science normally concentrates on types rather than tokens of these types.) This means that members of a class must for purposes of scientific analysis be considered as essentially the same. Anthropologists describe the behavior of the Ilongot in its typicality not the behavior of individual Ilongot tribe members. In this and like cases individual differences are ignored or placed in the background. Science stresses similarity.

This in itself does not entail holism: holism is not simply a matter of focusing on the traits of most individuals or of typical specimens. But the impetus to describe phenomena in general terms supports a holist approach when buttressed by a second factor, the explanatory aims of science. Science doesn't just want to describe its objects of study; it also desires to explain why they are the way they are. Science typically accomplishes this by discovering the causal forces which operate on a type of entity and which make it act as it does. Following this pattern, social scientists quite naturally look to explanations which invoke social phenomena as causal forces. With respect to questions of identity, for instance, what better explanation for similarities within a certain type than that its members have been enculturated or socialized by a particular social group or culture? The upshot is an inherent disposition in the social sciences to see individual identity in holistic terms as a function of the individual's culture or society.

Certain features of contemporary life reinforce holism and its concomitant separatist view of social entities. Group identification has become a very significant factor in contemporary life. As modern states have incorporated a wider and wider range of types of people into the body politic, members of these groups have come to insist on their own cultural and social individuality. In particular, ethnic, racial, gender, and (in some places) religious identification have asserted themselves sometimes to the point of stridency. Members of these groups insist on their distinctiveness in part as a way of resisting the hegemony of more powerful groups. They resist acculturation into the broader public world, refusing to assimilate to either the so-called "melting pot" or the styles and norms of the dominant group; instead they emphasize what is different and distinctive about themselves. In this way they believe they affirm their own value and their sense of themselves. The effect of this is to reinforce the notion that group integrity shapes individual identity, and the idea that those of one group are fundamentally different from those of other groups.

Holism, therefore, has a firm footing in social scientific aspiration and practice, and is also reinforced by the exigencies of multicultural living in the contemporary world.

3.2   Difference and Group Membership

Before considering the truth of holism directly, consider an obvious point: not all members of a group are alike in all respects. I may be a member of the middle class, but I may differ in significant ways from other members of this class (they may be female, black, non-religious, rural, unschooled, and so on). Indeed, depending on how one looks at the members of any group the differences within the group can often be as great as the differences between its members and others not members of this group.

Thus, from a certain point of view, both black and white citizens of the United States form a specific group because they are part of a common political culture whose elements (a commitment to individual rights, for instance) shape their sense of government and citizenship. This culture gives them a common set of values and standards, and a common political vocabulary in terms of which they conceive and express their grievances and proffer remedies for them. That the "Gettysburg Address" by Abraham Lincoln (a white) and the "I Have a Dream" speech by Martin Luther King (a black) both employ many of the same basic ideas, and touch both black and white Americans, is testimony to the shared quality of being a US citizen. However, from another point of view, the differences between whites and blacks are profound – indeed, so much so that in many ways African-Americans are more like Jamaican immigrants living in the United Kingdom than they are like whites living in Nashville or Omaha. Blacks have been denied the full rights and responsibilities of citizenship for most of their history in the US; moreover, much of its political culture has been shaped by deeply racist attitudes. To be a black citizen of the United States is in many ways to be quite unlike being a white US citizen.

The same sorts of considerations can be raised regarding any number of differences within the group "US citizenry": male vs. female; urban vs. rural; rich vs. poor; Christian vs. non-Christian; and so on. Nor is there anything special about this group: the same points could be made about any group. Think of the groups "women," "Catholics," and "working class": the differences within them are enormous. Even smaller and more homogeneous groups like "Ashanti," "the Fay Family," "Psi Epsilon Fraternity" include members who from another point of view significantly differ from one another. All groups necessarily include distinctions (for example, between those with and those without authority) that introduce and reinforce differences within them. Thus, it is simplistic to think that groups are comprised of homogeneous units which are all alike in ways that radically distinguish them from members of all other groups.

The idea that groups are integral wholes comprised of homogeneous units derives in part from a common but false conception of the notion "group." Too often we tend to reify this notion, that is, to conceive of it as a solid, almost physically existing thing which makes all its members conform to it (as if a group were a lathe). This reified conception has some plausibility if one adopts a strong view of culture and/or society, a view which highlights the power of culture and/or society to shape and penetrate its members. But this strong view is problematic for two reasons. First, it fails to recognize what I will call the processural nature of culture and society; and second, it fails to grasp the importance of agency in social and cultural life. To understand why, we need to analyze the important ideas of "culture" and "society." Having done so, we will be in a better position to answer the question of whether culture or society make us what we are.

3.3   Culture

According to a standard view, a culture is a complex set of shared beliefs, values, and concepts which enables a group to make sense of its life and which provides it with directions for how to live. This set might be called a basic belief system (note that such a belief system can include items which are fully explicit and others which are not, and can include matters of feeling and deportment as well as discursive claims about the world). In perhaps the most influential variant of this standard view, culture is pictured as a text the vocabulary and grammar of which its members learn. Indeed, on this view, becoming a member of a particular culture is a process of enculturation conceived as learning to read the culture's basic text and making it one's own.

This standard view asserts the further claim that in becoming the carriers of a specific cultural tradition individuals become the people they are. That is, by internalizing a particular belief system and its attendant forms of feeling and interaction a person acquires the basics of his or her identity. A culture penetrates its individual members mentally (so that they possess a certain mind-set), physically (so that they possess certain basic bodily dispositions), and socially (so that they relate to one another in certain characteristic ways). This penetration produces in them their distinctive capacities and characteristics. In this holistic way identity is a function of enculturation.

Is this standard view accurate? To answer this, begin by considering what it is like to learn a language (the paradigm case of cultural learning). One might plausibly claim that our language penetrates us and that we belong to it in the sense that its semantics and syntax allow us to say what we do. Our language provides the resources on the basis of which we assert, question, demand, and judge. But this is not a one-way street: in the process of learning a language we affirm parts of it and reject others; we embrace certain elements, recombine others in novel ways, and create new forms. We do not just absorb; we transmute and extend and reinterpret. In this process language users change language even as it molds them.

Even the most cursory examination of the way English has changed in the recent past reveals this. New words, newly acceptable grammatical forms, and new metaphors expressing new ideas abound – the result of the profound alteration which English speakers have made to their language in the act of using it. Some of this has resulted from political and social developments (gender neutral language, for example, as the result of the increasing awareness and power of women); from changes in technology (the spread of BBC pronunciation as a result of the radio and television, for instance); from scientific advances ("black hole"; "gene"; "quark";

55

"charmed particle"); from creative use of language by poets and ordinary folk ("my main squeeze"; "cool"); from changes in social relations, including manners (permitting contractions in academic prose, for instance); and a host of other factors. This is a vast subject but its general outlines are clear: in learning and using their language people have an active role in shaping it as they adapt it to new situations, develop its resources, and alter its character as they try to suit it to their purposes.

Language use suggests that culture is never merely absorbed; more accurate to say it is *appropriated*. The reason for this derives from the nature of rule following. Cultural norms consist of rules which detail acceptable ways to speak, think, feel, and behave. But what is involved in following a rule? Rules give direction as to how one is to proceed. But no rule can anticipate all the conditions under which it is to be applied. Nor can its meaning be unambiguous (a rule can't have as part of itself another rule which tells its followers how it is to be understood, because this rule would itself require another rule, and this rule would itself require another, and so on ad infinitum). Both the meaning of a rule and how to apply it in a given case call for *interpretation* on the part of those who follow it. Indeed, one of the marks of being able to follow a rule is precisely the ability to interpret it when the occasion demands. Rule-followers thus do not simply "conform" to rules, but instead elaborate and transform them in the process of following them.

Consider a simple rule from a hypothetical club: "No relative of a member shall be a member." What does "relative" mean in this rule? Does it refer to those in one's immediate family or to one's extended family? Does immediate family include only blood relations or those related by marriage? How extended is one's extended family? Does a divorced woman count as a relative of her former husband? A son who has disowned his family? What does "member" mean in this rule? Does one have to be able to vote to be a member? Or be eligible to hold office? Are permanent guests members? What about underage children?. . . . These and countless other questions (many of which I cannot anticipate because I cannot imagine all possible situations in which the application of this rule may be problematic) fill the annals of clubs. They do so not because members are inherently obstreperous but because the nature of following a rule requires ongoing interpretation.

Couldn't this problem be solved simply by stipulating what a relative is? No, for two reasons. First, the meaning of the stipulated terms will themselves be subject to precisely the same difficulties as the term "relative." Second, the stipulated definition will have to be applied to new situations and these will call for creative interpretations. Stipulation doesn't end debate but only shifts its ground and provides further material for it. This can be clearly seen in cases of legal adjudication. Even a cursory glance at laws and their application reveals disputes about the meaning of stipulated terms, disputes which call for constant further articulation. Indeed, much of the business of lawyering consists in arguments about the direction of such articulation.

Interpretation of meaning and application to new settings reveal the active role culture-bearers must play. *Agents*, not mere objects, are "enculturated" (or, more accurately, "engage in the process of enculturation"). Agents not only draw on cultural beliefs, rules, and values to form their intentions and enact their projects, but through their activity culture itself is reconstituted. That is, culture is not only the ground of human activity but is the outcome of this activity as well.

The role of agency in the application of culture shows itself in the phenomenon of resistance. Cultural values and codes are often subverted, challenged, re-thought, rejected, and/or transformed. This is particularly true of those at the periphery who, though they acknowledge the power of a particular culture, resist it as corrupt or oppressive. Note, for instance, that in our own time certain key cultural ideas and ideals such as "woman" and "man" (and subsidiary notions such as "sexuality," "wife," "mother," "husband," and "father") are the subject of deep contention and opposition among significant numbers of the population (often those who do not or cannot identify with the dominant conceptions). As a result the meanings of a number of these terms have significantly shifted; they will continue to do so.

So far I have been speaking as if culture consisted of a coherent set of beliefs (a "text"). But this is a mistake. Any culture complex enough to warrant the name will consist of conflicting beliefs and rules which offer mixed, contested, and ambiguous messages to its followers. The reason for this derives in part from what I have already said about cultural rules and agency: rules require interpretation, and interpretation requires reflexive analysis and judgment on the part of agents. Besides, cultural beliefs and ideals apply to people in differential positions of power. The meaning of a rule for a powerful member of an elite often will not be the same for, nor will it have the same outcome on, a member of a group who is on the periphery. Moreover, cultural norms and ideals result from histories of struggle in which significant voices are silenced. As a result, various members in a cultural group will have heterogeneous histories, divergent interests, and antagonistic interpretations. Far from being coherent unities uniformly distributed throughout a society, cultures are rather tense loci of difference and opposition.

Take for example the notion of femalehood. Recent thought about this concept has distinguished between female sex and female gender. Sex, it is claimed, is a matter of biology, something given by nature; gender, on the other hand, is a matter of culture, something which is constructed by various cultures in different ways. Thus the question, "what does it mean to be a female?" can on this view mean either of two things: either "what characterizes the female sex?" (a question which calls for an anatomical and physiological answer); or "what is the meaning of the various modes of behavior, relation, and experience which comprise femininity?" (a question which calls for a cultural answer).

Consider the question of the relationship between motherhood and femalehood. Is femalehood to be defined in terms of motherhood (such that if one is not a mother one is not a full female)? If so, how is motherhood to be conceived? Does it require breastfeeding? Educating the young? Subordination to the father? These are cultural questions; cultural definition consists in answers to them and questions like them. Such answers are not ordained by nature but are constructions which result from social struggles as to how a cultural category should be understood. Thus, many cultures define femalehood in terms of mothering but some do not; more relevantly, some cultures once defined motherhood as essential but then came to reject it (perhaps this has happened in contemporary Britain and the United States). Or again, some cultures define motherhood in very restrictive terms (for instance, to be a full mother one has to breastfeed), while in others motherhood is a much looser notion (in them wetnursing one's baby need not be a sign of a failure at mothering, for instance). The meaning of the category "mother" is itself debatable and changeable, something about which different groups can and will have differing ideas. Which idea will predominate in a society is a result of a struggle among these groups. Indeed, one may not predominate: a culture may contain a number of antagonistic conceptions of motherhood.

That cultural categories are the subject of, and the result of, intense debate can be seen even in the example I have just given which draws a clear distinction between sex and gender. Recently a number of feminists have attacked this distinction as misleading and oppressive. They argue that not just gender but sex itself is a culturally constructed category. They maintain that what makes a person of the female sex is not (simply or primarily) a question of biology but is instead ultimately a cultural question. For instance, is sexuality a matter of having certain organs or having a certain directionality in one's sexual desires? If the former, then what about the phenomenon of those who claim to be females trapped in men's bodies? Of those who have had sex-change operations? Or of hermaphrodites? If the latter, are lesbians any less or more of the female sex? What of bisexuals? The people in these and other categories do not fit into the neat dichotomy "sex:biology: :gender:culture"; they seem to blow this categorization apart, to show that even sex itself is a cultural construction.

Those who criticize the conception of sex as somehow prior to culture seek to undermine this conception in contemporary culture. They believe this conception is oppressive and limiting, the imposition by some in power on others who find this way of defining identity confining and false to their experience. Will this critique have any effect, or will it die in silence? This question cannot be answered as of now. But this is precisely the point: the cultural definition of femininity is an open question, one continually in the process of being answered and challenged, imposed and resisted, defined and revised. (Of course, these are not merely semantic debates. The way certain key terms and categories are understood in a society is crucial to the way this society functions – in particular, to how particular modes of behavior and relation are judged and to how social benefits and burdens are distributed.)

The process of cultural definition and re-definition is a process of social, cultural, and political struggle for dominance among elements in a culture vying with one another over the terms of personal and social identity. Thus, what "woman" means calls forth a number of different possibilities; some of these will come to pre-eminence (to be altered at a later date?) and others will drop by the wayside (to be resurrected in other times?), the result of collective struggles. Indeed, the conception of womanhood (and manhood and citizenship and authority and labor and death and prayer and love and . . .) which currently has supremacy (if indeed one does) is itself the sedimentation of such past struggles.

Another important fact about cultures is that they are essentially open. Cultures are ideational entities; as such they are permeable, susceptible to influence from other cultures. Wherever exchange among humans occurs, the possibility exists of the influence of one culture by another. (Even when such influence does not occur it is because those in one culture consciously reject the foreign or strange culture: but this rejection is itself another way the alien culture interjects itself into the home culture.) Human history is in part the story of the ways different cultural groups have rearranged cultural boundaries by expanding contacts, tolerating outsiders, and fashioning interactive arrangements. Even the creation of stricter boundaries involves mutual impact. The human world is not composed of a motley of independent, encapsulated, free-floating cultures; rather, it is one of constant interplay and exchange.

Thus, the slaves on southern plantations watched their white masters dance and then promptly transformed these European steps into something distinctly their own. Whites, now beholding this new form of dance, promptly incorporated it into their own repertoire and thereby changed their dance style. Blacks, no longer slaves but still distinctly oppressed, incorporated the newer forms of dance developed by the whites into their dancing. Through this interchange blacks and whites made something distinctively American. But this distinctively American form of dance became itself subject to influences from the world of classical ballet: with the advent of George Balanchine modern American dance assimilated the old Russian world into itself. This process goes on and on as new styles, insights, musics, and cultures come into contact with one another, alter the possibilities participants see for themselves, and transmute the vocabulary of bodily movement.

Interchange and appropriation are evident everywhere. Think of the foods you eat, the clothes you wear, the games you play, the books you read, the music you listen to. But more subtly, consider the deeper cultural rhythms by which you live. Your conceptions of time, of space, of power, of beauty, of agency, of sociality, of knowledge have all been deeply affected by importing, responding to, transforming, and borrowing the cultural meanings and values of others different from you. In 1907 an exhibition of African sculpture was held in Paris. That such sculpture was in a gallery was itself already a transformation of the nature of objects whose original meaning was intimately connected to tribal and religious practices. Those in attendance came to view these objects not as religious symbols but as aesthetic objects. But I doubt any of them had any appreciation of the way these objects would forever change western sculpture. In the audience was the young Picasso whose idea of the meaning of art and of beauty and artistic expression was radically altered by these African pieces. He started carving and molding artworks which were unlike anything then in evidence in western museums and galleries, and through him (among others) the entire aesthetic of the twentieth century in western art was altered. Not only that, but so also was the conception of art held by Africans themselves: for they began to make distinctions (between religion and art, for instance) which heretofore they had not made which allowed them to conceive and produce new sorts of artworks.

Far easier to think in simple categories: "black culture"; "white culture"; "western culture"; "African culture." But these are all dangerous simplifications deeply untrue to the reality of those who live in terms of these categories. People in them – real flesh and blood people, not the abstractions of the ideologues, politicians, and some social scientists – are blends of characteristics typical of one category or another. Moreover, real people listen to others, they try out new ideas and ways of living, rejecting some and incorporating others (always in their own manner). People learn from others, and change on the basis of what they have learned.

Allow me to summarize the remarks about culture I have been making. Cultures are neither coherent nor homogeneous nor univocal nor peaceful. They are inherently polyglot, conflictual, changeable, and open. Cultures involve constant processes of reinscription and of transformation in which their diverse and often opposing repertoires are re-affirmed, transmuted, exported, challenged, resisted, and re-defined. This process is inevitable because it is inherent in what it means for active beings to learn and apply cultural meanings, and in the ideational nature of culture itself.

Earlier I said that a standard model of culture conceives of it as a text to be read. This metaphor is possibly misleading: it may suggest a picture of culture in terms which are too static, too integral, too closed, and too given. In order to avoid these mistakes inherent in the metaphor of culture as a text Kenneth Burke proposed viewing culture instead as a conversation:

> Imagine that you enter a parlor. You come late. When you arrive others have long preceded you, and they are engaged in a heated discussion, a discussion too heated for them to pause and tell you exactly what it is about. In fact, the discussion had begun before any of them got there, so that no one present is qualified to retrace for you all the steps that had gone on before. You listen for awhile, and then you decide you have caught the tenor of the argument; you then put in your oar. Someone answers, you answer him; another comes to your defense; another aligns himself against you, to either the embarrassment or gratification of your opponent, depending on the quality of your ally's assistance. However, the discussion is interminable. The hour grows late, you must depart, with the conversation still in progress. (Burke, 1957, pp. 95–6)

Notice some of the key features of this little scenario: the conversation involves the active participation of the conversants, each of whom has something distinctive to contribute; the conversation is important – it is an argument and not a lighthearted chitchat; the argument in part requires that one gain allies who may or may not advance any members' ideas (indeed, such alliance building will almost certainly produce alterations in any position); the conversation is a continual round of challenge and response; and the course of the conversation is open and fluid, but not arbitrary or unstructured – a member enters an ongoing concern, but can challenge the terms or direction the conversation will assume.

Burke's metaphor of culture as a conversation is a decided improvement on the metaphor of culture as a text. It captures the dynamic nature of culture as an ongoing process in which agents and not automatons appropriate and alter the terms by which they live. Nevertheless, Burke's metaphor as he details it has some serious shortcomings, failing to capture certain elements of culture which we have already noted. In particular: the power differentials among the members is not mentioned; how members insert themselves into the conversation is not problematized (indeed, it seems as if no barriers to participation exist in Burke's conversation); the outcomes of the conversation appear to affect only the conversation itself and not other elements of the participant's lives; the ways in which certain "decisions" as to the direction of the conversation foreclose certain options is not acknowledged; the nature of the conversational units ("arguments"; "answers"), or the location of the conversation (a "parlor"), are not themselves explicitly made open to challenge ("parlor" is an especially misleading term because it suggests that the conversation is genteel and well mannered); the conversation appears to be univocal, with just one conversation going on at a time. In the "conversation" of culture some are often systematically excluded, differences of power favor some over others, and the results preclude life-options vital to some if not all. (Think, for instance, of what has happened to the Native-Americans in the "cultural conversation" of mainstream America. Note, too, that the culture of America includes a plethora of simultaneous conversations not all using the same terms.)

Moreover, Burke's metaphor as he outlines it makes it sound as if the conversants enter the conversation already able to converse. This is seriously misleading. To be able to converse a potential member must acquire certain conversational skills (concepts; ways of communicating) already present in the conversation itself. Potential conversants become actual conversants only by internalizing the terms of the ongoing conversation. Even ways participants may question or object are themselves shaped by the terms already in operation in the conversation. In insisting on the agency of cultural conversants, Burke's account shortchanges the way culture both enables certain kinds of agency and at the same time limits it.

Burke's metaphor thus needs significant amendment so that it more realistically portrays the rough and tumble nature of the cultural struggles from which certain potential participants are excluded and others are differentially placed with respect to power, in which all come to be participants by internalizing certain terms of this struggle, and in which the outcome shuts off certain possible life-options for participants and their offspring. Such struggles are multi-voiced, distinguished by starts and stops, intimidation and threat as well as patient argument, occasional shouting, and sometimes a lot of noise.

Burke's metaphor does capture the dynamic, fluid, contestational nature of culture. For Burke "culture" is not a noun but a verb; it refers to a process in which agents don't just reproduce the terms by which they live but extend, alter, and sometimes transform them. Culture is thus an evolving connected activity, not a thing. But Burke's metaphor fails to take account of certain key features of cultural struggle: power differentials; silencing; and the way culture itself forms the identity of the conversants. But Burke's metaphor could be suitably modified. If this were done, it would more accurately portray the interplay between, on the one hand, the activity of its members as they appropriate and alter cultural meanings and, on the other, the enabling and limiting role of culture as it shapes these agents and their activity.

3.4 Society

A standard holistic view of society conceives it as a system which determines how its members behave and relate. *Systems theory,* for instance, portrays society as a set of functionally interrelated units bound together by a flow of information generated by environmental demands and internal exigencies. According to this theory no fundamental difference exists between, say, a heating system, the endocrine system, and a social system: of course, at some level these are all quite different, but ultimately they are all structures organized around informational flows whose outcome is the maintenance of certain relationships among its various parts and with its environment. Thus, in a heating system the air communicates its temperature to the thermostat which in turn communicates this information to the boiler whose output alters the air temperature to the point at which the thermostat tells the boiler to shut off. Similarly, in a political system the populace communicates its demands to the allocative mechanism which responds with certain outputs (governmental policies, for instance) designed to generate support so that the demands of the populace subside. On this view political systems are like heating systems: open, homeostatic systems in a steady state employing various channels of information and feedback loops to maintain themselves in equilibrium.

The problem with this approach is that it plays fast and loose with the concept "communication" and its cognates. The thermostat communicates with the boiler in a radically different way than voters communicate to their elected officials. In the former case, information exists only in some metaphorical sense: neither the thermostat nor the boiler aim to communicate anything, nor are they aware of each other. In the latter case, communication is intended by the parties, and the information communicated is the result of the conscious appropriation of meaning. Thermostats don't *mean* to produce specific signals to the boiler, nor do they *intend* to tell the boiler to turn on, nor do they *desire* to raise the temperature in the room. The boiler doesn't *understand* anything either: its behavior is

63

strictly mechanical. But an elected official must understand the demands of the electorate and knowingly respond to them. (Analogously, I am communicating with you, reader, in a way that I cannot communicate with my computer: it can't know anything because it is literally mindless.)

It might seem picayune to insist that the use of "information" and cognate concepts like "understanding" is different in the cases of a heating system and a political system, but a great deal rides on making this distinction. The difference between communication between people and communication between parts of a mechanical system highlights the fact that society is composed of *agents* and not mere interrelating parts. Agents but not thermostats act on the basis of their intentions; agents but not thermostats are aware of their world and attempt to respond to it on the basis of this awareness. Agents perceive their situation, reason about it, form motives, knowingly act on the basis of this reasoning, and reflexively monitor their action to see whether it produces the desired result. Agents are capable of reflection – explaining, evaluating, justifying, and criticizing their actions – and altering them on the basis of this reflection. Agents but not thermostats are conscious and possess the capacity to think. Agents cannot, therefore, be mere cogs in an ongoing system; societies of agents are composed of competent performers who consciously learn their roles and sometimes alter them in pursuing their ends.

This is not to say that social rules or roles do not shape the behavior of the members of a social group. A priest saying Mass must follow certain procedures and formulations spelled out by liturgical rules. The rules dictate what the priest must do; indeed, if certain rules are violated no Mass takes place no matter what the priest may wish. The role of Mass-sayer is quite narrowly circumscribed by Church rules, the role of priest somewhat more loosely, the role of Catholic more loosely still. But in all these cases an agent's behavior is enabled and molded by social rules and roles.

These rules and roles can be one of two types: either regulative or constitutive. *Regulative rules and roles* indicate what behaviors and relations are permitted or prohibited; *constitutive rules and roles* make certain forms of activity possible. For instance, the rule in chess "if you touch a piece you must move it" is a regulative rule which indicates that players are not allowed to provisionally move a piece to a square in order to inspect its vulnerability to attack. But the rule "if the king is captured the game is over" is a different sort of rule. It doesn't so much regulate moves in the game as make the game of chess possible. This rule underwrites chess as the activity it is, such that without this rule chess-playing would not exist. Some (constitutive) rules of chess provide for the possibility of activities

64

like castling and checkmating, while other (regulative) rules spell out permissible limits to these moves. As regulative, rules constrain behavior; as constitutive, rules enable it. Following Anthony Giddens (whose thoughts about society I am mining here) we may call these enabling and constraining rules and roles the *structure* of a society.

But we should not be misled by the term "structure": structures are not physical entities which act over the heads of those they influence. Rather, as providers of rules and roles structures require interpretive activity on the part of those who act in terms of them in order for the structure to be realized. Structure provides the conditions for the possibility of action and guides as to how actions are to be performed, but it is agents who produce and reproduce this structure by means of their activity. The rules of chess, for instance, operate in a given situation because two players have understood them and made them their own (they may well alter them, too). Social structures do not operate like programs determining the movements of mechanical robots; rather, they require the activity of thinking and feeling agents who must appropriate these structures in order for them to exist.

Structure and action are thus not antithetical to one another. On the one hand, social structures don't dictate to utterly compliant automatons with no will of their own; on the contrary, social structures require intelligent agents to be realized. On the other hand, actions are only possible because they are enabled by certain social structures and constrained by others. The intrinsic connection between structure and action involves a constant interplay between them as structures underwrite actions which sometimes reinforce and sometimes undermine the structures which authorize them. Structures enable actions, and actions produce and reproduce structures. (Giddens calls this interplay between action and structure "structuration." He uses this verbal formulation to suggest the active and diachronic nature of society.)

Where does all this leave us with regard to the notion of "society"? Society on this view is not a thing at all but a process – a process of structuration and the patterned consequences of this structuration. On this view society doesn't "do" anything: it is not a *thing which has* power but is rather a *process in which* social practices are ordered through time. (In this way, "society" is like "culture": it is not a noun but a verb.) Societies are essentially temporal entities (like football games, trials, and Catholic masses), not things which mold and shape other independent things. Indeed, society just *is* the dynamic working through of rule and role-governed patterns of interaction among agents whose identity and relative position change constantly partly on the basis of the way these agents interpret the rules and roles.

65

3.5   Determination and Agency

Does our culture or society make us what we are? The answer to this depends in part on how "culture," "society," and "make" are defined. Holists answer this question affirmatively by conceiving of culture and society as *things* which *determine* their members rather like the way dies stamp out metal products. But our analysis of culture as a discordant conversation and society as a process of structuration calls this holist way of thinking into question. In particular, it highlights the way holism fails to provide an adequate role for human agency.

Enculturation is not a process of memorizing or mimicking or reproducing: it is rather a process of active learning and modification (what I have called "appropriation"). Cultural meaning is not imprinted on people like a tattoo: they must understand it, know how to employ it, apply it to new circumstances, alter it when situations change, and make it their own. Unlike a tattoo, culture requires its bearers constantly to ratify it or revivify it on the basis of reflection and judgment if it is to be effective in regulating feeling, thought, and action. Culture is not self-executing the way a computer program is: it requires reflective competence in order for it to be effective.

The holist view of culture as a text to be learned exaggerates the integrity of any cultural tradition and its power to inscribe itself on its members. Holism fails to take adequate notice of the active way individuals learn a particular cultural tradition: it misidentifies learning with mere absorption. Cultural learning is a process of contested appropriation in which cultural meanings are continually re-interpreted and re-inscribed by those who make them their own. Members of cultures are not mere sponges which simply soak up their contents. For this reason cultures are rich amalgams of only partially coherent definitions, rules, and ideals, the result of ongoing inner struggles and external influences.

The same is true for society. It is a process of structuration in which organized sets of rules and roles are embodied in ongoing practices through the interpretive and willful activity of conscious agents. Conceived this way a society cannot be an independent thing operating over the heads of its members, automatically producing their behavior in the way some machines take raw materials and churn out duplicate copies. Structuration like enculturation involves active appropriation by human agents.

Yet we must be careful here. Human activity always occurs within a cultural and social setting, a setting which agents did not create simply by their own activity, and which continues both to provide the resources in virtue of which their activity is possible and to limit the range of this activity in important ways. As Marx so well put it: "Men make their own history but they do not do so just as they please; they do not make it under circumstances chosen by themselves, but under circumstances directly encountered, given, and transmitted from the past" (Marx, 1977 (1851), p. 300).

Our original culture and society are imposed on us in that we did not, and could not, choose them. We acquired the capacities necessary to be agents in and through being enculturated and socialized into a particular culture and society. Moreover, the particular concepts, ways of thinking and feeling, rules and roles through which we are the particular persons we are have been given to us willy-nilly.

Further, our cultures and societies continue both to enable and to constrain us. Our culture provides the conceptual and affective resources by means of which we act – including the ways we resist, manipulate, and create new meanings and rules. Without certain constitutive rules and roles certain forms of identity are impossible. Moreover, regulative rules and roles delimit the range of permissible activity, penalizing behavior and thought which falls outside them, depriving violators of adequate resources, and sometimes preventing certain prohibited or shocking behavior or thought through imprisonment, shunning, or commitment to a psychiatric ward.

In any case, agency is a relative trait: one can have more or less of it. Some people are more "agential" than others by virtue of their place in the social order, their skill, their dispositions, and so on. All people in so far as they are interpreting and responding creatures are agents. But they may enact their agency in more or less direct, more or less effective, ways. For instance, traditionally the agency of peasants has been severely circumscribed because their society and culture afford them little room in which to affect their social arrangements. Indeed, these arrangements are often designed by those in power to undermine the peasants' capacity to act, even trying to hide from the peasants that they are indeed agents.

Part of being an effective agent consists in recognizing that one is indeed an agent. This is Paulo Freire's (1972) point: even the oppressed are agents, but because they don't recognize this fact about themselves they enact their agency in hesitant and ineffective ways. He calls for the appropriate "pedagogy" to aid them to recognize their powers of agency, so that, recognizing these powers, they will be able to express them all the more forcefully and proficiently.

All this suggests that in examining the relation between active creatures and their culture and society the key notion of "make" needs to be sharpened up. A number of possible relations are suggested by it; among them are the following:

1   enable (by providing necessary resources);
2   constrain (by limiting the range of possible options);
3   select (by favoring certain ranges of outcomes);
4   mediate (by shaping the way one element affects another);
5   prevent (by thwarting certain kinds of changes);
6   determine (by establishing definitively the nature, kind, or quality of).

In some senses of the term "make," society and culture do make us what we are even on the processural view of culture and society which insists on the importance of agency. Our culture and society shape our personal and social identities by enabling and constraining us, by selecting, mediating, and preventing certain sorts of activity and outcomes. But they do not make us in the sense of determining who we are – that is, in the sense of establishing definitively our nature and qualities such that how we behave, think, and feel is simply a function of the culture and society in which we happen to live. In the processes of enculturation and socialization humans are not parrots. Or, to employ another metaphor, we are not just products of a process which stamps out people the way a cookie-cutter produces cookies.

3.6   Summing Up

Given that culture and society are processes in which agents actively participate in the production and reproduction of meaning and ongoing patterns of relation, it follows that neither culture nor society are the sorts of things which can determine the character or nature of their members. Cultures and societies aren't separate entities which mold and shape their members; indeed, they just are the ongoing interactions of their members. They have no power independent of the participation of those they influence.

It follows from this that to be a member of a certain culture or society by virtue of being socialized and/or enculturated into it is not to become a clone of every other member. Membership does not imply similarity. As agents we appropriate culture, and as members of a society we continually produce and reproduce it by the way we interpret its meanings and embody its rules. Consequently cultures and societies are forever changing through the creative and innovative power of their members.

Thus holism as I have defined it cannot be correct. We are not mere reflections of the culture and society to which we belong. No cultural entity or social group is so fixed, closed, or coherent that we can be a reflection of it; indeed, group definition is an ongoing process in which its members struggle with one another to find a suitable place for themselves within a structure of beliefs and rules whose power depends on their interpretive activity. So there is no reason to believe that, just because we have been enculturated within a certain culture or socialized within a certain society, that we are thereby trapped within it or determined by it.

However, we must not exaggerate in this. Cultural and social activities are both enabled and constrained by certain cultural concepts and beliefs and social rules and roles. Agents become agents only by being enculturated and socialized into a particular culture and society – processes which pre-date them, and which continue to provide the means in and through which agents can act. Both cultural and social practices license certain forms of behavior and identity. Moreover, these ongoing patterns of interaction provide resources to their participants and in this way affect them, both constraining and rewarding certain forms of activity.

So does our culture and society make us what we are? The answer cannot be a simple yes or no. If by "make" you understand "enable and/or constrain" then our culture and society indeed make us (though we must be careful not to picture this making as the operation of a press which forces material into a particular mold). But if by "make" you mean "determine" then our culture and society do not make us what we are: in the process of enculturation and socialization we are not passive entities upon which cultural imperatives and social rules are impressed as if we were a wax tablet (though we must be careful not to picture our appropriative activity as unconstrained or as possible absent the resources provided by our culture and society).

Conceive of culture as a process of appropriation and society as a process of structuration in which meanings and rules are applied through the interpretive and willful activity of conscious agents. Doing so will reveal the ways culture and society can shape their members without their being independent things operating over the heads of their members, automatically producing their behavior as if they were mindless cogs in an elaborate machine.

In the last two chapters we have examined two approaches which appear to be the antithesis of each other. Atomism insists that the basic elements of social analysis are individuals; holism counters that, on the contrary, individuals are the products of cultural and social forces, and that therefore culture and society must be the bottom-line units of analysis. Usually philosophers of social science and social theorists have argued for one *or* the other of these alternatives, emphasizing either the individual *or* culture/society.

But we have seen that neither of these alternatives is acceptable because they are both one-sided. Atomism insists on the uniqueness and agency of individuals without adequately appreciating the way individuals need others to be what they are. Holism steps forward here, providing insights into the way culture and society both enable and constrain individuals, their thoughts, feelings, and actions. But holism goes too far in this, neglecting the fact that humans are agents and that enculturation and socialization are ongoing processes of appropriation. Also, holists reify culture and society, making them into things which have power, rather than ongoing processes in which power is expressed and enacted. The result is that holism is as one-sided as atomism only in the opposite direction.

A more satisfactory view is to combine both atomism and holism or, more accurately, to take from atomism and holism their principal insights and combine them in a way which avoids their excessiveness. This is what Giddens's theory of structuration accomplishes, as does Burke's conception of culture as a conversation (provided it is suitably amended). Atomism correctly insists on the importance of agency in human social life; holism correctly insists on the importance of the ways culture and society shape human activity. Understood in these terms atomism and holism are not necessarily competing views. Do we make our culture and society, or do they make us? The correct answer is not to accept the false dichotomy operative in this question; the proper answer is, therefore, "both." We both make our culture and society and they in turn shape us. The choice is *not* culture/society *or* individual agency, but culture/society *and* agency.

If you conceive of culture and society in the processural terms detailed in this chapter, and if you think of the self in similar processural terms outlined in the preceding chapter, this more inclusive and compatibilistic viewpoint, which combines agency with cultural and social power, will be much easier to appreciate.

Further Reading

The perspective of this chapter has been heavily influenced by Anthony Giddens (1976; 1979; and 1991), and Renata Rosaldo (1989). On Giddens, see Held and Thompson (1989), and Bryant and Jarry (1991). For further discussion of the topics of this chapter, see also Burke (1957), Clifford (1988), and Bhabha (1994).

For a useful discussion of various approaches to culture, see Alexander and Seidman (1990). Jenks (1993) also offers an excellent overview of the idea of culture.

For an example of a processural view of class, see Thompson (1963); of desires as they figure in economic theory, Lindblom (1990); of blood feuding, Keiser (1991); and of world history as a whole, McNeill (1995).

For holism, see James (1984) and the readings collected in part VI of Martin and MacIntyre (1994). For systems theory, see Easton (1965). For structuralism, see the readings collected in de George and de George (1972), and Petit (1977). See also Lévi-Strauss (1967 and 1970), and Althusser (1970).

The degree to which Foucault was a structuralist is a debated point. Dreyfus and Rabinow (1982) offer a view closer to the one I provide, insisting that the *Archaelogy of Knowledge* "shares certain fundamental assumptions with the structuralist approach" (xxiv), and that Foucault's later work "preserves the structural technique of focusing on both discourse and speaker as constructed objects" (xxvii). For an alternative reading of Foucault's *oeuvre*, see Rouse (1994).

For rule following, see Wittgenstein (1968, sections 172–242), and Kripke (1982). For the distinction between constitutive and regulative rules, see Rawls (1955).

For a discussion of modes of determination, see Wright (1978), chapter 1.

For a discussion of sex and gender, see Butler (1990), Giddens (1992), and Devor (1989).

71

4
Do People in Different Cultures Live in Different Worlds?

4.1 Perspectivism

Perspectivism is the dominant epistemological mode of contemporary intellectual life. *Perspectivism* is the view that all knowledge is essentially perspectival in character; that is, knowledge claims and their assessment always take place *within* a framework that provides the conceptual resources in and through which the world is described and explained. According to perspectivism knowers never view reality directly as it is in itself; rather they approach it from their own slant, with their own assumptions and preconceptions.

Perspectivism replaced *positivism* as the dominant view. Broadly speaking, positivists thought that it is possible, if one follows the so-called "scientific method," to attain fully warranted, objective knowledge. Positivists reasoned that if scientists could rid themselves of their biases they could grasp directly the facts about reality, and could objectively test various theories to determine which best explained these facts. Positivists believed that empirical observation and testing freed of preconceptions are the means by which facts are ascertained and explained. Hence they emphasized techniques of observation, measurement, and quantification, and they required scientists to ground their theories in overt behavior which is observable. (For a more detailed characterization of positivism, see "Further Reading" at the end of this chapter.)

Why does positivism gradually yield to perspectivism? Begin with the fact that even on a positivist view science cannot consist simply of the piling up of more and more facts. If this were the case, the *New York Telephone Book* or the *Guinness Book of World Records* would be candidates for the Nobel Prize. Science is explanatory as well as descriptive, and scientists ask questions about reality ("why did that happen?"; "how does that work?") as well as report on its states of affairs. Because science wishes to explain events in the world it must focus its attention on certain aspects of it. This means that scientists must sort facts not just gather them – must be rather more like mushroom cullers (in which varieties must be classified) and rather less like cherry pickers (in which mere quantity is the goal).

Imagine yourself being asked to describe an automobile accident you just witnessed by confining yourself just to the facts about it. The result would undoubtedly be an incoherent jumble of descriptive statements. If your only guide is to confine yourself just to the facts you have no way of distinguishing significant facts from insignificant ones. Consequently you would have no way of sorting facts into appropriate levels: the gross would be indiscriminately mixed up with the minute because you would have no way of telling which was which. Nor could you tell the superficial from the deep because you would have no principle which would select out those which are telling from those which are not.

Descriptions are only possible if describers can select the significant facts, can match facts as to their appropriate level, and can distinguish the deep from the superficial. But in order to do this they must be in possession of principles on the basis of which they can make these sorts of judgments. Thus, for example, you must already know what constitutes normal car operation before you can tell that the blue car losing a wheel is a significant fact whereas insects being struck by its hood (bonnet) are not.

Facts are not just states of affairs which present themselves immediately sorted out and identified. Think of these facts about the accident: "the blue car lost its front wheel"; "the red car swerved to the right"; "the side of the red car was crumpled and covered in blue paint." Each of these facts consists of phenomena picked out and grouped under a particular description. Note here that it is never phenomena themselves which are the facts but *phenomena under a particular description*. Facts are linguistically meaningful entities which select out from the stream of events what happened or what exists. But this means that in order for there to be facts at all there must be a vocabulary in terms of which they can be described. Without a prior vocabulary which a describer brings to a situation there would be no facts whatsoever.

Where does this vocabulary come from? Describers must possess some scheme of terms to provide the basic building blocks for their factual descriptions. Without such a scheme they would literally be mute, unable to say anything at all. (Imagine picking out the facts of an accident without any words!) Put succinctly: facts are rooted in conceptual schemes.

This is obvious in the natural sciences. The scattershot maps which result from collisions of subatomic particles yield descriptive statements about bosons and muons only because of highly developed atomic theory, which is the basis both for particle accelerators and for the vocabulary in terms of which observations are made and reported. But the same is true in social science as well. Only through the eyes of Marxian theory can we observe surplus value and therefore exploitation; only through the psychology of moral development can we identify a person's response as "post-conventional"; only through rational choice theory can we link a series of actions together as part of a strategy and describe them as "satisficing."

So description requires a scheme consisting of terms by means of which facts will be constituted, and principles of significance on the basis of which facts can be sorted and related. Without such a scheme even the most ordinary descriptions of the most mundane events could not take place. This is exactly what perspectivism claims: without an organizing conceptual scheme no intellectual activity, even something as basic as simple description, can occur. Descriptions always take place *within* a framework which provides the conceptual resources in and through which reality (or events and objects in it) is described.

What does the dependency of facts on such schemes reveal about the nature of facts? It shows, in the first place, that all facts are what has been called "theory-impregnated." A fact about an auto accident is a fact only because describers of it possess a prior conception or theory as to what is and what is not relevant to the performance of automobiles, and because they have a theoretical vocabulary in terms of which they can report their observations. It follows that no hard and fast distinction exists between facts and theories. Indeed, because facts are theory-impregnated it is more accurate to say that facts are themselves theoretical entities, albeit of a low-level, usually observational variety. Thus, facts might be best defined as "low-level theoretical entities unlikely to be contested."

The theoretical nature of even the most humdrum facts explains why there are so many different ways to describe the same event (indeed, what constitutes the same event will itself be a matter of the conceptual scheme in terms of which an event is individuated). It also explains something about the nature of scientific progress. The history of science consists in part of the emergence of different kinds of descriptions: from descriptions which are relatively implicit and coarse to those which are explicit and refined (from "that country is wealthy" to "that country has a GNP of . . ."); from those which are relatively obvious to those which are relatively recondite (from "inherited trait" to "recessive allele on chromosome 14"); and from those which are relatively subjective to those which are relatively objective (from "cold" to "3 degrees Kelvin"). Scientific advancement takes place at the level of description not just because as science progresses more sophisticated observational equipment becomes available, but also because scientists develop more complex, more precise, and more general conceptual schemes which provide more sophisticated and more precise descriptive terminology.

Just as descriptive statements are rooted in theories, theories themselves are nested in larger conceptual structures. Science aspires to link individual theories together to form a network of theories. The theories of the unconscious, of dreams, of psychosocial development, and repression are all linked together to form the Freudian theory of the psyche; the theory of capitalism is only part of a much larger set of Marxist theories which includes theories of ideology, society, politics, and history. That theories are so linked derives in part from the nature of science: it seeks to explain a divergent and extensive range of phenomena in terms of a few basic principles. (The culmination of such links might conceivably be a single comprehensive theory which would explain all phenomena deemed significant – the so-called "Theory of Everything" (TOE).)

Theories are also linked because individual theories are themselves explained by higher level, more general theories. For example, the theory of consumer behavior in neo-classical economic theory is itself explained by the more abstract theory of preference; the theory of voting behavior in political science is a special case of the theory of rational choice; the theory of manifest and latent functions is explained in terms of the larger theory of structural-functionalism. Science's answers to particular "why" questions do not stop inquiry but spur it on to ask further why questions about the answers themselves: Why x? Because y. But why y? Because z. But why z? . . .

But the most important reason why individual theories are linked into networks is that they ultimately draw upon fundamental assumptions and concepts for their articulation. All theories presuppose some basic commitments as to the fundamental building blocks of a subject, to the basic concepts by which to identify and describe these building blocks, and to basic claims about the nature of these building blocks. They do so for two reasons: first, these commitments provide the guidestar for theory development, indicating what can and cannot be changed as various modifications and developments in a network occur. Thus, no matter what revisions are proposed in Marxian theory, the notion of class cannot be abandoned if it is to remain Marxist. Or the notion that social systems are comprised not of individuals but of roles cannot be forsaken if systems theory is to be true to its core.

Second, scientific theory presupposes basic conceptual commitments because these commitments provide the material on the basis of which theories are formulated. Any highly developed theory of human behavior and society, for instance, will rest on certain basic assumptions about human motivation, sociality, and rationality, which are its core. This core might best be likened to a volcano: from it spews the materials out of which various formations will be molded and shaped. Think, for instance, of neo-classical economic theory: it derives from certain basic notions of humans as rational utility maximizers; or of Marxian theory: it derives from certain deep assumptions about the nature of human labor; or of systems theory and its assumption that human societies operate independently of individual intention and will.

Notice how far we have moved from positivism. Descriptions are shot through with theoretical material, are indeed (low-level) theories. Individual theories are nested in theoretical networks. And such networks are themselves rooted in basic concepts and assumptions out of which explanatory theories and descriptions are fashioned. Let us call a complex of interrelated, hierarchically arranged basic assumptions and concepts a "conceptual scheme." The characteristic scientific activities of observing, identifying, classifying, and explaining thus all take place within a conceptual scheme which communities of scientists bring to their work. Conceptual schemes provide the framework within which all scientific thinking occurs.

This is the way perspectivism portrays science. Human knowers cannot look at reality directly in some unmediated manner, no matter how much they try to purge their minds of prior ideas and concepts. It is a good thing that they cannot: for a blank slate is incapable of learning anything. Knowers have to bring to their experience a rich assortment of ideas and conceptual commitments in order even to describe what they see, i.e., in order even to have something about which to theorize. Without basic presuppositions, knowledge itself would be impossible. Thus, the positivistic ideal of knowledge as a mirror of the world as something which only reflects what is there but which in itself contributes nothing, is in error. All knowledge is a constructive activity in which knowers are active contributors.

4.2   Relativism

Perspectivism says simply that knowledge of the world is a function of the linguistic and conceptual framework within which particular knowers and agents live and operate. This claim found its first expression in the philosophy of Kant, who argued that certain categories of thought such as causality and temporality were necessary conditions for the possibility of any experience of the world. Nothing in perspectivism requires there be fundamental differences among frameworks; indeed, Kant thought that the conceptual framework underlying all human experience was the same for all, that it was shaped by a single universal set of categories.

But what if conceptual frameworks are radically different? Contrary to the Kantian idea of the universality of the basic categories, an important body of thought insists that neither in the notion of experience nor in the relation between the world and our ideas is a specific or unitary conceptual framework implied or required. Indeed, this way of thinking insists that conceptual schemes express fundamental commitments which can be deeply different among different cultures, time periods, and communities. The conceptual scheme of the Hopi people seems utterly different from that of modern Euro-Americans, the basic assumptions and categories of Aristotelian physics fundamentally at odds with those of Newtonian physics (which itself seems irreconcilable with Einsteinian physics).

The possibility of alternative and competing conceptual schemes provides an avenue by which perspectivism can be transformed from a fairly innocuous philosophical position into something quite provocative and powerful. Perspectivism combined with an insistence on radical conceptual difference contains within itself the seeds of relativism. *Relativism* as I will use the term is the doctrine that either experience (in the case of epistemological relativism) or reality (in the case of ontological relativism) is a function of a particular conceptual scheme. Thus, in the case of *epistemological relativism* the content, meaning, truth, rightness, and reasonableness of cognitive, ethical, or aesthetic beliefs, claims, experiences, or actions can only be determined from within a particular conceptual scheme. According to epistemological relativism no cross-framework judgments are permissible. In the case of *ontological relativism* reality itself is thought to be determined by the particular conceptual scheme of those living within it.

Begin with epistemological relativism. The simple perspectivism I described in section 4.1 claimed merely that our (scientific) *descriptions and explanations* of our experience and the world are perspectival in nature. This claim is compatible with our experience of the world being an independent basis on which to judge which descriptions and explanations are better than others. But what if *our experience itself* is also shaped and colored by our conceptual commitments? That is, what if the materials on the basis of which our experience is constituted derive in part from our particular conceptual scheme? In this case it would seem that we could not appeal to an independent criterion – human experience – by which to judge the merits of particular descriptions and explanations, since this criterion would itself be a function of the conceptual framework which underlay these descriptions and explanations. (Thus, we could not determine the relative merits of witchcraft as opposed to psychotherapy in the treatment of strange behavior – to describe such behavior as "psychic illness" would already beg the question – since how strange behavior is experienced would itself be shaped by whether one lived and believed in witchcraft or modern psychology.)

One of the most influential versions of the idea that our experience is a function of our conceptual scheme is the Whorf hypothesis. Benjamin Whorf studied the ways in which people in different linguistic groups experienced their world; on the basis of this study he concluded:

> We dissect nature along lines laid down by our native languages. The categories and types we isolate from the world of phenomena we do not find there because they stare every observer in the face; on the contrary, the world is presented in a kaleidoscopic flux of impressions which has to be organized by our minds – and this means largely by the linguistic system in our minds. (Whorf, 1954, p. 213)

Here Whorf concentrates primarily on sense experience, on our perceptions and sensations. His thesis is that what we sense is a function of the linguistic system within which we operate as cognitive beings. In order for there to be genuine experience, and not just a "bloomin, buzzin confusion" (to use William James's famous phrase), sensations must be organized into something focused and coherent. This is precisely what linguistic systems do: they provide the organizing principles on the basis of which an indiscriminate flow of stimulation is organized into true sense experience. But the interesting point is that each linguistic system organizes the flow of sensations into its own unique patterns so that those in different linguistic systems literally experience the world differently. Whorf himself claimed, on the basis of his study of the language of the Hopi Indians, that the Hopi conceptualize, and therefore experience, time and space quite differently from modern Europeans. Likewise, E. P. Thompson argued that only after the proletariat was subjected to the work discipline of capitalism did it begin to experience time in a linear fashion. And we have all heard the example of the Eskimos who have twenty-four words for snow, and who therefore supposedly see the winter landscape differently from those whose descriptive terminology for snow is less extensive.

Epistemological relativism claims not only that our perceptions are organized differently according to the linguistic or conceptual system to which we belong, but also that our ways of thinking are also determined by our conceptual scheme. What constitutes acceptable ways of cognizing and drawing inferences is a function of the conceptual scheme under which we live. Take for example Levy-Bruhl's idea that "primitives" think in a "pre-logical" and mystical manner. As he put it:

[Primitive thought] is not constrained, above all else, as ours is, to avoid contradictions. The same logical exigencies are not in its case always present. What to our eyes is impossible or absurd, it sometimes will admit without any difficulty. (Levy-Bruhl, 1931, p. 21)

This is a very powerful claim. It asserts not just that our sensations are fundamentally different from those who live in different conceptual schemes, but that so are the very ways we think. The laws of logic, for instance, which we may naively assume are universal, are nothing of the sort: the principles which govern my thought may be radically unlike the principles governing the thought of non-western or primitive peoples. Levy-Bruhl emphasized the poetical and analogical character of so-called primitive thinking, and contrasted it with the logical, scientific nature of western European thought.

Levy-Bruhl's is a particular instance of the thesis that epistemic principles are derived from one's particular conceptual scheme. By "epistemic principles" I mean second-order beliefs about which (first-order) beliefs are acceptable. Examples of epistemic principles are: "accept only those beliefs for which extensive empirical evidence exists"; "accept only what the Koran says"; "accept what tradition has told us to be the case." Relativists claim not only that epistemic principles vary from group to group, from age to age (this seems an obvious point), but that they have no foundation other than the practices of a certain cultural or historical setting. In so far as epistemic principles differ and are merely historically given in accord with a conceptual scheme it is impossible to evaluate and judge the relative merits of one scheme against another. For the principles of judgment would themselves be internal to one scheme or another, and thus any such exercise would merely beg the question at issue.

Up to now I have been describing the way epistemological relativism depicts our experience of, and thought and speech about, reality. But for ontological relativists this has implications regarding the nature of reality itself. In brief, the argument for ontological relativism goes like this. Our only access to reality is our experience of it; we can say nothing more about it except what our sensations, thoughts, and words can tell us about it. But this implies that ultimately there is no basis to distinguish between our experience of reality and reality itself. But since our experience of reality is conceptually scheme-dependent – assuming epistemological relativism to be true – then it would seem to follow that *reality itself is also conceptually scheme-dependent*. The reality of those in one conceptual scheme (and not just their thought about this reality) would consequently be different from the reality of those living in a different conceptual scheme. Put succinctly: if reality is a function of our experience, and if our experience is a function of

79

our conceptual scheme, then our reality is a function of our conceptual scheme. This is precisely what ontological relativism claims: people inhabiting different conceptual schemes do not just think about or experience the same world differently; instead they live in different worlds.

That epistemological relativism leads to ontological relativism can be seen explicitly in the work of the thinker most responsible for the idea that scientific thinking necessarily occurs within a conceptual scheme, Thomas Kuhn (see Kuhn, 1970). In *The Structure of Scientific Revolutions*, reflecting on the emergence of the idea of oxygen during the late eighteenth century, Kuhn wrote:

> Lavoisier . . . saw oxygen where Priestly had seen . . . dephlogistinated air and where others had seen nothing at all . . . At the very least, as a result of discovering oxygen, Lavoisier saw nature differently. And in the absence of that hypothetical fixed nature that he "saw differently," the principle of economy will urge us to say that after discovering oxygen Lavoisier worked in a different world. (Kuhn, 1970, p. 118)

Here Kuhn begins with a certain epistemological belief, namely, that the way the world appears ("Lavoisier saw nature differently") is a function of particular conceptual commitments (here, the existence of oxygen). He combines this belief with a philosophical principle ("the principle of economy") that ultimately all that can be said about the world is how it appears. From this conjunction it is an easy step to the conclusion that with a new oxygen-based conceptual scheme "Lavoisier worked in a different world." Pushed hard enough, epistemological relativism leads to ontological relativism.

Epistemological and ontological relativism taken together imply that so deep are the differences which separate those within different frameworks that their experiences and beliefs would be fundamentally incommensurable. By *incommensurable* I mean that no common measure can serve as a bridge among different conceptual schemes. Those inside one conceptual scheme would be living in their own reality, one different from those living in other conceptual schemes; and the experiences of the respective members would be so different that no basis could exist on which to understand each other. Indeed, translation between different conceptual schemes would be impossible, since the meaning of the terms located within one conceptual scheme would differ as a result of their location within this conceptual scheme. No neutral language could exist in virtue of which one conceptual scheme could be translated without residue or loss into the terms of another.

Moreover, none of these elements could be the subject of rational scrutiny from outside the particular conceptual scheme within which it is located. Rational inquiry must itself be carried out in terms of the basic commitments of a given conceptual scheme because it is this framework which provides the criteria on the basis of which explanations, assessments, and judgments are made. Nor can the elements of a conceptual scheme be compared with some conceptual scheme-neutral reality to see whether it matches up or not, because there is no conceptual scheme-neutral reality. Thus one cannot change from one conceptual scheme to another on the basis of rational analysis. Such change must be like a gestalt switch or a religious conversion (to use two metaphors employed by Kuhn), a sudden shift away from one way of perceiving the world to another.

If relativism is correct, then what is true for those in one conceptual scheme need not be true for those in other conceptual schemes. Their realities would themselves be different, and what it means for an assertion to be true would itself be a function of the epistemic commitments of their conceptual scheme. For those in colonial Salem, therefore, it may well be true that there were witches, whereas for those living in contemporary scientific communities it is not true that witches exist. Magic is efficacious in magical terms in various parts of the modern-day Caribbean but not so in other parts of the world. In general, what is true for those in one conceptual scheme need not be true for others operating in terms of another. Relativism would have us abandon the notion of an independent truth, one that is true no matter what people think or feel.

Kuhn himself employed the notion of a paradigm to illuminate the practices of communities of natural scientists. But some thinkers have extended this notion to cover more extensive communities. In a looser and perhaps analogical sense, an entire culture might be considered a paradigm. After all, cultures provide the vocabulary, concepts, and epistemic dispositions in and through which people form their beliefs. Isn't becoming the person one is in large part becoming enculturated within one's own culture, and doesn't this culture structure one's (possible) experience? Isn't it in terms of one's own culture that one's basic commitments, one's fundamental assumptions, one's primary dispositions are formed? And isn't it on the basis of these that one sees the world and judges others in it? Indeed, isn't one's world a result of one's culture – the world of the Ilongot headhunter fundamentally different from the world of the California surfer?

In so far as the world in which we live derives from our conceptual framework, and in so far as fundamentally different frameworks are incommensurable with respect to each other, it follows that those within radically different frameworks live in different worlds which are radically separate from one another. This is the final picture of relativism: isolated groups trapped inside separate spheres unable to understand or share or communicate with others in different groups. *Relativism ends in separatism.*

How ironic, since one of the deepest motivations behind relativism, and one of its most attractive features, is its recognition of difference and its respect for it. Relativists are deeply impressed by the variation in belief, desire, morals, reasoning – in short, conceptual schemes – of people from age to age and group to group. Relativists want to avoid *ethnocentrism* which thinks that everybody is just like us. Relativists want not just to tolerate difference; they want to trumpet it and to celebrate it.

But instead of joining us to others in ways that are respectful and appreciative, relativism separates us into enclaves of mutual incomprehension. Motivated by a deep appreciation of the ways people are different from one another, it ends up making it impossible for us to recognize and appreciate this difference. Something has thus gone very wrong with this line of reasoning. Is there a way to recognize difference without making it into a wall of separation?

4.3   The Argument From Translation

Relativism claims that we live inside radically different and incommensurable conceptual schemes which shape not only our knowledge of the world but our world itself. According to relativism people living in different conceptual schemes live in different worlds. But do they? Is the relativist picture correct?

Assume that all knowledge *is* perspectival, resting on fundamental commitments and presuppositions. Assume further that deep differences exist among competing conceptual schemes and that this explains why discontinuity is a mark of the history of science, the history of thought, and the history of cultures. Is relativism entailed by these assumptions? No it is not. In a moment I shall present an argument – "the Argument from Translation" – to see why not. Relativism's biggest mistake is failing to see that difference requires a background of deep similarity; as a result it overemphasizes difference while failing to appreciate what is shared.

But note first the strangeness of Kuhn's relativism in the context of natural or social science. For Kuhn paradigms are in competition with one another: the Newtonian paradigm versus the Einsteinian paradigm in physics, or the Keynesian paradigm against the monetarist paradigm in economics, for example. Kuhn claimed that paradigms are incommensurable in that claims made within one paradigm cannot be translated into claims made within another without significant loss, nor can they be neutrally judged as to their cognitive merits. Kuhn also maintained that "the proponents of competing paradigms practice their trades in different worlds" (Kuhn, 1970, p.150). But doesn't this render the notion of competition utterly nonsensical? If Keynesians and monetarists lived in different worlds, then their paradigms wouldn't refer to the same thing and so they could not compete with one another. Moreover, if these paradigms were literally incommensurable, then Keynesians could not know what monetarists claimed, and vice versa, so that they couldn't tell how their ideas about inflation or unemployment or other economic phenomena differed from the monetarists'. In order to be in competition paradigms must refer to the same object, and they must be sufficiently inter-translatable to be offering divergent explanations of the same phenomena.

And why shouldn't competing paradigms be about the same world and be sufficiently intertranslatable? Can't different paradigms overlap in certain respects, especially in their observational components? Isn't what occurs in the world in some important way independent of our paradigms? Can't different paradigms submit to the same evaluative criteria despite their differences? Surely both Keynesians and monetarists can both agree that the price of tomatoes is $1.79/lb. at the corner grocery store, or that tomato futures are selling at $2.10/lb. in the Chicago commodity market. This they can do for three reasons. First, despite their conceptual differences both have access to a similar stock of descriptive terms and observational techniques (that is, they both can go to the corner store, or call the commodity market, to ask the price of tomatoes, and they can both use terms like "price in dollars per pound" to report what they learn). Second, they can agree because the price of tomatoes is a fact about the world, not a construction of either Keynesianism or monetarism. Third, both Keynesians and monetarists can and do subject their explanations and predictions to the same sort of scientific scrutiny because, despite their differences, they share a common commitment to canons of empirical theory testing.

Our ideas do not *constitute* our world, as ontological relativism would have it. The universe after 1543 did not suddenly change shape because Copernicus published *De Revolutionibus Orbium Coelestium* claiming that the earth was not its center. Moreover, if in 1542 an astrophysicist operating within a Ptolemaic conceptual scheme claimed that the earth was the center of the universe and in 1543 a follower of Copernicus asserted that it was not, this does not mean that they were not referring to the same object (the earth), nor does it mean that each claim was true (because truth is relative to conceptual scheme) – unless of course the universe physically changed in 1543. Our thoughts about reality do not make it what it is. (We might even define reality as that which resists us, as that which jumps

83

up and bites us despite our beliefs, desires, and the deep presuppositions of our conceptual scheme.)

Taken to its logical conclusion the notion of radically different scientific paradigms competing with one another implodes on itself. Competing paradigms must be about the *same* world, and must share sufficiently similar vocabulary and canons of investigation, in order to be in competition with one another. One might say that disagreement among paradigms presupposes a fundamental background of agreement.

This same conclusion can be reached in a more general way, one that is not restricted to the world of science and competing scientific explanations. The Argument from Translation shows that we cannot interpret others both as operating within a conceptual scheme and at the same time as massively different from ourselves. But this is just what relativism asserts: it declares that others can live and work within radically different conceptual schemes which are incommensurable. Thus, if the Argument from Translation is correct, relativism of the sort described in section 4.2 is in error.

The Argument from Translation is derived from the work of Donald Davidson (1974). It consists of seven steps:

(1)   *To claim that others live in a different conceptual world from us is to claim that they speak and think.*

This is obvious: to inhabit a conceptual world just *is* to think and speak.

(2)   *To claim that others speak and think we need to know that they are actually saying something (and not just producing noises).*

Automobiles, guided missiles, and automatic teller machines make noises at regular intervals, sometimes followed by changes in their behavior. But none of them actually thinks and speaks. Bees, dolphins, chimpanzees in the wild, chimpanzees trained by human linguists, schizophrenics, and human babies also make such noises followed by changes in their behavior. Whether they are thinking and communicating is less clear because it is difficult to ascertain whether in their noisemaking they are actually saying something or not.

Squiggles on a piece of paper, vibrations of the air, blips on a computer screen, electro-chemical processes in the brain – these and many other phenomena may or may not be instances of actual thought and communication. Only if they are can we consider them as instances of operating within a conceptual scheme.

(3)   *To know that others are saying something we need to know at least some of what they mean.*

How can we know that others' utterances are more than just some elaborate chain of auditory causes and effects? Consider a group of aliens

84

discovered on another planet whose members are constantly squawking. Are these noises genuine talk? Sometimes the noises are followed by changes in behavior; but the same could be said about the squeaks in your automobile, or the interactions among the elements of your heating system. In order to know that the aliens' noises are genuine acts of communication in which various aliens say something to one another, we must know that they mean something by them.

But how do we know this? We might assume on the basis of the complexity of the interactions that meaningful communication was occurring, but this would be insufficient: complexity in itself does not show meaningfulness. (Think of the complexity of the interactions between two supercomputers even though no meaningful talk occurs between them.) Only if we can plausibly interpret the meaning of at least some of the noises and marks do we have good reason to believe that the noises are part of a system of meaningful interaction. (Think of the position of psychiatrists who cannot make heads or tails of any of the mutterings of a psychotic patient; in this case they cannot determine whether this murmuring is genuine talk or not.)

To conclude that the aliens mean something by their squawks we must be able to ascertain what some of these squawks mean; not to know what any of them mean is to be unable to assert that meaningful talk is occurring. (We needn't know, of course, what *every* utterance means in order to conclude that the aliens are indeed speaking a language.)

(4) *To know what others mean we need to be able to translate their utterances into our language.*

To answer the question, What does the utterance "squawk squawk squawk" mean?, we must be able to express in our language the functional equivalent of what is being said in the alien language. So "squawk squawk squawk" might mean "Earthlings are dangerous." Assigning meaning in this context is just translating from the alien language to the home language.

(5) *But to translate their utterances we need to ascribe to them various beliefs, desires, attitudes, and ways of connecting these mental elements.*

To interpret the meaning of a string of noises or marks we must determine what beliefs and/or desires are expressed by means of this string. Thus to ascertain that "squawk squawk squawk" means "Earthlings are dangerous" we need to assume something about the aliens' beliefs (that they know of our existence; that they think we come from earth; that they suppose we want to enslave them); their desires (that they don't want to be enslaved); their linguistic attitudes (that they hold their verbal reports to be true, and not, say, something just said in jest); and the principles by which they connect these various elements (such that a belief that certain entities are likely to enslave and a desire to avoid slavery when combined will lead the aliens to conclude that these entities are dangerous). Meanings constitutively arise out of beliefs, desires, and principles of thought such that altering the interpretation of any one of them will require adjustments in how (some of) the others are interpreted.

(6) *But to ascribe such mental elements to them we must assume that they share with us a background of common beliefs, desires, and principles of thought, that we live in the same world.*

This is the key move in the Argument from Translation. We cannot take a first step in ascribing mental states to others unless we start with an assumption of general agreement in perception, belief, desire, semantic attitude, and principles of thought. In the example, only if we assume that like us aliens do not want to be enslaved can we ascribe to them the belief that earthlings are dangerous. Only if aliens connect belief with judgments of danger, and only if we assume that they mean what they say, do we have reason to claim that "squawk squawk squawk" actually indicates a judgment of danger on the part of the aliens. To assign any sort of meaning to their utterances we must assume a rough similarity in their mental life to ours; otherwise, we would have no basis on which to begin assigning any sort of meaning to their noisemaking.

This of course does not mean that the assumption of similarity cannot be violated at least within a limited range. As with people, aliens presumably have beliefs, desires, and principles of thought different from ours. They must make mistakes too, not always connecting the elements of their mental life in a way we or they would judge as proper. They must have their share of error. But these differences cannot be too great, for then the entire enterprise of determining the meaning of what they say (and consequently whether they are saying anything) would grind to a halt: we would have no basis upon which to proceed.

Consider two principles of thinking that govern communicative uses of language, the principle of non-contradiction, and the principle of evidence. Any language in which asserting occurs must distinguish between saying "p" and saying "not-p": if this distinction were unavailable then no referential communication of any sort could occur. (For example, if "it is snowing now" did not rule out "it is not snowing now" then "it is snowing now" would tell us nothing about whether it is snowing or not; it would say nothing.) But this means that any language sufficiently rich to include assertions must operate according to the principle of non-contradiction. (which says that "p" cannot imply "not p").

Moreover, any linguistic system which permitted assertions must also contain rules which connect experience and belief. Without such rules no notion of evidence is possible, and without a notion of evidence no distinction between "true," "seems true," and "false" – or between "ought to believe" and "ought not to believe" – can be drawn. But these distinctions are essential if assertions are to be made. (Thus, the assertion "it is snowing now" is the assertion it is – a claim about the weather at this moment, and not a claim about how one would like the weather to be, or what form one thinks the weather ought to take, or what one guesses the weather conditions are – because it implies evidence available about the weather conditions.) For a statement to be an assertion it must at least implicitly invoke evidence and thereby indirectly certain rules on the basis of which this evidence warrants such an assertion. In this way assertion-making presupposes a principle of evidence.

These two cases show that speakers of a language must behave in accord with principles of deductive reasoning (here the principle of non-contradiction) and principles of induction. These principles therefore cannot be ethnocentric impositions by "Westerners" or "males" or "phallocentrists" on an unwitting world. They are necessary principles of interpretation which must be assumed in any attempt to understand what others – even others very different from us – are saying. For us to know others we consequently must assume that their thought is like ours in being governed by principles of thought (though of course what counts as a violation of these principles may vary from culture to culture). Shorn of this assumption they would stand before us as unintelligible as the finches and warblers outside my window.

The same is true for certain basic epistemic capacities. To be intelligible we must assume that other creatures feel pain and normally wish to avoid it; that they can for the most part perceive large obstacles in their path; that they can usually detect when others are present and can sort them into categories; that they want to live; that they can communicate with one another; that they have attractions and repulsions; that their interactions are rule-governed and intentional; and a host of other abilities and dispositions. Of course, as we proceed we may come to cease ascribing some of these to them, but only reluctantly and only for cause, and only to preserve ascribing most of the rest to them. Without these assumptions we could not even begin the process of assigning meaning to their utterances.

If we are to interpret others as operating within a conceptual scheme we must assume that we share homely truths about the world and ways of reasoning with them. Without this assumption we have no basis for giving their utterances any interpretation and so we have no basis for conceiving them as having a conceptual scheme in the first place. (In the next chapter

87

we will explore this point more deeply by considering whether and in what way we must assume others are rational.)

(7)   *But to have a shared background of epistemic capacity, belief, and principles of reasoning is to live in the same world as they do.*

We cannot ascribe meaningful interaction to others and not assume that we live in the same world and that their concepts and their use overlap with ours in significant respects. Grasping the ways that others differ from us thus presupposes that their outlook shares a great deal with ours, and that the world they live in is a world we share with them. So the thesis of relativism – that others can recognizably live meaningfully within worlds incommensurable with ours – is mistaken.

4.4   Summing Up

Many today are perspectivist in their epistemological orientation. They believe that all cognitive activity – even the most mundane, like describing states of affairs – occurs within and through a conceptual framework. Reality is never directly available to cognizers in some unmediated way; rather, reality is perceived only through cognitive lenses in virtue of which epistemic perception is possible.

From these humble perspectivist beginnings many have been led down the path of relativism of both an epistemological and ultimately an ontological sort. They have felt compelled to believe not only that radically different conceptual schemes exist but that those thinking and acting within them live in separate worlds unable ultimately to communicate with one another. Relativism focuses on the differences between conceptual schemes so ferociously that finally all it can see is difference.

The Argument from Translation challenges this one-sided emphasis on difference and in the process undermines the move from perspectivism to relativism with its separatist orientation. The Argument shows that others recognizably operating with a particular set of concepts must share with us certain basic capacities, beliefs, and principles of thought. If they did not we could not understand them and so we would have no basis for declaring that they were employing a set of concepts in the first place. To identify others as different thus requires that we also identify the ways we are similar. Another way of putting this is that difference can only exist against a background of sharing. Thus if differences are too great – if difference becomes paramount so that what is shared fades from view – then we would have no basis to attribute any understanding to others at all, and so no reason to suppose that they even had views, let alone different ones.

An analogy might help here, one drawn from Kant's moral philosophy. Kant claimed that the maxim "lie whenever it furthers your interest" cannot be a universal maxim guiding everyone's behavior. Why not? Because if lying were to become the rule rather than the exception people would never be able to know whether anyone was telling the truth or not when someone asserted a proposition, and so they wouldn't be able to assume that what one said was true. But this means that the entire practice of assertion-making would be jeopardized: since when you said "it is raining outside" they would have no reason to believe you were telling the truth, the assertion "it is raining" therefore would no longer have any meaning and so would no longer be an assertion. If lying were to become the norm, then assertion would become impossible and so lying would itself become impossible because lies are assertions (albeit false ones). Lying depends on a background assumption of truth-telling. The same is true for disagreement: if we disagreed about everything there would be insufficient basis to compare and contrast our differences and so the usefulness of the notion of disagreement would evaporate. Disagreement is only possible against a background of agreement and must itself be the exception rather than the rule.

Agreement in basic epistemic capacity, with the great bulk of our beliefs, and in norms of thinking is an unavoidable presupposition of any claim that a group of potential cognizers and agents is operating within a conceptual scheme. This means that the claim that a conceptual scheme is radically different from ours and therefore incommensurable is incoherent: it asserts radical disagreement but presupposes fundamental agreement.

But even as we insist on the necessary similarity of those in recognizably different conceptual schemes we must not make the mistake of relativism only in reverse by insisting that all humans are the same. Insistence on background agreement does not imply that we must all agree in all important respects, or that two communities cannot understand each other's language and yet disagree about large and important areas of life (particularly at the more abstract and theoretical levels). The Argument from Translation does not imply unanimity. It localizes disagreement but doesn't abolish it. (In the next chapter we will explore a particular instance of agreement/disagreement in more depth, that having to do with rationality.)

Indeed, sometimes we must focus on and even celebrate difference. Insistence on conceptual difference is a necessary antidote to the cavalier ethnocentrism which has marked most of human history (in which the most typical judgment is that others are just like us only stupider, lazier, more cowardly, or less morally, aesthetically, or politically good). But we must do so without degenerating into the grosser forms of relativism which end in utter separatism, judging others as utterly unlike us, as truly alien.

A mature synthesis is required here. If we insist too heavily on dramatic dissimilarity then we lose the capacity to understand others (and therefore the capacity to appreciate their difference). If we insist on their dramatic similarity, then we lose the capacity to appreciate and understand difference and therefore to see others as something not ourselves; in this case, we would only see ourselves everywhere we turn. In relating to others the choice is not difference *or* similarity; it is difference *and* similarity.

So to return to the question of this chapter: people recognizably living in different cultures cannot be living in a different world; but they may well be living differently in the same world.

Further Reading

The argument of this chapter is heavily indebted to Davidson (1974) and to Lukes (1970; 1982). See also Turner (1980) for a good discussion of the matters discussed in this chapter.

The definition of positivism given at the outset of this chapter was purposely loose: in contemporary thought the term "positivism" has come to refer to a broadly empiricist approach to knowledge rather than to the specific doctrines of Saint-Simon and Comte (the originators of positivism) or the logical positivists of the so-called Vienna Circle. Following Von Wright (1971), positivism can be more precisely characterized as consisting of three main doctrines: (1) methodological monism (that is, that there is one method for all inquiry); (2) the natural sciences provide the methodological ideal or standard for all inquiry; and (3) a "subsumption-theoretic" view of causal explanation (which we will discuss in chapter 8). Logical positivism more narrowly conceived proffered a number of contrasts – between metaphysics and science; logical and factual truths; facts and theories; description and explanation; and the verifiable and the non-verifiable – all rooted in a verifiability theory of meaning. Some or all of these doctrines or distinctions might be given up or modified and a position still be denominated "positivist" in the looser parlance of this chapter. For an excellent broadly positivist account of science both natural and social, see Hempel (1965); for social science, Rudner (1966). For a comprehensive examination of positivism, and the image of positivism, in cultural anthropology, see Roscoe (1995).

For the movement from positivism to perspectivism, see Rorty (1979). For perspectivism, see Lakatos (1970), Lakatos and Musgrave (1970), and Suppe (ed.) (1974), especially the introductory essay by Suppe. For perspectivism leading to relativism, see Kuhn (1970) and Lyotard (1984); for perspectivism that does not lead to relativism, see Laudan (1990).

On relativism, see the essays collected in Krausz and Meiland (1982) and Krausz (1989). Trigg (1973) provides a useful presentation and criticism of relativism.

On the Argument from Translation, see the relevant essays in Lepore (ed.) (1987) devoted to Davidson's work. See also the essays by Hacking, Newton-Smith, and Lukes in Hollis and Lukes (eds.) (1986).
On extending the notion of paradigm to include cultures, see Wolin (1968).

5

Must We Assume Others Are Rational?

5.1 Rationalism

Those attuned to the differences among people and various cultures and subcultures – those with multicultural sensitivity – usually try to avoid being judgmental. That is, they insist that different does not mean worse, that people should not be expected to do things the way "we" do (whoever this "we" is), and should not be judged deficient or evil because they fail to do so. Other forms of life have their internal integrity and must be viewed from within their own perspective if they are to be understood and appreciated.

An important truth lies in these admonitions. We all should feel queasy about claiming that those different from us are therefore morally unacceptable or irrational. Such claims bespeak a narrow provincialism. Worse, such attributions of immorality or irrationality have historically been covert ways of implying that others are inferior. On this basis they have justified paternalism, domination, and colonialism.

Multicultural sensitivism opposes the ethnocentrism which asserts that those different from "us" are thereby irrational. Instead it instructs us to explore what appears to us to be strange behavior and customs in a way that reveals their ultimate rationality. This instruction need not be based solely on the feeling of wanting to be respectful or compassionate or sophisticated. A philosophical justification for this instruction is available in what I shall call the rationalist approach to explaining human actions. According to *rationalism*, to explain human actions (as opposed, say, to the movements of stars or amoeba) is to provide their rationale; and to provide their rationale is to show how they were the rational thing to have done given agents' beliefs and desires. Rationalism asserts that human actions must be rational at some level, and it enjoins social scientists to discern this

92

rationality even in behavior which appears strange or even irrational. (Please note that the term "rationalism" has many other meanings in philosophy besides the one given here.)

In this chapter we will assess the merits and demerits of rationalism, in the process exploring the meaning of multicultural sensitivity. In order to do so, begin with the important distinction between *action* and *movement*. In his well-known essay "Thick Description" the distinguished anthropologist Clifford Geertz (Geertz, 1973) drew attention to a distinction made by the philosopher Gilbert Ryle (Ryle, 1949) between *thin* and *thick* *description*. Ryle imagined two boys whose eyelids rapidly contracted in a way that was identical as a physical movement. But in one case the movement was a twitch while in the other a wink. The difference between these two cases is fundamental. The twitch is not something the one boy did – it was not an action, but rather something that merely happened to him: suddenly his eyelid started fluttering. The wink, on the other hand, was an action by the second boy – it was something he did deliberately for the purpose of communicating some message. Ryle said that to describe the boys' behavior in terms of its physical movements alone is to describe it thinly; to describe it as an action is to describe it thickly – thickly because such descriptions involve mention not only of the physical movement but also the intentions of the person making the movement and the social rules which give it meaning (that a flapping of the eyes can convey a meaning requires social rules which specify that a particular sort of movement will mean some particular thing).

Ryle went on to consider even more complex acts which can be performed by fluttering the eyelids: parodying a wink, rehearsing the parody of a wink, faking a wink, and so on. But the point remains the same: a thin description of any of these acts would merely depict the physical movements involved, whereas a thick description would consist of intentional concepts which portrayed the intentions and rules expressed through the physical movement. There can be degrees of thickness. The intentions of the winker can be more and more fully characterized, and the rules which govern winking behavior can be more and more fully articulated. Some descriptions can be extraordinarily thick – a fully realized portrait of some act in all its complexity and depth. (Geertz claimed that much of anthropology consists of thick descriptions of the activities and relations of various groups of people. His most famous essay – "Deep Play" (Geertz, 1972) – is in fact a very thick description of the Balinese cock fight.)

The notions of thin and thick description call attention to a fundamental distinction in the social sciences, that between mere bodily *movement* and human *action*. A bodily *movement* is just what it says: the movement of a body part in some particular manner. *Actions*, unlike movements, are always something an agent does, something performed for a purpose. Actions are intentional and rule-governed: they are performed with an end in view often in conformity to social rules which specify that some act will have some particular meaning. Thus, my arm *rising* is a movement, whereas *raising* my hand to vote is an act because I did it to express my support for a candidate. An action, then, is not simply a physical occurrence; it has a certain intentional content which specifies what sort of action it is in terms of what it expresses or attempts to accomplish.

Unlike bodily movements, actions are not merely physically observable phenomena. Some actions, such as those of forbearance, do not involve any movement whatsoever. Even those acts which do include movements involve more than mere observation: they are the acts they are only because they express certain intentions and intentions are not observable. To ascribe a particular intention to agents – and therefore to characterize their actions – requires that we *interpret* their movements in a particular way, and to describe actions we must employ not physical terms which refer to overt movements but intentional terms which pick out the intentions and rules which define the acts they are.

The process of interpretation is quite complex. We will discuss it more fully in chapters 6 and 7. Suffice it to say here that in order to determine that an agent had a particular intention one has to assign to him or her a whole raft of other mental states or events relevant to that intention. Thus, to take a simple example, assume that person X flees an oncoming tiger and you describe this action as "X tries to escape from the tiger" because you judge that X has the intention to escape injury. But you can attribute this intention to X only on the assumption that X has *perceived* the tiger, that X *desires* to avoid injury, that X *believes* that tigers can injure, and so forth. Given a different set of beliefs, desires, and perceptions – say, that X believed the tiger was a toy programmed to play hide and seek – on the basis of the same movements an entirely different intention and therefore action would be ascribed (for example that X intended to hide in order to win the game, and that X's action was therefore not one of escaping but of a move in a game). The ascription of intentions and the determination of what actions are being performed always involves fitting together into a coherent scheme a raft of agents' mental states and events.

How are intentional actions explained? Consider the case of a potential car buyer who bargains with an automobile dealer; why does the buyer do this? The obvious answer is that the buyer wishes to purchase the vehicle as cheaply as possible, and the buyer thinks dealers will lower prices if pressured to do so. In this case the bargaining results from the buyer combining certain of his or her beliefs and desires, which together enjoin a particular sort of action. We might summarize this by saying that intentional actions are explained by giving agents' *reasons* for doing what they did.

Rationalist philosophers have concluded from this that all actions to be actions must be rational at some level. According to them to uncover the reasons for an action is to discover the beliefs and desires which warrant the act from the agent's point of view. In this way they *rationalize* it in the sense of showing that it was the appropriate thing to have done. As A. R. Louch expressed this rationalistic thesis:

> Desires and emotions, pleasures and pains are identified in ourselves and others in the light of what we regard or infer or see as desirable, appropriate, or entailed by the situations in which we find ourselves. As a consequence, such terms explain actions, not by showing a regular connection . . . but by seeing the situation as entitling the action. And this . . . provides the formula for an account of what has more traditionally been thought of as reasons for acting. (Louch, 1966, p. 93)

William Dray, perhaps the most articulate spokesperson for rationalism, put this point even more sharply:

> Reported reasons, if they are to be explanatory in the rational way must be *good* reasons, at least in the sense that if the situation had been as the agent envisaged it . . . then what was done would have been the thing to have done. (Dray, 1957, p. 126)

In these remarks both Louch and Dray assert that any attempt at understanding an action no matter how initially puzzling or peculiar must consist in showing how the act rationally follows from the agent's beliefs and desires. Human agents, they claim, are necessarily rational.

5.2 Reasons and Causes

Let's assume with the rationalists that actions require reason-explanations. Is it true that reason-explanations presuppose that agents are rational? Careful analysis shows that they do but in a much more limited way than rationalism contends. This analysis will comprise the next three sections of this chapter.

Begin by noticing that a reason-explanation seeks to pick out the *reason which actually evoked the action* rather than picking out reasons which merely *accompanied* it or were simply *compatible* with it. Imagine the following situation. A man proposes marriage to a wealthy woman, and the question is, why? Any number of possible reasons may be the correct answer to this question: her wealth will bring him a life of ease; she is lovable; she is a valuable status object; she is his father's choice; and so forth. But we are not interested in all the reasons for which the man *might* have proposed; we are interested in the *actual reason* why he did it. In this we must distinguish between the man's having a reason – indeed, even being consciously aware that he might have such a reason – from his actually being moved to action by his having such a reason. Thus, it may be that the man actually had all the reasons given to marry in the sense that he saw them as warrants for his behavior; and yet it may also be that only one of them was actually responsible for his proposing (though, of course, this needn't be so: many acts are the result of mixed reasons). Thus, though he had as *a* reason his desire to obey his father, this may not have been *the* reason why he in fact proposed; he proposed because he found her lovable. In this and all reason-explanations of actions we must distinguish between those reasons which the agent actually had but which were not causally efficacious from those which were.

Actually, to say that a reason-explanation seeks to provide the person's reason which actually caused him or her to act in a particular manner is misleading in a crucially important way. A "reason" is an abstract structure consisting of certain propositions which serve as premises and others as conclusions; as such, it is nothing more than the content of a person's thinking expressed in particular sentences. It is *what* the agent thinks or feels. But what an agent thinks or feels must be distinguished from his or her having a particular thought or feeling. Having a thought or feeling is a psychological state or process whereas the content of this process is not. *Having* a reason is not the same thing as the reason itself.

The confusion between having a reason and a reason, between a psychological state and the content of this state, is easy to make because psychological states are usually identified by their content. Thus we distinguish one belief from another by specifying the content of each belief – the belief that the earth is round is differentiated from the belief that it is flat by indicating what each belief claims about the world. The same is true about desires: I distinguish the desire I felt at the candy store yesterday – to eat a chocolate – from the desire I feel today – to lessen my sweet intake to lose weight – by what each desire is for. A confusion arises because the same term – "belief" or "desire" – can mean both "what is believed (or desired)" and "being in a psychological state of thinking (or wanting) that . . ." The same is true for concepts such as "intend," "motive," "emotion," and "perceive" as well as other intentional terms.

Distinguishing between a *reason* and *having (or acquiring) a reason* is crucial to clarify the nature of reason-explanations. Reasons in themselves cannot possibly be the cause of anything. They are not the sort of thing which could be a cause: the content of a thought is neither a state, nor an event, nor a process. Reasons cannot be causes. On the basis of this fact some philosophers have argued that reason-explanations are not a form of causal explanation. But this is a mistake. While the content of a thought cannot be a cause, having (or acquiring) a certain reason may be a cause; thus, while the proposition "p" cannot be a cause, assenting to the thought that p may be a cause. *What* an agent believes and wants is what constitutes his or her reasons; but *that* the agent believes and wants what he or she does is what provides the (causal) explanation of his or her action. Agents come to have a reason to act as a result of engaging in a practical reasoning process. A *practical reasoning process* is one in which agents' antecedent beliefs and desires are modified and brought together to form the basis for their actions. When we explain an action by reference to the reasons for which it was done we are actually explaining it as the causal outcome of a process of reasoning on the part of the agent. That is, to specify agents' reasons for their actions is always to specify the reasoning process that led them to behave as they did. Reason-explanations are a type of causal explanation because they explain an intentional act as the effect of an antecedent reasoning process.

Practical reasoning processes take the general form of an argument in which an inference is made from propositions which express the contents of wants and beliefs to propositions which express the content of the action that is thought to be entailed given these propositions. Schematized, practical reasoning processes typically take the following form:

(1) Let it be the case that X.
(2) But X iff *a* (where *a* is an action).
(3) Therefore, let it be the case that *a*.

Here the conclusion of a practical reasoning process is a sentence which enjoins an action whose appropriateness is warranted by the premises which specify the agent's wants and beliefs. If the agent then performs action *a*, the performance can then be explained as the outcome of this reasoning process.

In general intentional acts are explained in terms of the "real reason" agents had in performing them where "the real reason" is understood to mean "the practical reasoning process which caused the act." This does not mean that for every act there is a single reason which caused it; practical reasoning processes can be quite complex, and many acts may result from mixed reasons. Moreover, not every act need be the result of conscious deliberation on the part of agents. A great many intentional actions are undertaken spontaneously (as in unself-conscious speaking) or on the basis of unconscious reasons hidden from agents themselves (as in acting in self-deception). However, nothing requires that the reasoning processes which cause agents to act be either conscious or amenable to recall or even verbalization by such agents. Practical reasoning processes may be unconscious or subconscious or non-verbal and still fulfill their explanatory role in reason explanations. Lastly, many actions are done habitually without apparent thought or attention; nevertheless, they too can be explained as the outcome of practical reasoning processes which have become routinized such that they accord with the principles of such processes.

5.3 Reason-explanations and Irrational Actions

For rationalists what appear to be irrational actions – irrational because they are done for no apparent reason or no apparent good reason – are ultimately rational in so far as they are actions. According to rationalism, by definition actions are rational so that irrational acts are ultimately just a subclass of rational ones. Thus rationalists believe that the job of investigators is to probe beneath the surface to ferret out the rational bases for acts, even ones which appear to lack such a basis. However, I shall now try to show that agents may act irrationally despite the fact that they act on the basis of a practical reasoning process. Thus, contrary to rationalism, agents may have reasons for their actions *even though these reasons may be irrational*; in this way their actions can be irrational and yet still be actions.

In the argument I used above to schematize a practical reasoning process the relationship between the premises and the conclusion is a logical one in the sense that the acceptance of the premises constitutes a logically sufficient reason for accepting the conclusion. But this need not be the case; an agent could reason illogically in the sense that the premises of the argument in which he or she engaged did not warrant a certain action. In this case the act performed would be irrational in the strict sense of being illogical. The following is a scheme of an illogical reasoning process in which its premises do *not* warrant the action not-a:

(1)   Let it be the case that X.
(2)   But X iff *a* (where *a* is an action).
(3)   Therefore, let it be the case that not-*a*.

Here in performing act not-a the agent acts intentionally on the basis of a practical reasoning process; but since this process is itself illogical (in the sense that its premises do not warrant its conclusion) the act is indeed irrational. Intentional acts can be either rational or irrational; the explanations of intentional acts which identify the practical reasoning process which caused them need not assume that these reasoning processes are always logically valid.

It is not the *validity* of a practical reasoning process which gives it its explanatory power; rather, it is that agents *have engaged in a certain inferential process and acted on this basis*. It follows that the methodological principle appropriate to explaining actions is not to find those practical reasoning processes which actually warrant an act, but rather to discover those practical reasoning processes which caused the agent to behave as he or she did (whether these processes contain valid or invalid inferences).

Any number of factors may cause an agent to reason incorrectly in the process of trying to decide what to do. The agent may not have had ample time; he or she may be incapable of sustaining the systematic or elaborate chains of reasoning which are often involved in complicated actions; he or she may be fatigued or distracted or intoxicated; he or she may have learned to make invalid inferences which he or she believed to be correct; or the agent may be subject to severe psychological pressure; and so on. One of the jobs of social psychology is to study the conditions in which good and bad reasoning occurs.

(For simplicity's sake I will confine irrational acts to those which result from mistaken reasoning processes such that the agent's beliefs and desires do not warrant the resulting action. However, acts may also be irrational if they result from beliefs and/or desires which are themselves irrational. An agent may believe "If I step on a crack I will break my mother's back" but have no ascertainable basis for this belief; or, more frighteningly, an anorexic may perceive herself as fat even though she is skin and bones; or a paranoid may believe despite all the evidence that even his best friends are out to get him even though they are invariably supportive and friendly. In these and countless other instances agents have irrational beliefs and desires. A full account of irrational action would have to delineate the criteria for beliefs and desires to be rational, and the conditions in which these criteria are unlikely to be met.)

The possibility of illogical inferences has a direct bearing on how to construe explanations of neurotic actions. To say that neurotic actions are actions is to say that they are intentional items of behavior which have a sense or point to them which derives from the reasons they express. As such, neurotic actions call for reason-explanations. Rationalists have thought that just because it is intentional, neurotic behavior must be rational and that an explanation of it must show that it is warranted. Indeed, sometimes this is precisely how such actions are explained. Acts which appear odd and inappropriate (for example, sticking pins in dolls to injure one's enemies) may be shown not to be so once certain arcane or hidden beliefs and desires which rationalize these acts are uncovered. (In

99

the example, once it becomes clear that the doll-stickers conceive themselves to be witches who believe in supernatural forces which can be released in certain ritualistic ways, their pin-sticking is revealed not to be irrational.)

However, not all reason-explanations of apparently neurotic behavior show it to be ultimately rational given heretofore recondite beliefs and desires. Thus, while it is true that some of Freud's explanations of neurotic behavior consist in discovering the requisite intermediate beliefs and desires which rationalize what was apparently an irrational act (as when he explained an act as an attempt to satisfy a forbidden or unknown sexual desire, for example), this is not always the pattern of his explanations. Instead, sometimes he showed that actions were the result of unconscious thought processes which do not operate according to the rules of rational inference, so that no logical connection exists between an agent's beliefs and wants and his or her actions. Much of Freudian explanation consists in showing that beliefs and desires are connected to actions by means of "primary processes" of the unconscious, processes of association, symbolization, condensation, and so forth, which flaunt the principles of logic. In these cases the explanation of neurotic action will not consist in showing that it is rationally warranted if one takes into account certain hidden beliefs and/or desires of the agent, but rather will show how the reasoning processes which caused the act connect the agent's beliefs and desires to his or her acts through rationally unwarranted chains of thought.

Consider Freud's explanation of one of the compulsive behaviors of Paul Lorenz, the famous "Rat Man." One summer, while vacationing with his girlfriend and an English cousin, Lorenz decided he was too fat (German "dick"), and he consequently embarked on a compulsive and suicidal regime of dieting and exercise supposedly in order to lose weight. However, Freud says that the real reason for this behavior was that getting rid of this fat signified for Lorenz getting rid of his English cousin whom he wanted to kill because of his intense jealousy of the man's relationship to his girlfriend. Getting rid of his fat ("dick") could carry this symbolic meaning just because the Englishman's name was "Dick."

In this case Lorenz's dieting and exercising were clearly intentional actions, actions caused by a particular reasoning process. But the reasoning process involved an illogical inference upon Lorenz's part such that his actions were not warranted given his beliefs and desires. The illogicality consisted in the substitution of a homonym in one premise for one of the fundamental terms in another premise; the relevant reasoning process might be reconstructed in this way:

100

(1) Let it be the case that I get rid of Dick (the English cousin).
(2) But the best way for getting rid of dick (fat) is to run and diet.
(3) Therefore, let it be the case that I run and diet.

Here the reason for the performance of the action does not rationalize the act – it does not show that, given Lorenz's beliefs and desires, the act was warranted. This would have been the case if Freud had attributed to Lorenz the requisite intermediary beliefs which would rationally connect dieting and taking care of his rival (such as the belief that by slimming he would be more appealing to his girlfriend and in this way best his rival). But this is precisely what Freud does not do. Instead, he shows that Lorenz's actions were the causal outcome of an illogical reasoning process. Indeed, only because the reasoning process was illogical could it have the causal force that it had (because only by being irrational could slimming provide the substitute gratification that it did).

Now to this example a possible rationalist retort might be that, although Lorenz's behavior was not rational in the sense that his thought processes were not strictly logical, they were nevertheless still "rational at some level." Even the confused reasoning of the Rat Man had some symbolic sense, it might be claimed, and therefore the actions it caused were appropriate given the peculiar principles on which the unconscious operates. In other words, goes the objection, given the principles of associative reasoning that guide the unconscious, and given the constraints under which the Rat Man was operating, one can see that his behavior "makes sense" and is therefore "rational."

Something is obviously correct about this retort. But to see precisely what let's examine an analogous case of deductive reasoning which includes a logical mistake. Suppose a student's thinking went like this:

(1) All spirits are angels
(2) Whiskey is a spirit
(3) Therefore, whiskey is an angel.

One could argue that this bit of illogical reasoning was really "rational at some level" because the mistake it contains still makes "symbolic" sense. But all this just means that, though the reasoning is illogical, it is easy to see how someone might think it logical and so be emboldened to make such an argument. In this case, and in the case of the Rat Man, the character of the (invalid) reasoning process serves, not as an explanation of the act, but as an explanation of how a person might think it rational.

It should come as no surprise that mistakes in practical reasoning, like mistakes in theoretical reasoning, by and large fall into patterns which share important similarities with the patterns of logical thought, such that the principles of illogical thinking make it appear "like rational thought." In cases of both logical and illogical reasoning the person engaged in them must *believe* them to be valid in order for them to be effective, and given that he or she lives in a community in which valid reasoning is far more prevalent than invalid reasoning (a point I shall take up in section 5.3), it is likely that a person would unwittingly make mistakes and act on them only if they bore a strong resemblance to rational thought processes. Thus, it is likely to be the case that invalid reasoning processes borrow patterns that are in an important sense derivative from the patterns of valid reasoning processes, and therefore that they make some "sense."

The rationalist retort to my analysis of the Rat Man's slimming is useful in so far as it draws attention to the fact that typically in order for an intentional action to be intentional the agent must think that his or her reasoning processes are correct, and to the fact that in most cases these reasoning processes will bear strong resemblance to cases of rational inference. In this sense, even irrational actions, and especially systematically irrational ones, will have some point or rationale to them, and therefore be like rational actions. But it is a mistake to conclude from this that there are not important differences between actions performed as a result of rational as opposed to irrational thought processes; for in the former case, the agent's beliefs and desires do rationalize the actions in the sense that they warrant his or her acts, and actually are means to the agent's ends given his or her view of the world, whereas in the latter case they are not.

This difference can be of profound importance to agents themselves. Many times in acting irrationally agents do not feel themselves to be agents: their behavior, though intentional, occurs despite their conscious wishes and cannot be stopped at will (obsessive-compulsive behavior, for example). Assuming these are instances of action – that is, something the person does – nevertheless the agent feels victimized and disabled in performing them, in part either because they seem to make no sense or because they are not responsive to rational persuasion. The agent's conscious rational thought does not appear to touch the source from which the activity springs. In these cases reason-explanations can help to restore to the agent his or her powers of agency by showing: (1) that these acts are indeed actions in the sense that they result from the agent's (usually unconscious) thought-processes; (2) that they are irrational acts in that the thought processes which underlie them are irrational; and (3) that their irrationality is purposeful, allowing the agent to address some desire or need which cannot be addressed in more standard rational ways.

By rendering these underlying thought processes conscious and by revealing their functional role in the agent's psychic economy, reason-explanations which explicitly recognize the irrational character of the thought processes involved can make them more amenable to the will of the agent. (It is something like this process which Freud meant to capture in his famous description of the goal of therapy: "Where there was id, now there is ego" – better translated as: "Where *it* was, now *I* am.")

To sum up: in explaining intentional actions we need not assume that agents are rational in the sense that their practical reasoning processes logically warrant their behavior. Irrational actions can and should be explained by reason-explanations (just as rational actions are), but reason-explanations need not presume that an agent's reasons are rationally warranted. To explain an intentional act is to pick out the practical reasoning process which caused it, and this process can be illogical and still play its explanatory role. Contrary to rationalism, a commitment to explaining intentional actions by giving the reasons for them does not require that we believe that all actions are rational at some level. Intentional activity is not restricted to the domain of the rational.

This has important consequences for the kind of explanatory theory permissible in the social sciences. In their commitment to interpreting human behavior intentionalistically, the social sciences need not be blind to the absolutely central role which irrational intentional actions have played, and continue to play, in human societies and human history (as we shall see in section 6.4, where we will discuss the role of critique in explaining human behavior and relationships). A social science committed to viewing its subjects as agents who behave on the basis of thought processes can still view them as engaged in systematically irrational behavior.

5.4 Rationality in Reason-explanations

Rationalism is wrong in that in any *particular* reason-explanation the agent need not be rational. Nevertheless, as I hope to now show, the presumption that most agents most of the time are rational must be an operating assumption of the whole endeavor of explaining human behavior by giving the reasons for which it was done. Thus, *in general* reason-explanations must assume that actors are by and large rational. In this more limited sense rationalism is correct.

To begin, it is surely a sound methodological rule to assume that agents are acting rationally given their wants and beliefs, and therefore to seek explanations of their actions which construe them as rational. An agent's acting irrationally is less likely to be the case than the observer's inability to discover the underlying reason which warrants the behavior. Failure to appreciate the rich diversity of reasons which can serve to rationalize actions of the (apparently) most peculiar sort is all too easy. A stricture to assume rationality until the opposite is demonstrated is a good protection against the parochialism of calling everything for which you cannot give reasons of your own an instance of irrational behavior.

However, making the presumption of rationality merely a counsel of wise methodological prudence does not go nearly far enough in linking together the notions of "action" and "rationality." For the assumption that people generally are rational creatures, and that their behavior is indeed rationalizable, is in fact a constitutive principle of the whole enterprise of explaining actions by finding the reasons which produced them. In other words, in order to explain human actions in terms of the reasoning processes which caused them, one must presume that in general people are rational.

Why? Unless one assumes agents are rational no way would exist to determine a person's beliefs and desires because without the presumption of rationality there would be no limit on the kinds of interpretation one could give of agents' psychological states. If there were no rational relationship between what an agent does, wants, says, and believes, there would be no way of ascertaining what the agent believes or thinks or does – no way of knowing what signified what, or what was related to what. Thus, for example, if it were generally the case that having the belief that carrots need to be cooked to be enjoyed together with having the desire for sleep could cause the action of putting on galoshes, then the very possibility of ascertaining what people intended when they did something would disappear: any act could as equally well be connected with any belief and any desire.

If people generally behaved in ways that were rationally unconnected with their beliefs and wants, then the whole point of, and the basis for, the category of intentional action would disappear, and with it the need and the possibility of reason-explanation. It is for this reason that in trying to discover the psychological causes of actions one must assume that *in general* people are rational, and why the explanation of actions in terms of reasoning processes which are rationally construed must take a supervenient place in any theory of action. This fact provides the justification for the currently standard procedure of trying to seek out beliefs and desires which rationalize prima facie irrational action. That is, when anthropologists come upon a tribe which acts in apparently irrational ways, the appropriate methodological rule is to assume the behavior is rational and therefore to look for (arcane) beliefs and desires which in fact do warrant the behavior rather than to look for mistakes in the natives' reasoning ("primitive thought," etc.). Only if this procedure fails should mistakes in reasoning be sought.

5.5   The Principle of Humanity

Rationality and intentional action are inextricably bound up with one another. Actions are caused by practical reasoning processes, and are explained by reason-explanations which in general must presuppose a rational connection between agents' beliefs, desires, and actions. This connection between intentionality and rationality has sometimes been expanded into a stronger thesis concerning the rationality of others' thinking. Donald Davidson's *Principle of Charity* asserts that the enterprise of interpreting the meaning of others' doings and sayings presupposes not only that they are rational but also that their beliefs are largely similar to ours. As Davidson put it:

> The methodological advice to interpret in a way that optimizes agreement should not be conceived as resting on a charitable assumption about human intelligence that might turn out to be false. If we cannot find a way to interpret the utterances and other behavior of a creature as revealing a set of beliefs largely consistent and true by our own standards, we have no reason to count the creature as rational, as having beliefs, or as saying anything. (Davidson, 1986a, p. 137)

The reason that Davidson claims that charity is forced on anyone bent on interpreting the behavior, including the verbal behavior, of others ought to be clear from our discussions in the last chapter and this. Actions express beliefs and desires; to determine the meaning of an act one must determine the relevant beliefs and desires behind it. How can this be done? Davidson asserts that only by assuming that beliefs and desires of others are connected in the ways we connect them, and only by assuming that most of their beliefs and desires are like ours, do we have any basis for assigning belief and desires to them, and therefore do we have any basis for determining the meaning of what they do.

Take as an example our earlier case of person X fleeing the tiger. We see a tiger approach X and we see X run away; what is the meaning of X's movement? By asking this question we already assume that this movement is indeed an intentional action performed for some reason. But X's reason for moving consists in a combination of his or beliefs and desires, so that explaining the act of moving requires that we determine what X believes and desires. How can we do this? We must possess some constraint on what we can ascribe to X, otherwise we will be utterly stymied. Davidson claims that we must assume that the way X puts together his or her beliefs, desires, and acts must generally follow the principles of rationality as we understand them, for it is these principles which tell us the way these elements are combinable. Moreover, he also claims that we must further assume that X possesses "a set of beliefs largely consistent and true by our standards"; if we don't assume this, he asserts there will be no constraint on what beliefs and desires we can assign to X. Thus, if X is healthy and the tiger looms large in X's field of vision we must assume that X sees the tiger, and if X moves away from the tiger we must assume that X desires to get away from the tiger because X fears it. On the basis of simple assumptions about X's perceptions, beliefs, desires, and the way X puts these together, we can then describe X's movement as the intentional action of fleeing the tiger. If the Xs of this world generally perceived in ways utterly unlike the ways we perceive, or generally possessed desires radically different from our own, or generally thought in logically bizarre ways, we couldn't interpret the meaning of their acts or their utterances.

But we must be careful here. For as we have seen in section 5.3, people may act in irrational ways. Moreover, they may at times have beliefs and desires which are strange relative to our beliefs and desires. This presents a problem for interpretation *only if we cannot explain and therefore anticipate these differences.* That is, in order to interpret the meaning of what others do and say we do *not* have to assume they are roughly like us if we have good reason to explain why and in what way they differ from us. If we can do this then we can factor these differences into our interpretations.

Consider the case of perceptions. We need not assume that others perceive as we do if we have reason to believe that their perceptual apparati are quite different from ours. Someone may run a red light; on the assumption that he or she sees as we do and believes that red means stop we may interpret this act as one of lawbreaking. We might then look for some desires which would rationalize this act. But the person may in fact be color-blind and consequently be unable to distinguish between red and green lights in certain situations. If we came to know this fact about the driver's perceptions, then our interpretation of this act and other acts involving responses to green and red colors would be quite different. Of course learning this fact about the driver is not always easy because in many situations he or she may be able to function as if able to see as most do; the color-blindness may reveal itself only in special circumstances. (An astonishing fact is that color-blindness was discovered only in the eighteenth century. For millennia interpreters of others' behavior assumed that color perception was roughly the same as their own. Here interpreting in accord with the Principle of Charity would actually have misled interpreters.)

We can generalize from this case. Sometimes it is more understandable that others disagree with us than that they agree. We may hold some beliefs that they could not have acquired; in these cases we would do better to attribute to them what we consider explicable falsehoods rather than baffling truths. Moreover, sometimes we have good reason to ascribe irrational reasoning processes to others, perhaps because their actions are so self-defeating or oddly connected to their apparent beliefs and desires, and because we have a theory which can explain why they think in illogical ways. In these cases the Principle of Charity is too restrictive. Enjoining interpreters to "interpret others as maximally like us" forecloses the possibility of difference which is explicable and which can therefore be factored into reason-explanations of their actions.

To remedy this defect in the Principle of Charity, Roger Grandy (1973) reformulated and expanded Davidson's principle into what he called the *Principle of Humanity*. Rather than requiring that all agents be broadly similar to us, it demands only that we assume that their behavior be intelligible. Only those beliefs, desires, and ways of thinking should be imputed to agents which we can make sense of their having. Sometimes this will be a matter of their sharing beliefs, desires, and patterns of thought with us, but other times it will not; in either case we must be able to understand why they agree or why they differ from us. The Principle of Charity says: "Count them like us"; the Principle of Humanity says: "Count them intelligible."

Intelligibility can occur in at least one of three ways. First, when agents are rational by our lights or share most of our beliefs and desires ("It's obvious why X fled the tiger – who wouldn't run from a dangerous beast?"). Second, when agents' rationality is vindicated by imputing to them some arcane though understandable beliefs or desires ("now I understand why X didn't run – she was temporarily blinded by the sun and so didn't see the tiger"). Or third, when the mistakes in reasoning of agents are explicable in terms of the agents' past conditioning or present situation ("now I understand why X froze: he never could think clearly on his feet"). In practice the Principle of Humanity will amount to the counsel "Count them like us unless we can't explain their being like us, or can better explain their being different from us."

The Principle of Humanity commands interpreters to minimize unintelligibility (rather than minimize disagreement with us as does the Principle of Charity). But "intelligibility" is not a fixed notion. Specifically, we cannot assume that what we initially take to be intelligible encompasses the entire range of what constitutes intelligible behavior.

As interpreters of behavior of those apparently alien to us we must be prepared to have our concept of intelligibility challenged and perhaps expanded even as we obey the injunction to interpret others as intelligible.

This point has been made most forcefully by Peter Winch in a number of famous essays (see Winch, 1964 and 1970). An example from "Understanding a Primitive Society" will show the force of this point. The Azande perform a certain activity when harvesting their crops; we might describe this activity as a crop-rite. What are the reasons for this rite? The most obvious answer – one many anthropologists have given – is that the crop-rite is a (magical) attempt to produce good harvesting conditions by assuaging the gods. Given certain beliefs about the power of the gods and the way this power can be unleashed, together with the easily understood desire for a successful harvest, this interpretation of the crop-rite clearly makes the Azande's actions intelligible: the rite is an instrument by which to achieve the goal of good harvests. Intelligibility here consists of an instrumental connection between means and ends. This sort of intelligibility is quite familiar to Euro-Americans – it is the basis for technology, and is therefore widespread in our technological society. It is thus probably not accidental that an interpretation of the Azande crop-rite which explicated it as an instance of instrumental rationality should have commanded so much respect in our society.

But Winch claims this interpretation of the Azande crop-rite is in error. He maintains that western anthropologists have mistakenly equated intelligibility with being instrumentally rational, thereby foreclosing other forms of intelligibility. According to Winch, anthropologists have misinterpreted the meaning of the Azande crop-rite precisely because they worked with a restricted concept of intelligibility, that they projected onto the Azande an instrumental connection between their beliefs, desires, and actions which simply is not present in the Azande crop-rite.

As an alternative Winch proposes what might be called an expressive conception of intelligibility:

> A man's sense of importance of something to him shows itself in all sorts of ways: not merely in precautions to safeguard the thing. He may want to come to terms with its importance to him in quite a different way: to contemplate it, to gain some sense of his life in relation to it. He may wish thereby, in a certain sense, to *free* himself from dependence on it. I do not mean by making sure that it does not let him down, because the point is that, *whatever* he does, he still may be let down. The important thing is that he should understand *that* and come to terms with it . . . He must see that he can still go on even if he is let down by what is vitally important to him; and he must so order his life that he still *can* go on in such circumstances. (Winch, 1972, p. 39)

Winch thinks that the crop-rite is an Azandean way of dealing with their dependence on the harvest different from the technological way of trying to ensure that the harvest is successful. The crop-rite is an expressive, not technical, activity in which dramas of possible misfortune are symbolically represented and the ability of the tribe to continue in spite of these misfortunes is reaffirmed. In this way the Azande contemplate their dependence in a manner that frees them from it.

Note that Winch's expansion of our understanding of the Azande must still in the end be intelligible to us. That is, though he stretches the notion of intelligibility he doesn't abandon it altogether; his reading of the Azande crop-rite shows how it makes sense even as he deepens our notion of what it means to make sense. To demonstrate this, Winch appeals to practices in our own culture which analogously compare with the technological and the expressive modes of rationality. Thus he contrasts two Judeo-Christian prayers: (1) "Lord, please give me what I want and I will perform the following good deeds . . ."; (2) "Lord, not what I want but what You want." The former is a kind of technique in which promises are offered as a way of influencing the Lord to grant the outcome which the person desires; the latter is not an instance of technique at all – it isn't concerned with outcome but expresses acceptance of whatever outcome the Lord has in store. The former deals with contingency by trying to control it; the latter deals with contingency by getting free of it. Thus, the expressive rationality of the Azandean crop-rite is not altogether foreign to us.

The general philosophical point of this example is that the notion of intelligibility is neither a fixed nor a universal concept. *What constitutes intelligibility can vary depending on the particular form of life being investigated.* That is, actions can be intelligible in many ways; what counts as intelligibility is not identical for all societies or cultures. Modern westerners may more easily appreciate the kind of intelligibility involved in instrumentally rational activity. (Winch thinks this form of rationality is fundamental to an industrial form of life which copes with existential uncertainty and dependence by seeking methods of technical control to enhance power.) But this does not mean that many other forms of intelligibility do not operate in our own and in the vast array of other human cultures. Indeed, one of anthropology's major contributions is to reveal the many and varied ways intelligibility can be achieved.

All interpreters in the dispute about the Azande follow the Principle of Humanity. They assume that the Azande are rational in the sense that their actions are intelligible. But the Principle of Humanity must be augmented by an explicit sense of cultural diversity in which the ways intelligibility can be achieved varies from culture to culture. That we must assume that

109

other agents are rational in the sense of intelligible is a necessary presupposition of interpreting their actions; but of what rationality and intelligibility consist is something investigators must continually be revising and developing as they explore the variable and rich panoply of human arrangements.

5.6 Summing Up

Must we assume others are rational? The answer at which we have arrived in this chapter is complex, one which borrows from rationalism but does not accept it completely. I have assumed that "others" in the question means "agents who perform intentional acts." Agents get food for dinner, marry, vote for one candidate rather than another, migrate, argue, tell jokes, revolt against authority, and engage in all the countless other behaviors which are undertaken for a reason. The behavior of agents is explained by means of reason-explanations which pick out the practical reasoning processes which cause agents to act as they do. Such reasoning processes can be discovered only by assuming that agents and their activities are intelligible in that they make sense. But to make sense, beliefs, desires, and actions must in general be rationally connected. In other words, without the presupposition that agents are rational the entire enterprise of interpreting the meaning of their activity – and thus the point of describing their behavior as intentional activity – would be undermined. Therefore we must assume that agents are in general rational.

But the "in general" in this answer is important. In the first place, in any particular case agents may be irrational: their practical reasoning processes may be illogical. Such irrational processes may still be explicable and therefore the actions they engender intelligible, especially if their irrationality mimics in some way rational processes. In the second place, what it means to follow rational principles – and therefore of what intelligibility consists – may vary from cultural setting to cultural setting.

Therefore, though we must assume other agents are in general rational we need not assume that they are always so. Moreover, what can count as rational itself may vary across time and place.

Further Reading

The position adopted in this chapter is heavily influenced by Davidson (1986a and 1986b) and Lukes (1970; 1982). See also Roth (1987) for a clear-headed, insightful discussion of the matters discussed in this chapter. Henderson (1993), chapter 4, is a particularly impressive recent analysis of this ground.

For a general account of the notion of action, see Davidson (1963), Kenny (1963), Goldman (1970), Hampshire (1970), Danto (1973), Aune (1977), Bernstein (1971 and 1976), Ginet (1990), and Mele (1992). Anscombe (1957) is the *locus classicus* of this literature.

For the view that reason explanations are not causal, see Von Wright (1971); Dray (1957); Collingwood (1946); Melden (1961), Taylor (1964), and Louch (1966). For the view that they are causal, see Davidson and Goldman cited above, as well as Searle (1983). For a good collection of essays presenting both sides of the question and others, see Borger and Cioffi (1970).

On the idea of irrational action and its explanation, see Davidson (1982), Pears (1984), and Sutherland (1994).

For the Principle of Charity see Davidson (1986a); Grandy (1973); Cherniak, (1986); Stich (1990); and Henderson (1993), chapters 1–3.

For the notion of intelligibility and the way this notion differs from culture to culture, see Winch (1958, 1964, and 1970). For good anthologies of essays on this and related questions see Wilson (1979) and Hollis and Lukes (1986).

6

Must We Comprehend Others in Their Own Terms?

6.1   Interpretivism

Captain Cook lost his life in part because he didn't interpret the meaning of his sudden return to Hawaii from the natives' point of view. On his first visit Cook and his men were treated lavishly. Indeed

> There were mystifying ceremonies, processions, long harangues, which sometimes seemed to take the form of services, formal exchanges of apparently valuable gifts. Cook gathered he was "Orono" or, more likely, *an* Orono, for he thought this to be a kind of Hawaiian title: it was all part of very friendly and useful relations and otherwise meant little or nothing to him. (Villiers, 1967, p. 259)

Unfortunately for Cook "Orono" was in fact "Lono," a god who had long ago been exiled but who had been prophesied to return. The Hawaiians thought Cook was Lono, and adored him accordingly. At first this worked to Cook's favor: he refitted his ships and was wined and dined in the process. He departed on very favorable terms. But two weeks out to sea the mainsail of one of his ships developed serious problems, and Cook decided to put back into his old Hawaiian port. He had no reason to be suspicious; he thought his return a simple revisitation by an old friend. But to the natives this second coming demonstrated that Cook was not in fact Lono, that he was an intruder who had cost them dearly in food and other gifts. It never occurred to Cook that for the natives his return was an act of un-deification (to coin a term). For this mistake he paid with his life, for shortly after his return Cook was murdered in a riotous encounter on the beach.

The misadventure of Captain Cook in Hawaii is precisely the kind of event multiculturalism is meant to prevent. For if multiculturalism means anything it is the idea that we have to understand others from *their* point of view, not our own. Are social scientists like Captain Cook: do they ignore the meanings and self-understandings of their subjects at their own peril?

Interpretivists have answered this question decidedly in the affirmative. Indeed, so impressed are interpretivists with the necessity of paying attention to the meanings of their subjects' behavior and the products of this behavior that they claim that explanation in social science consists solely in uncovering this meaning and nothing more. (Thus *interpretivism* may be defined as the view that comprehending human behavior, products, and relationships consists solely in reconstructing the self-understandings of those engaged in creating or performing them. Put colloquially, interpretivists think that to comprehend others is to understand the meaning of what they do, and that to understand this meaning is to understand them simply in their own terms.)

It is not difficult to imagine the appeal of interpretivism. As we saw in chapter 5, many of the objects of social science are intentional phenomena, and even those phenomena which are non-intentional (like economic depressions) take place against a background of intentional phenomena. But intentional phenomena are meaningful in nature, and typically are individuated in virtue of their meaning. Thus the focus on meaning by interpretivists is not surprising.

Consider the cases of human actions, relations, and products. Actions differ from mere movements in that they are intentional and rule-governed: they are performed in order to achieve a particular purpose, and in conformity to some rules. These purposes and rules constitute the "semantic dimension" of human behavior – its symbolic or expressive aspect. A given movement is a vote, a signal, or a salute depending on this semantic dimension. Similarly, social institutions like the family, or human products like buildings, also possess a semantic dimension. They are not simply physical relations or objects, but have an intentional content which specifies what sort of institution or building it is, and which can be grasped only in terms of the system of meanings in which they are situated. A building is a church because it is set apart for public worship; a social unit is a family because its purpose is raising children and establishing lines of descent.

The same is true of psychological states and events. As intentional, these states are what they are in virtue of what they are about. The belief that Captain Cook was murdered is the belief it is because of what it is a belief about, the death of Captain Cook. Similarly, the identity of the desire for beer is fixed by what it is a desire for: beer (and not wine or juice). The fear of heights is distinguished from the fear of the sea by the object that is feared. The same is true for perceptions, moods, and motives:

they are individuated by their content. In general, psychological states and events derive their identity from the propositional contents which they instantiate.

A crucially important feature of the description of intentional phenomena in intentional terms is that, because their identities are distinguished and classified in terms of their content, these descriptions must capture the conceptual distinctions and intentions of the agents involved. An act is one of voting and not marriage or bank depositing precisely because the agent him or herself possesses particular intentions (themselves located within a particular cultural setting) which make the acts what they are. But this means that the social sciences are constrained as to the kind of descriptions they can employ. Put bluntly, they must operate in terms of the meanings of those they study.

The reason for this lies in the failure of substitutability among intentional contents. "X believes p" is not equivalent to, and cannot be substituted by, "X believes q" even though p and q are logically equivalent. Thus, that Jim believes that Ronald Reagan was a poor president does not mean that Jim believes that the fortieth president of the United States was a poor president even though Ronald Reagan and the fortieth president of the United States are identical. The same is true of the contents of all intentional states and events – perceptions, desires, motives, and the relations and products of these states and events. The upshot is that the propositional contents of intentional states and other intentional objects can only be identified and described *in terms of how they appear to and are conceived by the agents involved*.

According to interpretivism this marks an essential methodological difference between the study of humanity and the study of nature. Concept-formation in the natural sciences is governed by two related sets of considerations – those of theory and those of measurement. Natural science requires concepts which permit the formation of testable laws and theories, and other issues – e.g., those deriving from ordinary language – may simply be set aside. But in the human sciences another set of considerations exists as well: the concepts used to describe and explain human activity must be drawn at least in part *from the social life being studied*, not from the scientists' theories.

Scientific concepts thus bear a fundamentally different relationship to social phenomena from that which they bear to natural phenomena. In the social sciences, concepts partially constitute the reality being studied, while in the latter case they merely serve to describe and explain it. An event can be an "order" only if the *social agents involved* have the concept of an order and of such related concepts as obedience, authority, etc.; but the natural event we call lightning is the same whether it is conceptualized as an expression of Zeus' anger or as an atmospheric electrical discharge: its identity is not a function of its meaning or intentional content (though, of course – as we saw in chapter 4 – its description is a function of the conceptual scheme on which it draws).

The interpretation of the meanings of actions, practices, and cultural objects is an extremely difficult and complicated enterprise. The basic reason for this is that the meaning of something depends upon the role it has in the system of which it is a part, and this system may be exceedingly complex and rich. In order to know the meaning of certain overt movements interpreters must understand the beliefs, desires, and intentions of the particular people involved. But in order to understand these, they must know the vocabulary in terms of which they are expressed, and this in turn requires that they know the social rules and conventions which specify what a certain movement or object counts as. Moreover, in order to grasp these particular rules, they also have to know the set of institutional practices of which they are a part, and how these are related to other practices of the society.

Nor can interpreters stop here. The conventions and institutions of a social group, as Taylor (1971) has convincingly argued, presuppose a set of fundamental conceptualizations or basic assumptions regarding humanity, nature, and society. These basic conceptualizations might be called the "constitutive meanings of a form of life," for they are the basic ideas or notions in terms of which the meanings of specific practices and schemes of activity must be analyzed. For example, the social practice of banking can only occur given the shared constitutive meanings of (say) a conception of property, a notion of being an individual social unit, and an idea of exchange value. An adequate account of the practices of a particular society, by setting out the basic ideas and conceptualizations which underlie these practices, will show how various aspects of the social order are related to each other, and how (or the extent to which) the social order constitutes a coherent whole.

The need for such a deeper level of interpretation may be missed if one confines oneself to studies of one's own culture by other members of it. In these situations, social scientists needn't make explicit their interpretive scheme in order to identify and characterize the class of actions and institutions in which they are interested. Economists, as well as their readers, already know what banks are and what depositing funds means, so they needn't engage in a depth analysis to elucidate the constitutive meanings in virtue of which they are what they are in order to theorize about them. However, this point should not be pushed too far, because the implicit self-understandings of interpreters may be inadequate for the tasks of social science either because they are superficial or because they are

115

often mistaken. Social scientific accounts even of the societies of the social scientists themselves must ultimately probe beneath the surface of shared self-understandings to uncover their deep structure and presuppositions. Some of the very best work in social science consists in explicating the sets of shared rules and constitutive meanings which underlie social practices.

The need for interpretation is most evident in anthropology. Anthropologists usually do not have an insider's implicit understanding of the society or culture they study, and so they must develop an explicit scheme of interpretation if they are to do any explanatory work at all. And even in studies of their own society or culture anthropologists seek to uncover the deep presuppositions of practices they as agents merely take for granted. It is thus no accident that anthropology has developed the interpretive enterprise most highly, producing ethnographies of great sensitivity and sophistication to capture "worlds" greatly different from their own. Evans Pritchard's *The Nuer*, or Robert Redfield's classic *The Primitive World and its Transformations*, show just how rich a nativist-inspired social scientific account can be.

The idea of constitutive meaning shows that interpretivism is more sophisticated than at first it might appear. Interpretivists do not claim that all social scientists need do is ask those under study what they are doing. Such survey research can play an important role but is not in itself sufficient. Some elements of the conceptual structure which informs agents' social lives – specifically, its constitutive meanings – are not necessarily immediately available to the agents themselves. Constitutive meanings are the *presuppositions* of activities (including speaking), and as such are not automatically known by those who operate in terms of them. Bankers may presuppose a concept of individuality in their work but to be capable bankers they need not be able to elucidate this concept.

In this regard one might distinguish three sorts of concept: (1) those we use *in thinking*; (2) those we think *about*; and (3) those we think *with*. Bankers may use the concept "depositor" in their work to refer to various people; for these bankers "depositor" is a first sort of concept. These same bankers may from time to time examine the concept "interest" in order to define it more sharply (undoubtedly to save the bank money!); here "interest" is a second sort of concept. But neither the first nor the second type of concept requires the bankers to be aware of the concepts they are thinking with in order to employ these two types of concept. Thus, they needn't recognize that they implicitly utilize the concept of "individual" when they think about "interest" or use the term "depositor," nor need they be able to clarify this concept in order to do so. Thus, economic anthropolo-

gists interested in banking – and therefore ultimately in the deep constitutive meanings which it presupposes – must do more than simply ask
their banking informants as to the nature of their institution and its
activities. Anthropologists have to engage in their own interpretation in
order to uncover the third type of concept and its meaning in this case.
(This sort of interpretation is consistent with interpretivism because the
third type of concept is still possessed by *the bankers themselves*, though
tacitly.)

But, a critic of interpretivism might retort, can't social scientists employ concepts which are not operative in the world of those they are
studying? For instance, mightn't anthropologists employ categories of
thought – say, those describing kinship relations – about which those they
are studying are totally ignorant? Surely members of a tribe may not
possess the notions of matrilineal descent or leviratic marriage even though
these terms may accurately describe their kinship patterns. Or
businesspeople may function quite successfully without the concept of
liquidity preference even though this concept captures some important
dispositional aspect of their economic lives and economists use it to understand some of their economic behavior.

To this objection interpretivists have a convincing reply. They do not
deny that social scientists may employ technical concepts of their own by
which they group together various sorts of behaviors or relations, or by
which they pick out aspects of social interaction or mental life about which
the agents involved are imperceptive. Instead, interpretivists deny that
social scientists can employ these technical concepts independently of the
intentional vocabulary of those under study.

They do so for two reasons. First, people may "have" a concept without
being able specifically to identify it. In the case of matrilineal descent, for
instance, an interpretivist might plausibly argue that even though no such
term exists in a tribe's language, the tribespeople nevertheless possess this
concept because they make the distinctions and draw the conclusions this
concept underwrites.

Second, interpretivists claim that social scientific terms must be logically related to, and therefore translatable into, the terms of those under
analysis. As the most articulate spokesman of interpretivism put it:

> Although the reflective student of society, or a particular mode of social life, may
> find it necessary to use concepts which are not taken from the forms of activity which
> he is investigating, but which are taken rather from the context of his own investi-
> gation, still these technical concepts of his will imply a previous understanding of
> those other concepts which belong to the activities under investigation. (Winch,
> 1958, p. 89)

Why? The identity of intentional entities conceived as such depends upon the concepts and self-understandings of social agents. If social scientists wish to go beyond these self-understandings by introducing concepts which transcend or are at variance with them, they face the problem of relating these new concepts to those employed by the agents themselves. Failure to establish this relationship would result in the scientists failing to capture the phenomena they wish to explain, the events in question potentially slipping through the conceptual net the scientists had constructed.

For example, consider political scientists bent on making some general claims about the nature of politics; assume further that they employ a technical concept of politics which defines politics in a highly theoretical manner. But to what does this technical concept apply? The nature of social activities including politics depends on the intentions which the agents within a realm at least implicitly share. But this means that whether some behavior falls under the political scientists' technical concept "political" depends on how the agents of this behavior conceive of politics. The nature of behavior can profoundly differ depending on whether the activity occurs in an African tribe, an ancient *polis*, Elizabethan England, or twentieth-century America. Political scientists cannot know the extent to which an activity is indeed political by their definition without paying strict attention to the deep concepts, beliefs, and practices of those whose behavior they are studying.

Some political scientists have taken explicit cognizance of this fact, attempting to unearth the meanings which are partially constitutive of particular political practices and to show how these meanings underwrite particular forms of political life. For example, Samuel Beer's classic *Modern British Politics* shows how the periods of political life in modern Britain have been discontinuous in important ways because each of them has been structured around different understandings of the nature of the political. Or Takeo Doi's *The Anatomy of Dependence* demonstrates how the peculiar character of Japanese politics derives from the basic Japanese concept of *amae*, a derivation which renders Japanese political life qualitatively different from that found in other cultures. This kind of work is crucial because it shows that any categorization of behavior (such as "political" or "economic" or "religious") must be sensitive to the differences in the nature of the behaviors being counted as instances of this categorization. Otherwise, the categorization will be crude and inaccurate.

So social science in so far as it studies intentional phenomena intentionalistically described must be interpretive, and as such must be rooted in the distinctions and concepts of those it studies. Social science cannot simply ignore or replace the distinctions of its subjects with its own technical concepts. In this way interpretivism is correct. But because social scientists are thus bound in important ways to the concepts and terms of those they study, does this mean that they must understand others solely in their own terms?

The next three sections will explore ways social science must go beyond the self-understandings of those whose lives it attempts to explain, and in this way must transcend interpretivism. The point of these sections is not that interpretivism is wrong – indeed, we shall see that causal, competence, and critical theories all presuppose grasping the self-understandings of those being studied. Rather, interpretivism is one-sided because it omits important elements of social scientific analysis.

6.2   Causality

Social phenomena are not just abstract structures of meaning; they are also events and objects which occur in the world. For this reason to understand them requires more than just knowing *what* they mean; we must also know *why* they occurred. For example, to understand a speech act we must know not only what it says (in order to identify the type of speech act it is) but also why the speaker said it (to be able to explain its occurrence). As we saw in chapter 5.2, explaining actions, including speech acts, is to provide a reason-explanation of them, one which picks out the practical reasoning processes which caused them. Put succinctly, to comprehend intentional acts we need to know more than just their meaning; we also need to know their cause.

This can be generalized to cover social phenomena more widely. Thus, an interpretation of the content of a society's world-view or its constitutive meanings, though it reveals *what* this worldview is, does not explain *why* the society has the worldview it has, or why this worldview has evolved as it has, or why it reinforces certain social relations and not others, or why people of a certain sort seem to support it more avidly than others. To answer these questions we need answers which are, broadly speaking, causal. The fixation of interpretivism with the meaningful dimension of human action has prevented it from developing an account of the causal questions and answers so important in social science.

Also of causal interest are the effects of certain actions, relations, or arrangements. In particular social scientists are concerned with general regularities which, though resulting from particular actions, are not intended by their agents. For example, economists have discovered the "paradox of savings," which occurs when an increase in peoples' rate of savings leads to a fall in national income and thus eventually to a decline

119

in the aggregate level of savings. Here, though the fall in savings resulted from intentional acts of saving, it was not an intended outcome of these acts. Similarly, political scientists have shown that despite their leaders' wishes party platforms inevitably tend to the middle of the political spectrum in a two-party polity with a unimodal distribution of attitudes over the electorate. These are but two examples in which social scientists have traced patterns in the unanticipated consequences of intentional actions and social arrangements.

Another sort of causal explanation which concentrates on consequences is structural-functional in character. Here certain forms of social relations (such as the nuclear family or the democratic polity), or cultural products (a particular ideology or symbol, for instance), are explained by showing how they contribute to the well-being of the society of which they are a part, and therefore to their own continued existence. Here a certain structure is explained in terms of its functional role in an ongoing system. In this sort of explanation the function is not a purpose in the minds of the people concerned, but a result of their activities and relations which occurs whether they know it or not. An example of such an explanation is Evans-Pritchard's account of the blood feud as having the function of maintaining the segmentary balance in Nuer society (Evans-Pritchard 1940, chapter 3). The participants in the feud do not intend to reinforce the balance of their social order, but this is the effect of their feuding – an effect which reinforces their tendency to feud.

A third kind of causal explanation which concentrates on effects is inspired by the work of Foucault. Foucault believed that our selves and our bodies, as well as the "discursive regimes" within which we think and relate, result from what he calls "the endlessly repeated play of domination," which is what he thought comprised human history. Accordingly, understanding who we are involves unearthing the mechanisms by which we have been produced; this unearthing he called genealogy. Genealogy seeks to understand how "the subject" has been constituted out of particular systems of subjugation by tracing the tortuous paths by which this constitution occurred.

Of particular importance for the question of whether social science is restricted to the terms of its subjects, Foucault maintained that this process is not the result of either a conscious or unconscious motivation on the part of the shapers or the shaped. Power for Foucault is not confined to cases in which an individual or group deliberately imposes its will on others. Rather, power concerns how actions affect the field of possible future actions. So understood, power is constitutive of all social interaction such that no matter what their subjective intentions agents are in fact implicated in relations of power: the effects of their activity are always delimiting or empowering, coercive or defining. Ultimately for Foucault power does not work through the intentions of agents but emanates from their every act by the ways the effects of their acts enable and constrain other acts.

Moreover, Foucault also thought that certain types of power do not function through the meaning of acts or utterances. Peoples' bodies and dispositions to act can be shaped directly without the intermediary of meaning. For example, the arrangements of desks in a classroom can directly affect the bodies of students and teachers, and consequently their forms of interaction, without any mediating ideas entering the heads of either the students or the teachers. As Foucault put it:

> What I want to show is how power relations can materially penetrate the body in depth without depending even on the mediation of the subject's own representations. If power takes hold of the body this isn't first through its having to be interiorized in peoples' consciousness. (Foucault, 1981, p. 186)

Given a non-subjectivist account of power, and given that certain forms of power bypass "the subject's own representations," genealogists do not focus on the meanings which social agents attach to their activities nor on the implicit meanings which underlie given social practices or ways of thinking. Instead, the genealogist seeks to explore how certain micropractices restrict and license certain effects on the bodies and dispositions of those they subjugate.

Uncovering the genealogy by which subjects are constituted is like the other explanatory endeavors we have been considering: like discovering the conditions which produce a worldview or a form of interaction or a characteristic way of perceiving or feeling; like analyzing unintended consequences; and like discovering the functions of social structure, genealogy is a form of causal explanation. But how do causal explanations work? I will answer this question more fully in chapter 8; for present purposes a simplified account will suffice. Causal relations differ from relations of mere conjunction; that is, "c caused e" is fundamentally different from "c occurred and then e occurred." That c occurred and then e happened to occur does not imply that c caused e; to say that c causes e is to say (speaking very roughly) that c's occurrence is a necessary and/or sufficient condition for the occurrence of e: if e could have happened without c, and/or if c could have occurred and e not occur, then c did not cause e.

To put the matter slightly differently: causal statements license subjunctive conditionals ("*if* c were to occur, e would occur") or contrary-to-fact conditionals ("*if* c had not occurred, e would not have occurred"). But in order for causal assertions to license these inferences they must indicate some reason why c and e are more than accidentally related. Thus, unlike statements of mere conjunction causal statements must be able to explain their instances.

Take, for example, the fact that in western Europe support for totalitarian parties is inversely related to education. Are these causally related or is their concurrence merely an accident or the result of some other cause? In order to claim that a relative lack of education causes support for totalitarian parties, social scientists must indicate how the former could be related to the latter in more than an accidental way. Thus, for instance, they might explain this finding by observing that in western Europe less educated people tend to have authoritarian personalities, and that people with authoritarian personalities tend to support authoritarian political movements. However, this putative connection is somewhat undeveloped. What is it about people with authoritarian personalities that leads them to support anti-democratic parties? Is it just a coincidence that they do, or is their behavior somehow necessitated by their having the kind of personality they have? If we could change a person with an authoritarian personality, would his or her political preferences change as well? And is it a lack of education which spawns an authoritarian personality, or is it the other way round: do people with authoritarian personalities tend to eschew education? Can we prevent the emergence of authoritarian personalities by educating people more? Or is education really not a causal factor in all of this?

To answer these and similar sorts of questions causal theories are required. Theories provide a systematic account of a diverse set of phenomena by showing that the events in question all result from the operation of a few basic principles. A causal theory shows precisely how two or more events are related causally by specifying the basic entities which constitute the phenomena to be explained and their modes of interaction such that one of them produced the other(s). Thus, a causal theory gives the grounds required to enable subjunctive conditionals or contrary-to-fact conditionals. Causal ascriptions ultimately must be backed by causal theories; this is why causal explanations of particular occurrences inevitably lead onward to causal theories.

Theory is also needed for another purpose besides legitimizing particular causal explanations. As social science attempts to become more rigorously scientific, it necessarily attempts to organize its various causal explanations and the theories upon which they rest by systematically interrelating them, and by subjecting them to experimental and other empirical verification. In this process, the self-conscious development of "grand scale" theory – a sort of theory of theories – is absolutely crucial. The sciences of behavior have developed such grand theories of the wide scope and power they have for precisely this reason. (Examples of such grand theories include rational choice theory; structural-functional theory; neo-classical economic theory; Freudian theory.)

The relevance of this for the question of whether we must comprehend others in their own terms ought to be obvious. Causal theories will undoubtedly transcend the conceptual and cultural resources of their subjects, employing categories of thought and establishing connections about which these subjects are entirely ignorant. The categories of causal social analyses derive from social science, not from the social agents being analyzed. Interpretivism is correct that to know what people are doing or creating we need to know what their activities and products mean for them; in this we must pay strict attention to the terms of the agents themselves. But interpretivism fails to acknowledge that social science also needs to ascertain the causes of these doings and creations beyond the agents' own practical reasonings, and that in this endeavor social scientists will inevitably develop terms different from those of the agents themselves.

6.3 Competence

The social sciences typically seek to explain phenomena conceived in terms different from those in the natural sciences: intentional actions and the products of those actions described in terms of their meaning. The result is that theories in the social sciences have jobs to do different from those in the natural sciences. Specifically, the social sciences require competence theories as well as causal ones.

Intentional actions are both rule-governed and rational. They are rule-governed in that their identity derives in part from principles of thought and behavior which they instantiate. In order for an agent to be an agent, and in order for an act to be an act of a certain kind, agents' performances and products must embody these principles in some standard or publicly recognizable manner. A speech act is one of greeting only if the greeters express themselves in an appropriately identifiable way. You are checkmated in chess only if your opponent moves in a manner permitted by the rules of chess; more generally, you and your opponent are playing chess only if you observe the rules which comprise it. As we said in chapter 3, constitutive rules enable the performance of intentional actions and their products.

Besides being rule-following, intentional actions are also generally rational. They result from practical reasoning processes which relate means to ends and which express psychological states. Intentional activity is intentional because it embodies certain procedures and norms of rationality (for example, as we saw in chapter 5, it must conform to certain norms of intelligibility).

Rule-following, rational behavior is irreducibly normative in character. That is, it can be assessed as more or less correct or perspicuous depending on whether the rules are followed well or poorly, whether the rules themselves conduce to their goal or purpose, and whether these goals and purposes meet certain criteria. Thus speech acts, because they are performed in accordance with linguistic rules, can be assessed as grammatically correct or not. Checkmating, promising, and voting succeed or not depending on whether they accord with the rules which enable them. And all instrumental actions can be assessed as more or less rational depending on the extent to which they are likely to realize their intended aims.

Because of the normative character of intentional activity and its products, a distinction can be made between the competence of agents and their actual performance. An agent's *competence* is his or her mastery of the rules or norms of rationality which apply to a particular activity; an agent's *performance*, on the other hand, refers to the agent's actual behavior, which is determined in part by his or her competence but also by other factors including degrees of attention, perception, learning, and the like. Thus an agent may be a competent speaker of English, but any given actualization of this competence – the performance of a speech act – may or may not adequately reflect this competence. That is, the speaker's utterance may be syntactically and/or semantically correct or not.

Corresponding to the distinction between competence and performance is a distinction between two types of theory. A *competence theory* attempts to model the capacities and processes of an idealized agent who is perfectly rational or who has perfectly mastered the relevant rules which underlie specific sorts of action. Such a theory seeks to disclose the system of rules and norms of rationality which enable the production of meaningful symbolic activities and their products. A *performance theory*, on the other hand, while making use of or presupposing a theory of competence, is designed to explain what agents actually do, and so it encompasses causal factors in addition to certain competencies which bear upon their behavior.

Competence theories abound in the social sciences. In the theory of transformational grammar, for example, Chomsky (1965) attempts to set forth the basic rules or principles which generate all grammatically well-formed sentences of a language, and only such sentences. Chomsky's is a competence theory because it seeks to model the ideal speaker's mastery of his or her language, his or her (potential) capacity to utter and to recognize well-formed sentences. Habermas's (1979) theory of universal pragmatics seeks to lay bare the epistemic and pragmatic conditions presupposed in all forms of communication (a form of social interaction which is oriented towards mutual understanding). Habermas's is a competence theory because it ventures to explicate the rules, structures, and capacities the command of which underlies the ability of agents to convey meaning in their actions, expressions, and productions. Piaget's (1970) genetic epistemology is also in part a competence theory. It endeavors to disclose the perceptual and cognitive skills necessary for adult (and ultimately scientific) perception and cognition, as well as the principles of growth which underlie the progressive unfolding of these skills. Kegan's (1982) constructive-developmental theory in the psychology of development tries not only to describe and categorize the stages of the evolution of the self (in this it is a performance theory), but also to account for this evolution by means of an inner logic of capacities which underlie this evolution (in this it is a competence theory).

Perhaps the most developed and influential competence theories in the social sciences are those which undergird rational choice theory. This theory is at the heart of modern economics; it has also inspired important work in sociology, anthropology, and political science. Rational choice theory seeks to explain behavior in terms of agents maximizing their expected utility. As an explanation of actual behavior it is of course a performance theory. But because it conceives agents as instrumentally rational in the sense of attempting to choose the best means available to achieve their ends, rational choice theory needs a theory of instrumental rationality; this it gets from two competence theories: decision theory and game theory.

Both decision theory and game theory attempt to formalize utility-maximizing strategies given certain basic assumptions and conditions. Decision theory spells out the processes of decision-making in various situations of choice (of degrees and reliability of information; of probabilities of outcome; of kinds of end; and the like). Game theory outlines processes of practical rationality given certain constraints imposed by the interdependency of choices of other utility-maximizers (including degrees of trust, kinds of outcome, degrees of interdependency, and so forth). Taken together, decision theory and game theory attempt to model the thought processes of perfectly rational agents seeking the best course of action to attain their goals in various kinds of situations all marked by the presence of other utility-maximizers. These competence theories figure in rational choice theory when the behavior of actual agents is explained as more or less replicating these perfectly rational thought processes.

Even though the performances of agents derive at least in part from their competencies, agents themselves may be totally unable to specify the nature and content of these competencies. Indeed they may be totally ignorant of them. In order to speak proficient English you do not need to know anything about the structure of its deep grammar or whether this structure shares formal features with all other grammars. You needn't know the pragmatic conditions in virtue of which you are able to communicate with others. As an agent you can be very much like the student who was speaking prose all the time but didn't know it. Acting and speaking subjects know how to perform and produce a variety of actions and objects without explicitly adverting to, or being able to give an explicit account of, the underlying skills, principles, and rules on which these performances and productions are based.

Thus, competence theories are not constrained by the terms of their subjects. All kinds of theoretical terms abound in existing competence theories which go far beyond the practical knowledge which even the most adept agents possess in performing and producing. Consider some of the terms of decision theory and game theory (competence theories which are closer than most to ordinary experience!): Bayesian criteria of maximization; utility function; prisoner's dilemma; bounded rationality; satisficing; co-ordination equilibria; maximin or minimax principles of choice; payoff matrices; revealed preference. These technical terms undoubtedly transcend those of even the most successful utility maximizers. They are part of a conceptual armory developed by social scientists, not by the agents themselves.

But although competence theories employ concepts which go beyond those of their subjects, this does not mean that these theories can simply ignore their subjects' behavior and the terms in which it is expressed. Competence theories are ultimately tested against the intuitions of competent agents. In linguistics, for instance, proposals must, in the words of Chomsky (1965, p. 20), "meet the empirical condition of conforming, in a mass of crucial and clear cases, to the linguistic intuitions of the native speaker." How else to ascertain whether a given utterance is well-formed except by consulting native speakers' intuitions?

Competence theories attempt to uncover certain basic skills and knowledge tacitly possessed by competent agents, and to make these skills and knowledge explicit and formalized. Thus their ultimate test must be, does the theory make explicit what is already present in practice (though in an implicit and not fully realized form)? Habermas tellingly calls competence theories "rational reconstructions" of basic capacities (to speak grammatically; to think in instrumentally rational terms; to communicate; to perceive and think scientifically; and so on). Such theories *re*-construct what is already present, though in a tacit and impure form. In this way competence theories must still attend to the activities and products of their subjects and especially to the terms by which these activities and products are

126

conceived, even as they employ concepts and terms which transcend those of the agents themselves.

6.4 Critique

Interpretivism claims that social science ought to consist in laying out the structure of the reasoning processes which cause intentional actions and the schemes of meaning within which these processes and their results occur. This does not mean interpretivists believe that social scientists need only ask agents the meaning of their activities. Any given agent may be ignorant of the meaning of his or her acts, and may be unable to articulate the schemes of meaning on which he or she draws. Interpretivists desire to learn not what actual agents know but what a fully self-knowledgeable agent would be able to provide if there were such a person. They put this point by claiming that social scientific explanations should consist of the self-understandings of an ideal informant in a given society.

Unfortunately, this claim ignores crucial elements of human life. Even ideal members of a society may systematically misunderstand their own motives, wants, values and actions, as well as the nature of their social order, and these misunderstandings may underlie and sustain irrational forms of social interaction. Further, these misunderstandings may derive from fundamental inadequacies or incoherences in a culture's schemes of meaning. In these cases even ideal agents' self-understandings may mask social reality as much as reveal it. Social scientists thus cannot confine themselves to explicating even ideal agents' concepts and self-understandings because these may be essentially confused. Sometimes social scientific explanation requires identifying this confusion and its results; in these cases social scientists must go beyond the scheme of meaning operative in a given culture.

Consider the European witch-craze of the early modern period in Europe and North America. As Trevor-Roper (1969) has argued, the belief in witches was not necessarily irrational in the intellectual context of the time. But the witch craze involved more than a belief in witches. What distinguished the witch-craze, and what requires explanation going beyond the self-understandings of even ideal agents of the time, are the sudden and dramatic increase in the number of putative witches who were discovered and condemned, the ferocity of the persecutions, and the geographic and social patterns of persecution. By focusing only on the concepts available to the agents involved social scientists would be unable to explain these phenomena adequately: it would certainly not do to explain the witch-craze as the result of a sudden increase in the number of witches!

Confining analyses to the terms of those of the period would prevent setting the witch-craze in the context of the social tensions of the period and the scapegoating that served to deflect these tensions. By explaining the witch-craze only in terms of the system of beliefs and values of which it was a part, social scientists would miss what was essential to the social reality of the witch-craze.

Mental states, actions, and their products which result from confused or incoherent schemes of meaning are not uncommon. Compulsive and other neurotic behavior, violent prejudicial conduct toward minority groups, and recurring self-destructive patterns of social interaction are all too frequent in human experience. Nor is such behavior always an isolated feature of peoples' lives. It may be systematically related to a wide range of their emotions, beliefs, relations, and actions. Moreover, the very basis of peoples' self-understanding – the terms in which they talk about themselves in their most lucid and reflective moments, and the fears, aspirations, beliefs, passions, and values which they ascribe to themselves at these times – may be fundamentally mistaken. As a result they may be unable adequately to explain their behavior to themselves or others. Worse, as a result of such misunderstanding they may pursue ends they cannot achieve, and the goals they reach may not be satisfying. Such frustration may lead them to intensify their efforts and so to perpetuate their misery.

Moreover, just as individuals may be systematically mistaken, so whole forms of life may be based upon such self-misunderstandings or what Marx called "false consciousness." Whole groups may have institutionalized patterns of belief, desire, and action which are incoherent, self-defeating, or unwarranted. Worse, such patterns may be inexplicable given the terms available to the agents themselves. Trapped in a fundamentally limited and inadequate scheme of meaning, agents may be unable to gain self-knowledge or knowledge of the ways their social lives are inherently frustrating; they may even be unable to perceive that they are in fact trapped. For this a scheme of concepts different from their own must be employed to describe and explain who they are and what they do. This is the picture of human life classically painted by Marx and Freud, and more recently portrayed by Brown (1959), Laing (1960), Marcuse (1964), Becker (1973), and Habermas (1975).

Crucial in this regard is the distinction between manifest and latent content. An activity's manifest content is its meaning understood from its own vantage point. Its latent content is its actual meaning which can only be ascertained by transcending the vantage point of the agents' themselves. The manifest content obscures latent content. In these cases elements of the manifest content must be treated as ciphers for the latent content, ciphers which can only be understood by re-interpreting the manifest content from outside its own realm.

Thus, according to Marx, Christians pray to God because they desire to be complete and whole human beings, and they believe that God will provide this fulfillment. The manifest content of prayer is its meaning as delineated by Christian theology: a form of worship of the Supreme Being. But all this, says Marx, is an illusion: God is not a separate being; rather He is just an idealized picture of human beings fully actualized. By praying, humans imaginatively partake in God's power (which is to say, they imaginatively exercise their own potential power); this is the latent content of prayer. Marx argued that the satisfactions afforded by prayer are ersatz satisfactions because in prayer agents only seem to express who they potentially are, they don't actually do so. Only the development and exercise of their productive capacities in forms of cooperative social labor can provide genuine satisfaction. The reason why they content themselves with the illusion of power rather than its reality (that is, with prayer rather than cooperative social labor) is that their current social conditions preclude them from exercising their power, prevent them from being the agents they could be.

The relevant point here is not the correctness of Marx's diagnosis but the nature of this diagnosis and what it shows about social theory. Marx's theory claims that as long as people conceive of their lives in religious terms they will remain alienated from themselves, though they will not understand this alienation and so will not understand their desires or their actions. Moreover, as long as social scientists confine themselves to the manifest meaning of religious practices they will systematically fail to understand what these practices are all about. For that they need to employ a scheme of concepts different from those engaged in these practices (in this case, a Marxist scheme).

The identification of the latent content of ways of acting and thinking is sometimes called "ideology-critique." The schemes of meaning operative in a society, but which offer inadequate resources for comprehending the characteristic ways people think, act, and relate in that society, are said to be ideologies. To understand an ideology, precisely because it is inherently deficient and misleading, requires that social scientists reveal this deficiency and the way it functions to frustrate those in its grip. Doing so demands not only that the manifest content of this ideology be uncovered, but that this be translated into its latent content; further, the mechanisms by which ideologies acquire their symbolic import and with it their causal power, and yet remain hidden from agents' views, must also be identified. All this will inevitably involve a full-scale account of the systematic ways people are deluded and frustrated because of this delusion; such a full-scale account is called *critical theory* (the classic examples of which are those of Marx and Freud; some contemporary feminist theory is also of this type.)

In the case of ideologies a culture's scheme of meaning possesses a sense quite different from what it seems even to ideal informants. Another way schemes of meaning can be different from what they seem has been explored by Jacques Derrida by means of his concept of *"différance."* According to Derrida for everything affirmed there is an "other" that contrasts with it which, though ostensibly absent, is in fact contained in it as a deferred meaning. *Deconstruction* is the critical procedure by which this supposed other is unearthed and shown to be an operative if invisible element in an ongoing scheme of meaning. Derrida urges that not only texts, but actions, practices, relations, and cultural products be "deconstructed" to reveal their full complexity and internal tensions.

An example will make this clear. Assume a heterosexually dominated society in which the principles which organize the society and the self-understandings which underlie them are heterosexual. In such a society, homosexuals are conceived as "non-heterosexuals," defective and only of negative value. Homosexuality is thereby intended to be excluded from the self-understandings of this society. But is it? In such a scheme heterosexuals gain their identity only by distinguishing themselves from what they supposedly are not; they define themselves as the antithesis of homosexuality, and they try to shut it out of their lives. But in so doing they unwittingly include homosexuality in their own self-conception: homosexuals are intimately related to heterosexuals as the image of what they are not, and therefore they function as an essential reminder to heterosexuals of what they are. Heterosexuals therefore need homosexuals even as they attempt to subjugate or shut them out of their experience. Heterosexual identity is thus parasitically dependent on homo-sexuality in the act of excluding and subordinating it.

Worse, perhaps such exclusion is necessary because homosexuality may not be so external to heterosexuals after all. Perhaps heterosexuals have homosexual elements in themselves which, because they define themselves as not-homosexuals, heterosexuals have to repress, deny, and expel from their own being. Thus they may relegate homosexuals to inferior regions and vigilantly police these regions as a way of protecting themselves from their own homosexual impulses. Or they may engage in rituals intended to re-affirm their heterosexuality in which they demonstrate to themselves as much as to others that they are thoroughly heterosexual. In these ways what is pushed outside is actually something inside, even though heterosexuals may have no conscious knowledge about this.

This same pattern may be present in other dichotomies operative in social life. Consider the antinomies of man vs. woman, white vs. black, colonizer vs. colonized, sane vs. mad, civilized vs. barbaric, the religiously saved vs. the damned or the pagan. In these the former terms are usually privileged, but the same pattern of the presence of the term's opposite is often evident. In these and other cases deconstruction attempts to show how the clear conceptual boundaries which constitute a scheme of meaning are not as clear cut as they appear to those who live and act in terms of them. In particular it seeks to show how such oppositions inadvertently invert or collapse or spill over into one another. Schemes of meaning, despite their apparent coherence, often embarrass their own ruling conceptual logic; deconstructionists fasten on points of tension, ellipses, silences, or margins to discover the ways these schemes come unstuck or contradict themselves. Deconstructionists say that meaning is always confused, continually flickering, collapsing, and spilling out and around ostensible categories of thought and action.

Despite deconstruction's insistence that no hard distinction exists between literary and non-literary texts, it has been most successfully applied in the analysis of the former. Nevertheless, deconstruction – both as an individual technique, and as part of the larger enterprise of post-structuralist social science – has also figured in analyses of various forms of social interaction. For example, what is now called "cultural studies" seeks to unmask the self-contradictory elements operating in various forms of representation in popular culture (such as the tabloid press, soap operas, football crowds, popular movies, and the like). These "texts" (usually of familiar events or objects) are said to be "sites of contestation"; accordingly, they are "interrogated" to demonstrate how they distort, "occlude," or in other ways inadvertently reveal the ideological pressures which shaped them. (These pressures often are said to derive from the differential way power operates in a culture to the disadvantage of certain "marginalized" groups.)

Deconstruction requires social analysts to transcend the conceptual scheme of those being analyzed to reveal the ways this scheme betrays itself. Deconstruction aims to dismantle agents' notions of identity by exposing a heretofore concealed "otherness" which has been suppressed to preserve the illusion of a fixed, bounded self and a unified society rooted in a coherent, single scheme of meaning. Thus deconstruction is a form of interpretation which does not use the terms of even the ideal agent's self-understanding. It seeks out what is invisible even to the most aware participants whose cultural discourse unwittingly covers over the heterogeneity, discord, and systematic exclusions upon which it is based.

131

Particularly important when discussing both ideology-critique and deconstruction is not to misinterpret these two kinds of critique simply as forms of moral evaluation. Though ideology-critique and deconstruction involve assessing the rationality and unmasking the duplicities of forms of interaction and ways of thinking, *this assessment and unmasking are required for purposes of explanation.* Here interpretation involves making peoples' self-understandings clearer than they can be to themselves by showing that these self-understandings are illusory, contradictory, wrongheaded, or narrow. This critique is necessary precisely when peoples' behavior and relations derive from the illusory nature of their self-understandings; in these cases explaining the behavior and relations is inseparable from criticizing it, and explanation centrally involves forms of evaluation.

Human behavior is intentional in the sense of being undertaken on the basis of the beliefs and desires of those who perform it. But in situations in which systematic misunderstandings of the meanings of their activities reinforced by repressive mechanisms result in agents engaging in irrational behavior, the traditional interpretivist goal of understanding intentional phenomena in their own terms must be replaced by the need to critique these phenomena. The only way to understand irrational behavior is to lay bare the ways peoples' self-understandings mask the social reality which their behavior creates, and to demonstrate that the cause of their behavior occurs at a level beyond the capacity of the agents to appreciate, given the conceptual and emotional responses open to them. In doing this, social scientists must use concepts and conceptual distinctions which outstrip those operative in the social life which is being studied.

Still, this does not mean that in critiquing the behavior and self-understandings of even ideal agents critical social science can ignore these self-understandings. In the first place, the nature of the confusion and inadequacy of a particular form of activity or social organization cannot be demonstrated without careful attention to the ways it operates in its own terms. In the second place, critique requires that the self-understandings of agents be translated into those of the alternative scheme which more accurately reveals who agents are and what they are doing. Such translation requires detailed knowledge of the original scheme. This translation is particularly important for endeavors like ideology-critique and deconstruction which claim to know agents better than they do themselves, for without being connected to the self-understandings of these agents these endeavors can easily degenerate into ideological assertions themselves, unconstrained by empirical evidence. In the last analysis, critique depends upon its ability to illuminate the self-understandings of a group of people; thus, critique is dependent upon interpretation of what this group is doing from its own vantage point even as it transcends this vantage point.

6.5 Summing Up

The philosophy of social science has consistently been plagued by two related dichotomies: that between understanding and explanation, and that between cause and meaning. Interpretivism defines itself by means of these dichotomies: it insists that, unlike the natural sciences which seek to explain non-intentional phenomena by discovering their causes, the job of social science is to understand intentional phenomena by interpreting their meaning. Intentional phenomena are said to be essentially meaningful in the sense that they are what they are in virtue of the sense they have for those engaged in them. Uncovering this sense is the way intentional phenomena can be comprehended.

Moreover, interpretivists further insist that social scientific interpretations must be cast in the terms of those being studied. The identities of intentional phenomena derive from the constructions the agents themselves place upon what they live through and the scheme of meaning which underwrites these constructions. To grasp these identities, interpretivism argues, social scientists must thus interpret a culture from its own internal point of view.

But from the correct observation that social science must be interpretive interpretivism incorrectly concludes that social science is *only* interpretive. Interpretivism overlooks the fact that many noninterpretive theories have great importance in social scientific explanations: *causal theories* which explore the factors which produce cultures and their alterations, unintended consequences, functional interrelationships, and genealogical origins; *competence theories* which seek the capacities that underwrite various kinds of intentional activity; and assorted *critical theories* which aim to understand the mechanisms by which people become subject to ideologies and therefore engage in systematically irrational behavior. What is wrong with any view which focuses exclusively on one sort of theory is that it necessarily leaves certain types of question and therefore certain types of answer unaccounted for. Different explanatory modes in social science pose and answer different questions, and an adequate philosophy of social science must attend to all of them.

Besides failing to allow for the full range of questions in social science, interpretivism also incorrectly claims that all interpretations consist in grasping how others see the world. As we have seen, some forms of interpretation – such as ideology-critique and deconstruction – go beyond

133

the conceptual schemes of those under study. The range of theories in the social sciences which involve more than understanding meaning and which transcend the terms of those being studied is exceedingly wide. Interpretivism is thus not so much false as one-sided. It correctly insists that any acceptable account of social phenomena which conceives them as intentional must pay strict attention to the scheme of meaning in which they are located and on which they draw. But interpretivism mistakenly asserts that uncovering the scheme of meaning operative in a culture is sufficient. Social science does require understanding, but it *also* requires explanation; it consists not just of the interpretation of meaning of social phenomena but *also* the uncovering of their causes, the competencies which underwrite them, and the ways (if any) in which they are irrational. Social scientists therefore must not just master the conceptual schemes of those they investigate but also must master another more theoretical and technical vocabulary which employs conceptual resources which transcend the framework of those being studied.

If Captain Cook had included an anthropologist aboard he might have understood how the Hawaiians would interpret his return by grasping how it fit into their scheme of meaning. But he would have known more than this. He would also have then learned the conditions which produced this scheme, how it functioned in Hawaiian society, its unintended effects, its origins, its relation to certain social tensions, its ideological dimensions, and the ways it contained seeds of its opposite. He would have comprehended the Hawaiians both as an ideal Hawaiian informant would understand them, but also with a depth and from a perspective that not even the most self-knowledgeable of them could have had.

So must we comprehend others in their own terms? Yes, in the sense that we cannot grasp intentional phenomena and their products as intentional without ascertaining what they mean for those engaged in them. But No, in the sense that explaining these phenomena often will require outstripping the conceptual resources of those being studied.

Further Reading

This chapter owes a great deal to Moon (1975).

For a fine overall discussion of social scientific explanation, see Little (1991). For an excellent discussion of various explanatory strategies in the social sciences, and a sophisticated philosophy of social science in light of this, see Bohman (1991).

For a criticism of the notion that Hawaiian natives mistook Captain Cook for their god Lono as a cultural myth perpetuated by western scholars, see Obeyesekere (1992). For a spirited reply to Obeyesekere and a defense of the interpretation given in this chapter, see Sahlins (1995).

For interpretivism, see Winch (1958); Taylor (1971 and 1985b); MacIntyre (1971), Geertz (1973a and 1983), and the essays collected in Rabinow and Sullivan (1979).

For an account of the relation between interpretation and explanation different but related to that developed in this chapter, see Mahajan (1992) and Henderson (1993). See also Beattie (1964) and Ulin (1984).

For a discussion of cause and meaning in the social sciences, see Von Wright (1971), Jarvie (1972), Gellner (1973), and most especially Moon (1975).

Regarding the various sorts of causal theories discussed in this chapter: for a type of causal analysis which studies concepts in terms of their social and political contexts (*begriffsgeschichte*), see Koselleck (1985; 1988). For structural-functionalism, see Malinowski (1944), Parsons (1951), Radcliffe-Browne (1952), and Merton (1957). For genealogy, see Foucault (1977, 1978 and 1981), and Dreyfus and Rabinow (1982). For Foucault's notion that power affects bodies directly, see Fay (1987, section 7.2).

For competence theory, see Chomsky (1965). For rational choice theory, see the articles by Becker, Harsanyi, and Elster in Elster (1986); as applied to social conflict, see Hardin (1995); in economics, see Becker (1976); in political science, see Downs (1957); in sociology, Blau (1964); in anthropology, Barth (1959) and Bradley (1969). For game theory and decision theory in general, see Luce and Raiffa (1957); Schelling (1960); and Friedman (1986); Von Neumann and Morgenstern (1944) is the *locus classicus*.

For critical theory, see Horkheimer (1937), Habermas (1971 and 1988), Wellmer (1971), Bauman (1976), Held (1980), Geuss (1981), and Fay (1987). For a feminist perspective in this area, see Harding (1986) and Smith (1987; 1990). For cultural studies, see Hall (ed.) (1980), Grossberg (ed.) (1992), Ingils (1994), Jenks (1993), and Bhabha (1994). For deconstruction, Derrida (1973a; 1973b; 1981). For a useful overall analysis of this entire area, consult Eagleton (1983), Hoy (1982), and Seidman (1994).

For the importance of the category homosexuality/heterosexuality as a "social logic" which structures core modes of thought, culture, and identity in modern society, see Sedgwick (1991).

7

Is the Meaning of Others' Behavior
What They *Mean by It?*

7.1 Intentionalism

On the night of 10 January, 49 BCE Julius Caesar with one of his legions crossed the Rubicon, the small river which separated Italy from the province he governed. What was the meaning of this act?

That this is a question which must be put by historians ought to be obvious given the distinction we have already drawn in chapter 5 between mere movements (which can be described in purely physical terms) and actions (which as meaningful must be described in terms of the intentions they embody). Human actions are what they are precisely because of the meaning they express. The events in which social scientists are interested are essentially gestural in the sense that they communicate a message, enact a strategy, follow a principle, or advance an interest.

The clearest example of this is, of course, speech itself. In interacting humans emit sounds; but these sounds are not of the same type as the sounds coming from a squeaky wheel, or even of the same sort as the grunts, chirps, and squeals which comprise the sounds of biological urgency characteristic of lower-level non-human animals. (Whether higher-level non-human animals speak is an open, much debated question.) Human speech is intended to express something by standing for something else – it is symbolic. Thus, it may convey information ("A hunter is coming"), or express a desire ("I want to be held"), or indicate an attitude of mind ("I like you"), and so forth. By means of uttering sentences humans represent the world and themselves to themselves and to each other in a variety of ways; in this way these utterances are meaningful.

From the point of view of multiculturalism, the question regarding the meaning of others' behavior is one of the first questions which must be asked. As we have seen, one of the distinguishing features of multicultural

136

sensitivity is the awareness that others do things differently from the way oneself and those in one's group do them. You can't assume that what you mean by an act of speech or a gesture or a practice is what others mean by them. Consequently, a prime rule of multiculturalism is: when confronted by the behavior of others, don't presuppose that it means what it would if you did it; always ask, what is the meaning of that?, with the presupposition that this meaning is likely to be different from what it might at first appear. Questions of meaning are thus at the heart of multicultural experience.

They are also at the heart of social science. If much of the behavior of humans is what it is because of the meaning it contains, then social scientists and historians are required to do something their counterparts in the natural sciences need not do, namely, interpret the meaning of the behavior and its products which they observe. Social scientists must do this for both descriptive and explanatory reasons. Descriptively, in order to know what they are observing, social scientists must know the meaning of a particular act, product, or relation. An arm goes out from a person's side; what has occurred? a signal? a rude gesture? a rehearsal of such a gesture? a vote? a dance step? an attempt to strike a bothersome insect? In order to be able to say, social scientists need to ascertain what the act signifies or indicates.

Regarding explanation, in order to illuminate the nature of a meaningful act, product, or relation social scientists need to spell out its meaning in greater depth and detail. Even with behavior or texts whose surface meaning is relatively clear social scientists must seek to grasp its deeper meaning. Thus an act may be one of investing, but economic sociologists will want to probe the deeper assumptions which lie behind and enable such activity (by so probing Max Weber was led to the deeper senses of capitalist behavior, and thus to an exploration of Protestant theology – something which on its face seems quite removed from saving and investment activity). Or an act may be one of betting, but further elucidation of the meaning of this activity will force anthropologists to explore its purposes and significance more fully (in this way Clifford Geertz came to appreciate the Balinese cockfight as a text for Balinese society similar to the way *Macbeth* is for ours – again, a feature of it not readily visible).

It is no wonder, therefore, that social scientists and historians ask of human behavior, what does it mean? And hence the opening question of this chapter: what was the meaning of Caesar's crossing the Rubicon?

In order to answer this question we must know the meaning of "meaning." That is, what is it that is being asked for in seeking the meaning of Caesar's action? The root of the word "meaning" suggests one very plausible answer to this question. "Meaning" is derived from the German word *meinen*, which means "to have in mind." On this basis the meaning of an act, text, relation, and the like would be that which its author had in mind in performing or producing it – what he or she intended to express or achieve by it. This commonsense insight is the basis for a general philosophical theory of meaning called intentionalism. According to *intentionalism* the meaning of an act or its product derives from the intentions of its author. (This implies an answer to the question in the title of this chapter: the meaning of others' behavior is what *they* mean by it.) Thus the meaning of Caesar's crossing the Rubicon is precisely what Caesar intended by this act, that is, what he hoped to accomplish by it; and it is the historian's job to reveal Caesar's own intentions in performing this act.

How does intentionalism account for that most characteristic form of meaning, linguistic meaning? One of the most influential versions of intentionalism is to be found in the theory of linguistic meaning put forward by Paul Grice (1957). According to this theory for a speaker to mean something by an utterance is for him or her to make this utterance with the intention of producing certain effects on an audience. According to Grice, a speaker S means something by what he or she utters (U) if he or she intended to produce some effect in an audience A, and intends this effect to come about through A's recognizing that this is S's intention. Thus in the case of the utterance "it is raining outside," speaking this collection of words means what it does because by it S

(1)   intended that A should come to believe that it is raining;
(2)   intended that A should be aware of intention (1);
(3)   intended that the awareness in (2) should be part of A's reason for believing that it is raining.

Here linguistic meaning derives from a certain sort of communicative intention on the part of speakers.

In the philosophy of social science and history a number of intentionalist accounts of meaning have been proffered; it would be useful to examine at least one of these to appreciate more fully the nature of the intentionalist research programme. Here I am thinking about the theory of re-enactment proposed by R. G. Collingwood (1961).

Collingwood claimed that it was the task of the historian to "think himself into an action, to discern the thought of its agent" (1961, p. 213). According to Collingwood actions have an "inside" or a "thought-side" as well as an observable outside, an inside which distinguishes them from purely physical events which can be described and explained from the outside in purely physical, non-intentional terms. Thus, to identify actions we must ascertain the inner thoughts which they incarnate. For instance, to describe Caesar's crossing the Rubicon as a "crossing" – that is, as an intentional act as opposed to a mere occurrence (which might have been the case if Caesar had been unwillingly dragged across the river, or didn't know the river was the Rubicon) – is already to see it as having an inside, as in part constituted by Caesar's own thoughts which it expresses.

To understand intentional acts like Caesar's, Collingwood reasoned not surprisingly that we must uncover the thoughts which are operative in them. Collingwood put this by saying that an historian must "re-enact" an agent's thought in his own mind, "re-thinking for himself the thought of its author" (1961, p. 283). Thus, for example:

> Suppose an historian is reading the Theodosian Code and has before him a certain edict of an emperor. Merely reading the words and being able to translate them does not amount to knowing their historical significance. In order to do that he must envisage it as the emperor envisaged it. Then he must see for himself, just as if the emperor's situation were his own, how such a situation might be dealt with; he must see the possible alternatives, and the reasons for choosing one rather than another; and thus he must go through the process which the emperor went through in deciding on this particular course. Thus he is re-enacting in his own mind the experience of the emperor; and only in so far as he does this has he any historical knowledge, as distinct from a merely philological knowledge, of the meaning of the edict. (Collingwood 1961, p. 213)

"Re-thinking" thus means grasping the agent's conception of the facts of his or her situation; his or her beliefs and desires regarding it; his or her sense of the possible courses of action in light of these; and the process of practical deliberation by which the agent put all these together. In the terminology of chapter 5, it means discovering the agent's reasons for behaving as he or she did. In this way historians uncover the meaning of the act.

To return to Caesar, on a Collingwoodian view the meaning of his crossing the Rubicon derived from the purposes which Caesar himself thought he was fostering in so acting. What were these? The political situation in Rome in the fall of 50 BCE was extremely unstable. Deep distrust marked the relations between the two chief military players, Caesar and Pompey; deep divisions rendered the Senate ineffective; and fear beset the Consuls who did not wish Caesar to become a Consul himself when his term of service in Gaul finally ended in 49 BCE. Of course, Caesar himself was aware of all this, having spies and allies in the thick of things in Rome. In the midst of all this suspicion and uncertainty rumors broke out that Caesar was going to move against Rome; to protect themselves the Consuls called upon Pompey to save the State against Caesar. Having learned about this, Caesar moved with his characteristic dash, attacking

Pompey before Pompey could raise a proper army. So the meaning of the crossing of the Rubicon was to strike pre-emptively against Pompey and those who supported him.

Despite its usefulness, however, the Collingwoodian account of meaning is not entirely adequate even in its own intentionalist terms; it consequently needs to be emended. (In section 7.3 we shall see that intentionalism itself needs to be supplemented even further.) Consider the distinction prominently drawn by another intentionalist, Quentin Skinner, between the intention *to do* something and the intention *in doing* something:

> But to speak of a writer's intentions may be either to refer to his plan or design to create a certain type of work (his intention to do x), or to refer and describe an actual work in a certain way (as embodying a particular intention in x-ing). In the former type of case we seem (as in talking about motives) to be alluding to a contingent antecedent condition of the appearance of the work. In the latter type of case, however, we seem to be alluding to a feature of the work itself, and to be characterizing it, in terms of its embodiment of a particular aim or intention, and thus in turn of its having a particular point. (Skinner, 1972, p. 401)

The intention *to do* x is not necessarily the intention *in* what is done. The act may not in fact realize the conscious intentions of the agent. For example, the agent may make a mistake, or think that a certain act will accomplish x when in fact it will not, or perform an act which advances purposes the agent may not recognize as operative in this act. Moreover, the intention *to do* something refers to the agent's consciously entertained motives, but an act may embody intentions about which the agent is unaware or uncertain.

To identify intentions *in* actions involves not equating agents' conscious intentions with the acts they perform, and instead asking of an action, what is the intentionality contained in the act itself, not what is in the mind of the agent. The answer to this question involves placing acts into the wider context of the agent's life and the social setting in which they are performed, and by interpreting them in light of this wider context.

According to Collingwood historians merely re-enact the thought processes of the agent. But this ties the meaning of an act too closely to what the author consciously intended by it. It implies, for instance, that at least in theory the agent is the best interpreter of the meaning of his or her own acts. But intentionalism need not be committed to this thesis; that is, it need not deny that interpreters (including the agent at a later, more reflective time) can understand the meaning of an act better than the agent him or herself. This is possible because meaning is grasped not by a psychological process of re-living the thoughts of the agent (as

Collingwood would have it) but by an interpretive process which places the act into an appropriate context (as Skinner would have it).

As we saw in chapter 1, the difference between re-enactment and interpretation is important. Re-enactment is a psychological process of identification in which historians and social scientists re-experience the thought processes which went through the minds of agents as they performed various actions. In contradistinction, interpretation is not a psychological process at all; rather it is an explicatory process in which acts are situated within relevant social and intentional contexts – the agent's cultural world. In interpretation the point is not to discover the conscious thoughts which went through the mind of the agent but to decipher what the agent was doing in behaving in a particular manner.

So how might an intentionalist reading modified along Skinner's lines re-interpret Caesar's act? Despite the fact that at the time Caesar's thoughts in crossing the Rubicon were to pre-empt Pompey and thereby to protect himself, this act needs to be situated within the wider context of Caesar's own actions both prior and subsequent to the crossing, and to the wider political world in which these acts were located. So situated, it is not implausible to interpret the act of crossing the Rubicon as a step in Caesar's becoming an autocrat.

7.2   Gadamerian Hermeneutics

So far we have answered the question of the meaning of Caesar's act by describing it as a pre-emptive move against Pompey and/or as a step toward Caesar's becoming an autocrat. These answers focus on the intentionality of the act on the (intentionalist) assumption that this act's meaning is a function of Caesar's intentions. But consider three other characterizations of the meaning of Caesar's crossing the Rubicon:

1   Caesar's crossing the Rubicon marks the end of the Roman Republic (this is indeed how Cicero interpreted the meaning of Caesar's act);
2   Caesar's crossing the Rubicon put an end to the "empty formalism of the Republic," thereby taking the first steps necessary to "hold together the Roman world" and to provide a "new scene of achievement" for the genius of Rome (the quotations are from Hegel's *The Philosophy of History* (1956 (originally 1831), pp. 312–13);
3   The meaning of Caesar's crossing the Rubicon lies in the way it shows how the emergence of a powerful leader is to be expected when political situations become desperate through "the incompetence of the oligarchy, the unrestrained ambition of lawless men, and the failure to

create an efficient executive machinery of government and to link it with and subordinate it to the policy making authorities" (this from *Cicero and the Roman Republic* by F. R. Cowell (1962, p. 250)).

Note that none of these descriptions of the meaning of Caesar's act involves the intentionality of Caesar. Here, meaning is assigned on the basis of the event's later *effects*, and on its *significance* for later generations.

It is cases like these which have motivated another account of meaning, one utterly different from that provided by intentionalism. This account has been given its most lucid expression in the hermeneutical philosophy of Hans Georg Gadamer. ("*Hermeneutics*" comes from the Greek word *hermeneuein* meaning "to interpret"; it in turn derives from the Greek name for the god Hermes who carried messages for the other gods. Hermeneutics is the science of the interpretation of written texts. It originated in the modern period in reflections on what interpreting the meaning of biblical texts consists – a matter of urgency in the sixteenth century when Protestants and Catholics fought over answers to the meaning of the Bible. A number of hermeneutic theories have been developed over the past five centuries, but the most significant for our times is Gadamer's.)

According to *Gadamerian hermeneutics*, the meaning of an act (or a text or a practice) is not something which is in the act itself; rather meaning is always meaning *for someone* such that it is *relative to an interpreter*. According to it meaning never involves just one element (agents and their intentions) but two (that to be interpreted (acts, texts, and the like) and their interpreters). Meaning arises out of the relationship between an act and those trying to understand it – it is the product of an interaction of two subjects. This might be put by saying that meaning is only potentially present in any act, and that this potential meaning becomes actualized only in and through the process of interpretation itself. Thus, to answer the question of this chapter: on a Gadamerian hermeneutic account, the meaning of others' behavior or its products is *not* what they thought of it; rather, it is what we or some other interpreters make of what others have done.

On a Gadamerian account, meaning is both multivalent and dyadic: multivalent because any intentional act or its product will have many meanings depending on the interpreter(s) involved; and dyadic because meaning only emerges out of the relation between two subjects (the agent and the interpreter). This sharply contrasts with intentionalism, according to which meaning is both univalent (each act has a specific meaning) and monadic (this meaning results from just one subject, namely, the agent). Notice that according to intentionalism the meaning of the act is already contained in it by virtue of the intentionality it embodies. Meaning is something already present waiting to be grasped, a meaning which exists independently of those who seek to discover it. In this way meaning for intentionalism only requires an intentional agent acting intentionally in order to be produced; no other activity, and in particular no activity of interpretation, is required in order for it to be meaningful. Meaning derives from the activity of its creator, but not from the activity of its audience. This is why for intentionalism the meaning of an act is fixed at the time of its performance, in contrast to a Gadamerian account according to which meaning only emerges when it is interpreted, and continues to re-emerge with each new interpretation.

It follows from the Gadamerian account that understanding the meaning of intentional acts and their products cannot be the re-enactment or recovery of the past intentions of agents or ferreting out the intentionality in the acts themselves. Meaningful acts become meaningful only when they are placed in a specific interpretive context by a specific interpreter who in so doing actualizes their meaning. As the interpretive horizons of various interpreters change, new dimensions of meaning will show themselves. This implies that the meaning of acts and their products will not only change over time, but will never be definitively realized. The meaning of any intentional act or its product (the assassination of Lincoln, the signing of the Declaration of Independence, Aristotle's *Nicomachean Ethics*, Beethoven's *Ninth*, or the United States Constitution) will be different for different people. Thus it is no accident that the meaning of Caesar's crossing the Rubicon was different for Caesar, Cicero, Hegel, and modern-day historians like Cowell.

In part this will result from the different effects which Caesar's act caused – effects which continue to work themselves out over time even to the present day. And in part this will result from the different interpretive frameworks which later interpreters bring to Caesar's act. The significance of an act is in part a function of what it produced and in part a function of the concerns of those for whom it carries importance. Interpretation is the process by which the significance of an act or its products is revealed to a particular audience.

Such a revelation does not involve identifying with or re-creating the minds of past agents. Interpretation is not a psychological process of empathy. Rather it is a process of letting the significance of an intentional act or object reveal itself. Gadamer describes interpretation as a "fusion of horizons" in which a meaningful act or object emanating from one conceptual world is translated into terms relevant for another. By "horizons" Gadamer captures the situatedness of all interpretations occurring as they do within a tradition of discourse. Moreover, horizons move as those looking at them move; thus by "horizon" Gadamer also hopes to indicate the openness and flexibility of conceptual paradigms. By "fusion" *(verschmelzung)* Gadamer means to capture the process in which a past or foreign object speaks to specific interpreters situated in their own cultural milieu. Interpretation might thus best be understood as a process of translation.

"Fusion" is a good English translation of the German term *"verschmelzung,"* but it may also be misleading. (Note that in trying to explicate the meaning of *"verschmelzung"* I am trying to translate it into terms modern English users will understand. In so doing I am engaging in the same process as all interpreters of meaning, whether it be the meaning of a poem or an historical act like Caesar's crossing the Rubicon.) "Fusion" might suggest that the two horizons become one, that the differences between them are eliminated. But this is *not* what "fusion" means in Gadamerian hermeneutics. In interpretation a tension is maintained between a past or foreign act or object situated within its own conceptual context and the interpreters situated within their own conceptual contexts. The meaning of Caesar's act will never be exactly the same for Caesar as it is for Cicero or Hegel or Cowell, or for interpreters living in a time later than ours.

Care is required here. Gadamerian hermeneutics is *not* subjectivistic in the sense of claiming that a text is whatever an interpreter says it is. Even though Gadamer insists on the active role of interpreters in actualizing meaning, he does *not* suggest that interpreters simply read themselves *into* past events and objects so that interpretation becomes a form of mere self-reflection. The interaction of the interpreter with the interpreted elicits from the interpreted various dimensions of meaning which become evident as it is placed in new historical settings. Interpretation involves tapping new reservoirs of (potential) meaning hidden from those in other historical moments, including those who lived at the time of its production. In new contexts different aspects of meaning emerge; that which is interpreted speaks in new ways. (This is beautifully captured in the advice Pastor John Robinson gave to the Puritans as they set sail on the Mayflower for the New World: "There is yet more light to break forth from His Word.")

In this it is the interpreted speaking to interpreters in their own tongue, not the interpreters speaking to themselves using the interpreted as a mere stimulus for their own self-enclosed conversation. Interpretation, according to Gadamer, is *not* a hall of mirrors in which interpreters only see themselves in different poses and shapes depending on the shape and angle of the mirror which confronts them. Rather, interpretation is a process of listening to what others through their words and deeds have to say to us (in full recognition that what an act or its product says to us may well differ from what it says to others in different interpretive situations).

144

The difference between intentionalism and Gadamerian hermeneutics reveals itself in their different attitudes toward temporal distance. For intentionalism temporal distance is an enemy to be overcome. Interpreters must attempt to put themselves back into the world in which the act was performed, must try to recapture the cultural world and specific mindset of the agent as best they can. But for Gadamerians time is an ally not an enemy. Time gives acts and their products the means to produce their effects, and in this way to reveal what they are about. Moreover, time permits different sorts of interpreters to place these acts and their products into new interpretive contexts, thereby revealing different dimensions of their significance.

The contrast between intentionalism and Gadamerian hermeneutics also shows itself in the different ways each conceives the famous hermeneutic circle. (The idea of the hermeneutic circle has figured prominently in discussions of interpretation at least since the work in the nineteenth century of Schleiermacher and Dilthey.) The *hermeneutic circle* is meant to capture the movement which occurs in any act of interpretation. Traditionally this has been described in terms of the relation between part and whole: one can grasp the meaning of a part (say, a sentence in a novel) only by knowing the meaning of the whole (the entire novel); but one can ascertain the meaning of the whole only by knowing the meaning of its constituent parts.

Consider, for example, the famous opening sentence of *Anna Karenina*: "All happy families are alike, but each unhappy family is unhappy in its own way." The full meaning of this sentence only becomes apparent by the end of the novel when the reader has gained acquaintance with a number of families and with a sense of what Tolstoy meant by happiness. But a deeper appreciation of the meaning of this opening sentence will in turn change the reader's sense of the meaning of the whole novel, and this will lead to a further re-interpretation of the meaning of the novel's first sentence, and so on, as the meaning of part and whole continue to ramify indefinitely. This circularity can in theory go on forever: one's understanding of a part will alter one's understanding of the whole, but an alteration in one's understanding of the whole will alter one's understanding of the part, and so on.

The intentionalist construal of the hermeneutic circle conceives of the parts as actions (including utterances) within the whole life of their author. That is, interpreting the meaning of an act like crossing the Rubicon requires placing it within the larger context of Caesar's life, including the wider social and cultural settings within which this life was led. By so placing the act (the part) within the context of Caesar's life and times (the whole) its meaning can reveal itself. Of course, discovering the meaning of this crucial act in Caesar's life may alter one's sense of Caesar's life as a whole, and this re-figuring of the meaning of his whole life may lead to a re-interpretation of the meaning of his crossing the Rubicon. In this way the hermeneutic circle can continue as interpreters argue about the nature of the meaning of Caesar's act.

In Gadamerian hermeneutics the hermeneutic circle is explicated quite differently. Its parts consist of objects to be interpreted; the whole consists in the relation between these objects and their various interpretive audiences. In other words, in Gadamerian hermeneutics the hermeneutic circle is comprised of a continual ramifying between something to be interpreted and its interpreters. Since for Gadamer meaning is not a property of an object but a field within which an object is situated in interpretation, only in being related to its interpreters is the meaning of objects or events actualized; thus, the meaning of these interpreted entities will vary as their interpretive audience varies.

The interaction between a meaningful object and an interpretive community is not a one-off event. New interpretations will help to re-fashion the nature of the interpretive community, and the newly re-fashioned interpretive community will undoubtedly come to re-interpret the meaning of the original object afresh. The result is a constantly evolving process of interchange in which both the meaning of the object and the nature of the interpretive community change. Here the hermeneutic circle is a spiral of reciprocity as new interpretations of past meaningful objects change the nature of the interpretive community to which they are related which in turn changes the interpretation of the meaningful objects, and so on indefinitely.

That this is so can be seen in any history of the reception of a classic text. Certain new interpretations of the meaning of a text (take the Bible as a good example) will help to define a particular interpretive community (it might distinguish Protestants from Catholics, for instance); but such an identification can lead to new interpretations of the text (Calvinist interpretations instead of Lutheran, for instance), which helps to further define the interpretive community, and so on. The process of meaning-interpretation and identity-formation can continue indefinitely (as the history of the reception of the Bible and the various interpretive communities such reception has helped to fashion clearly shows).

The same is true of historically significant events like Caesar's crossing the Rubicon. This act has been interpreted and re-interpreted almost continually since it first occurred as it has been explicated by new interpretive communities. This is why historians even today can continue to debate the meaning of Caesar's act (and the meaning of the broader acts of which it was a part) two thousand years after the event occurred. Its meaning continues to change, and the appreciation of the way it changes is one of the contributing factors to the changes in the interpretive communities which approach it with ever original perspectives.

Moreover, this ongoing process of interpretation itself has a history which historians of the history of interpretations can write. Thus, an historian can compose an account of the various interpretations of Caesar's crossing the Rubicon. This history may itself help to re-define how this event comes to be reinterpreted. (Indeed, histories of the histories of interpretation may themselves change over time, and historians may tell the story of these changes as well. In the process the meaning of the histories of interpretation will itself change as they are situated in different interpretive communities. In short, the history of receptions itself has a history. In this way the hermeneutic circle continues to ramify indefinitely as the meaning of an event and its reception continues to "shed more light".)

7.3   Two Dimensions of Meaning

Intentionalism and Gadamerian hermeneutics each propose a theory about the nature of meaning. In this they are directly competitive: intentionalism argues that meaning is a matter of the intentions embodied in an act or its products, whereas Gadamerian hermeneutics eschews such intentions and looks instead to acts' significance. But we shall now see that each of these theories is better understood as focusing on only one aspect of meaning, and even then as needing insights from the other to be adequate. Thus, intentionalism necessarily requires elements from Gadamerian hermeneutics to adequately account for those aspects of meaning about which it is concerned; the reverse is also the case: Gadamerian hermeneutics must be complemented by elements from intentionalism to be true to its task.

In the first place, the antagonism between intentionalism and Gadamerian hermeneutics can in part be ameliorated if they are understood not as complete theories of meaning but as theories which employ two different senses of "meaning" and which address two different interpretive endeavors. Intentionalism focuses exclusively on answers to the question, "what intentions are expressed in act x?" Gadamerian hermeneutics spotlights answers to the question, "what is the significance of act x for some particular interpretive community?" These are different questions which require different accounts of what is involved in answering them. Intentionalism focuses on the first sort of question (though it conceives of itself as a comprehensive theory of meaning and interpreta-

147

tion); Gadamerian hermeneutics concentrates on the second sort of question and its answers (though it too poses as an exhaustive theory of meaning and interpretation).

The moral here is to avoid conceiving of these two theories as theories about the nature of meaning as such; instead think of them as accounts of different questions interpreters pose about intentional acts and their products. What did the agent want to do? What did the act mean for those in its original context? What meaning did it have for later historical events? What does it say to us today? These are all questions about meaning, but meaning understood in two different senses. They are thus different questions which support different accounts of what is involved in interpreting meaning. This suggests that intentionalism and Gadamerian hermeneutics are not necessarily competitive. The two theories focus on different interpretive questions which interpreters may pose to meaningful acts, texts, and objects.

However, even understood as accounts of only one type of interpretive question about meaning, both intentionalism and Gadamerian hermeneutics are still deficient. Intentionalism fails to account for the role translation plays in accounts of agents' intentions; consequently it needs to be supplemented by insights from Gadamerian hermeneutics. In its turn, Gadamerian hermeneutics is insufficient as a theory of meaning understood as significance because it overlooks the crucial role agents' intentions play in answers about acts' significance; thus Gadamerian hermeneutics must be amended to incorporate insights from intentionalism. Authorial intention and translation both play important roles in any and all attempts to ascertain the meaning of intentional acts and their products. Let me explain this.

Begin with the role of translation in answering questions about the meaning of an act or its product in terms of its author's intentions. The thoughts of others from different historical epochs and cultures become accessible to modern historians and social scientists and their audience *only by being translated into terms accessible to them*. Moderns cannot express the intentions of Caesar in Caesar's own terms because Caesar thought in Latin and because the Latin he knew contained distinctions, categories, and beliefs which are not the same as those, say, of twentieth-century academic English. The conceptual world of Rome was quite different from that of twentieth-century Anglo-America. The best historians can do is to render the terms of Caesar's thought into words and sentences in English hoping thereby to express in English what Caesar intended in Latin.

Thus the intentionalist idea that modern historians must express Caesar's thoughts "in his own terms" cannot be literally correct. The most they can achieve is to restate Caesar's thoughts as best they can in their own language, recognizing fully that something will be lost (and gained!) in this process because Caesar's culture and conceptual world will not map onto ours perfectly. This can be seen in Collingwood's own discussion of Caesar's crossing the Rubicon. In *The Idea of History* Collingwood described Caesar's crossing as an act of "defiance of Republican law" (and he characterized Caesar's assassination as "a clash of constitutional policy between himself and his assassins") (Collingwood, 1961, p. 213). But the terms "Republic," "law," and "constitution" are modern English terms to describe the political situation in Rome; indeed, in some ways these political terms are misleading. They derive their original meaning from modern constitutional democratic states and can only roughly be applied to the complex political arrangements of the Roman period.

To understand Caesar's crossing as an act of "defiance of Republican law" will thus require a fairly detailed analysis of precisely in what sense the Roman form of government was a republic, and how it is like and unlike a republic as we currently use that term. This in turn will require explications of related terms and ideas such as "citizen" and "representative" to make the notion of republic clear. In all of this English terms which have their home in modern political institutions will necessarily be used even though they will not exactly capture the distinctions and contents of political designations in ancient Rome. Indeed, even the designation "political" is itself somewhat misleading: we quite happily separate the political realm from the economic or the religious or the artistic; but these sorts of distinctions were not made in ancient Rome (and are not made in many other cultures). Note, for example, the political importance of soothsayers, omens, and the like in ancient Rome.

None of this is meant to argue that later interpreters cannot understand the intentions behind Caesar's behavior (or the intentions of agents from cultures even more removed from their own). Instead, it is meant to show that understanding another's intentions involves not only the agent but also the interpreter. Discovering the intentions in act x is dyadic in that interpreters must render the agents' thoughts into terms the interpreters can understand. Since in this example interpreters think in modern academic English and Caesar (and the Azande and medieval priests and even Americans of only a century ago) do not, understanding cannot be a *re*-thinking but at most a *thinking anew* as terms and ideas from conceptual schemes different from their own are translated into terms they can understand.

A Gadamerian point follows from this: there can be no single understanding of what Caesar did. Even if a broadly intentionalist perspective is adopted which insists that the meaning of Caesar's act consists in the intentions it embodies, the articulation of these intentions will vary from

149

one cultural and historical setting to another because such articulation requires elucidating these intentions into terms fitting for each particular setting. The translation of Caesar's intentions into terms appropriate for us today will not be the same as those for historians in eighteenth-century France or twenty-first century Japan. Thus, renderings of the meaning of Caesar's act will vary over time such that there can never be one "definitive" account of it. Each age will have to re-write the history of the intentionality inherent in Caesar's crossing the Rubicon putting it into terms accessible to it. The same is true for all other past intentional acts and their products, as well as for those in alien cultures.

But just as intentionalism must be supplemented by an element which finds its home in Gadamerian hermeneutics, so also Gadamerian hermeneutics must be enlarged by an element whose home is in intentionalism. The Gadamerian account is flawed because it overlooks the special role the intentions of the agent, and/or the intentionality of the act itself, play in ascertaining an act's significance. The identity of an act about which we ask its meaning requires a fundamental place for the act's intentionality. The intentions of an act or its product define the act or product to be the act or product it is; only in this way can their identity be fixed sufficiently such that we can inquire as to their significance. Put simply, we need to know the intentions embodied in an act or product in order to be able to ask about their significance.

Thus, the act of Caesar's crossing the Rubicon is the act it is – a deliberate strategic move by a Roman commander – because of Caesar's intentions. This was not an accidental maneuver, or the deed of a sleepwalker or someone drugged or otherwise unaware that he was indeed crossing a river with deep political significance. Even if the intentionality of the act transcended the conscious intentions of Caesar himself such that the intentionality *in* the act can be ascertained only by fitting it into the broader context of Caesar's life and the life of the Roman republic, this intentionality itself is vital in fixing the identity of the act about which later historians may inquire as to its significance either for Roman politics or its meaning for us today. That is, when the meaning of x is conceived in terms of its effects on later events or on its lessons for future interpreters, the x which has these effects and lessons itself is the x it is precisely because of the intentionality which it embodies.

Because of this importance of intentionality even in those interpretive endeavors best described in terms of Gadamerian hermeneutics (those concerned with the significance of acts and their products), this hermeneutics cannot overlook the insights of intentionalism which insists on the indispensability of recovering authorial intentions in the interpretation of meaning. Gadamerian hermeneutics must therefore be supplemented by elements from intentionalism: even when meaning is conceived in terms of significance, the intentionality in the act or its product must play a prominent role.

To conclude, therefore. Intentionalism and Gadamerian hermeneutics are best understood in terms different from the way they understand themselves. They are not complete theories of meaning. Rather, they focus on different aspects of meaning: intentionalism focuses on meaning understood in terms of past intentions; Gadamerian hermeneutics focuses on meaning understood in terms of present significance. These are different dimensions to the meaning of an act or its products, and any comprehensive theory of meaning must insist both on the distinction between them as well as the relevance of both. Conceived in this way intentionalism and Gadamerian hermeneutics are both correct because each highlights a different aspect of meaningfulness.

However, it is a mistake to overdraw the distinction between past intentionality and present significance. Past intentionality can be revealed only in terms of what is significant in the present, and the present significance of an act or its product can only be ascertained in terms of the past intentionality which establishes the identity of this act or product. In this way intentionalism and Gadamerian hermeneutics must be transcended, producing an account which includes elements of both of these theories.

7.4   Summing Up

We started this chapter with the question, what is the meaning of Caesar's crossing the Rubicon and what theory of interpretation (intentionalism or Gadamerian hermeneutics) best captures this meaning? It ought to be clear by now that this is a profoundly misleading question. It assumes that meaning is an independently existing entity, and that only one of these theories best characterizes it. But as we have seen, meaning can be conceived in at least two different sorts of ways. The meaning of acts or their products can refer either to what the agents intended by them or to their significance for those who feel their effects. The question of the meaning of an act like Caesar's crossing the Rubicon is thus really at least two questions.

Moreover, depending on which meaning of meaning is operative, two different sorts of possible answer can qualify as an answer to the question of an act's meaning. If meaning is understood in terms of the intentionality of an act, then an account of the agent's intentions is an appropriate response. However, if meaning is understood in terms of an act's significance for some community, then the agent's intentions are not enough.

Instead, a question of meaning understood as significance requires an account of an act's effects and their contemporary relevance. Intentionalism concentrates on the former construal of meaning, and Gadamerian hermeneutics on the latter. But since they are theories of different things – of different aspects of meaning – they are not necessarily in conflict.

Moreover, even understood as theories of one aspect of meaning each of these accounts is inadequate. Each fails to do justice to the insight of the other in explicating what is involved in ascertaining meaning. Intentionalism correctly insists that authorial intentions are crucial in the meaning of an act understood as the intentions it embodies; but it fails to accord a role for the way the intentions of past agents must be translated into the terminology of later interpretive communities in order for them to be intelligible. Gadamerian hermeneutics, for its part, correctly maintains that on one construal of meaning not authorial intentions but significance for an interpretive community is critical in determining an act's meaning; but it fails to recognize the critical role the agent's intentions have in fixing the identity of an act or its product. Thus, not only must intentionalism and Gadamerian hermeneutics be understood as accounting for different sorts of interpretive endeavor, but each of them must be supplemented by insights from the other in order for them to provide an adequate account of their respective interpretive enterprises.

With all this in mind we are ready to answer the question posed in the title of this chapter: is the meaning of others' behavior what *they* mean by it? The answer to this question is both yes and no. In the first place, if by meaning is meant the intentionality present in an act at the time of its performance, then clearly what the agent meant by it is crucial. But one should not be misled here: ascertaining agents' intentions requires translating them into terms interpreters in their own conceptual world can understand such that what they mean by an act must be translated into terms particular interpreters can appreciate. Thus, the answer to the question of an act's meaning understood as the agent's intentions cannot be answered solely in the agent's terms; rather, it must be answered in the agent's terms as translated into those of the interpreters. In this case the meaning of an act will not simply be what *the agent* meant by it but what he or she meant by it as rendered into *our* terms.

In the second place, if the meaning of an act or its products is understood to mean its significance for later agents and other interpretive communities, then clearly the agent's intentions do not constitute an acceptable answer to the question of meaning. Rather, meaning here consists of the relevance of the effects of an act or its products and/or what the act reveals to those who view it through their own historical experience and interpretive lenses. But one should not too quickly dismiss the intentionalist insistence on the relevance of agential intention in this endeavor. The identity of the act or its product is fixed in terms of the agent's intentions such that ascertaining the significance of an act or its product must include a crucial role for these intentions. In this case the meaning of an act will not simply be what it signifies to *us* but also what it meant for *the agent*.

To the question of this chapter (is the meaning of others' behavior what *they* mean by it?) both intentionalism and Gadamerian hermeneutics want to give simple, exclusive answers: the former answers the question in the affirmative, the latter in the negative. But both of these answers are simplistic. The meaning of others' behavior can refer either to its past intentionality or to its present significance, and depending on which of these is operative a different account of meaning is required. Moreover, no matter which construal of meaning is at work, both past intentionality and present significance will play a role. The chapter's question invites an either/or answer: either yes (as answered by intentionalism) or no (as answered by Gadamerian hermeneutics). But the best response is of a both/ and form. On one interpretation of the meaning of meaning, agents' intentions as understood by them are determinative; however, even here to state what these intentions are their significance for us cannot be overlooked. In this case, therefore, the meaning of others' behavior is what *they* mean by it but only as rendered in *our* terms. On a different interpretation of the meaning of meaning, not agents' intentions but later significance is critical; but even here the intentions of agents are pivotal in determining the identity of the acts whose significance is being sought. In this case, the meaning of others' behavior is not what they mean by it but what it as understood by *them* means for *us*. In all cases of meaning, therefore, what it means for them and what it means for us are both operative.

Further Reading

This chapter is indebted to Thompson (1993).

For good overviews of the material discussed in this chapter see Howard (1982), Hoy (1982), and Bernstein (1983). See also the essays by Hookway, Skorupski, and Dunn in Hookway and Pettit (1978), and the excellent collection by Hiley, Bohman, and Shusterman (1991), especially the essays by Rouse, Bohman, Hoy, and Roth.

For intentionalism, see Hirsch (1967); Skinner (1969 and 1972), and the book devoted to Skinner's thoughts edited by Tully (1988); Pocock (1971); and von Wright (1971). See also Outhwaite (1975) for a discussion of intentionalism through a consideration of the doctrine of "verstehen."

For hermeneutics, see Gadamer (1992 (1960)), and Weinsheimer's (1985) commentary on

Truth and Method. See also Barnes (1989), Hoy (1982), Bernstein (1983), and Ricoeur (1981). The essays collected in Shapiro and Sica (1984) are uniformly illuminating.

A crucial source for talk about meaning and the problems about such talk is Quine (1960 and 1973), especially his thesis of the indeterminacy of translation and his rejection of meaning realism. ("Meaning realism" is the claim that meanings are fixed entities existing independently of interpreters.) The position of this chapter is anti-meaning realist (though its anti-meaning realism derives more from Gadamer than from Quine). For a powerful discussion of Quine and his relevance to questions of meaning in the social sciences, see Roth (1987). See also the essay by Hookway in Hookway and Pettit (1978), and the essay by Newton-Smith in Hollis and Lukes (1986).

For a fine discussion of sociological explanation as translation, and a discussion of what translation involves, see Turner (1980).

8

Is Our Understanding of Others Essentially Historical?

8.1 Nomologicalism

Multiculturalism is rooted in the experience of apparent significant difference. That is, multicultural awareness arises when people are confronted by others who seem to be fundamentally different, strange, or even alien, when the comfortable provincialism that "everyone is just like us" runs up against ostensible diversity in ways of thinking and living. At these moments the question, are these differences real or only apparent?, can hardly be stifled. A deep question for multiculturalism is therefore, are people essentially the same, or are they essentially different?

This question can be addressed in a number of ways. For example, the analysis of chapters 4 and 5 in which the notions of different worlds and shared rationality were examined, is one way of addressing this question. In this chapter we shall explore another avenue to this question, an avenue which connects to a debate in the philosophy of the human studies which has been going on since Enlightenment thinkers and their critics began to dispute what it means to understand human beings, their actions and relations. I refer here to the debate between nomologicalism and historicism.

Inspired by the success of Newton and those who came after him, nomologicalism subscribes to a model of explanation in which the central role is played by scientific laws. Because of the centrality of law in this model it is called the nomological model of explanation, and the view which decrees that an adequate explanation must be based in scientific law *nomologicalism* (from the Greek word for law, *nomos*). In contrast, *historicism* argues that the identity of social entities and actions lies in their history such that to understand them is to grasp the historical development by which they came to be what they are.

As we shall soon see, nomologicalism involves seeing particular events and entities as instances of general patterns or laws; in this way, it requires investigators to transcend the particular in order to grasp what it shares with other particulars. Historicism, on the contrary, counsels strict attention to the specific process by which a particular entity or event is produced, and in this way highlights what is unique to it. On this seemingly narrow base of disagreement about the nature of the explanation of human doings and relations, nomologicalism and historicism blossomed into antithetical ways of viewing the world. Since the time of Kant and Herder nomologicalism and historicism have often been considered exhaustive, irreducibly different, and mutually incompatible alternative worldviews. Their opposition is revealed in a number of basic dichotomies which supposedly mark deep differences in epistemological perspective:

Nomologicalism	*Historicism*
Universal	Particular
Type	Individual
Recurrence	Novelty
Atemporality	Temporality
Sameness	Difference

From this it ought to be clear that nomologicalism supports an affirmative answer to the multicultural question, is everybody the same? By emphasizing that underneath the particular and the temporally situated lie general recurring patterns of which the particular are mere instances, nomologicalism suggests that at bottom people are ultimately the same. Historicism, on the other hand, answers the question regarding the similarity of people decidedly in the negative. By arguing that what gives an act or a social group its identity is precisely what makes it unique and different, namely, its own particular history, historicism suggests that people with different histories are not just different but are essentially so.

In this way the dispute between nomologicalism and historicism raises an issue which is directly relevant to the meaning of multiculturalism, namely, the ultimacy of the differences between people. Thus, though the question of this chapter (is our understanding of others essentially historical?) – a question meant to capture the dispute between nomologicalism and historicism – might not at first appear to be connected to multiculturalism, in fact it is so. Indeed, deeply so.

Let's begin with nomologicalism. According to it scientific laws are general in form, that is, they assert some invariant relation between members of one class of events and another. For example, Boyle's Law claims that at a constant temperature, the volume of a confined gas varies inversely with its pressure. Note that laws cover future instances, not merely those cases which have already been observed. Laws are more than mere generalizations of past observations ("In all cases of confined gases so far observed . . ."), but apply to all instances including those yet to occur ("For *any* confined gas whose temperature is constant, if its volume is increased its pressure will decrease"). Boyle's Law applies to all confined gases, even ones not yet observed or discovered. Thus scientific laws assert a relationship not between certain particular events but between certain classes of events, and they assert that this relationship is invariable. They therefore assume the form, "If C, then E" or "If no C, then no E" (where C and E are classes of events represented by the use of capital letters, to distinguish them from particular datable events c and e represented by small letters).

Scientific laws are slightly more complicated than this. Most laws make reference to some kind of standard conditions which must obtain in order for the relationship between C and E to occur. Examples of standard conditions are "in a perfect vacuum"; "at standard atmospheric pressure"; and "in markets of perfect competition." These standard conditions are symbolized by the capital letter S, so that the common nomological formula reads "Under S, if C then E." However, for clarity's sake I shall continue to employ the simpler formula "If C then E" with the phrase "Under S" being understood.

How do laws help to explain events? Say that e is a particular event which we want to explain. According to nomologicalism event e is explained only when we can see why e had to happen given certain explanatory events c (in this case c would be the sufficient condition for e), or why e could not have occurred without c (in this case c is the necessary condition of e). If c could have occurred but not be followed by e, then e is not fully explained by the occurrence of c; or if e could have occurred without c then the occurrence of e isn't explained by c either. Event e is explained by events c only when e is shown to be invariably produced by c and/or invariably prevented by the failure of c's occurrence. The notion of invariability is thus crucial for explanation. But this requires that c and e be instances of some invariable regularity – either of the form "If C, then E" or of the form "If no C, then no E." Seeing e as an instance of E, and c as an instance of C, and C and E as invariant patterns removes the puzzlement surrounding the occurrence of e.

The logical form of this type of explanation is the well-known *deductive-nomological model of explanation*. It relates a statement describing e to a series of statements about other events c and to one or more general laws L such that the statement of e (the explanandum) is logically deducible from the conjoint statement of c and L (the explanans). Given such an explanation, the e event could not have been other than it was – we see why it *had* to

157

be and thus we have explained it. Laws are the linchpin of this type of explanation. The deduction from the explanans to the explanandum is possible only because of the universal law which asserts that every case in which events of the type C occur events of the type E will also occur.

Of course this is only the bare bones of the deductive-nomological model of explanation. A more fine-grained account would introduce the different types of laws which can figure in nomological explanations (universal or statistical); the different criteria which C and E must meet to figure in such laws (they must be observable or connected via bridge principles to observation statements); the role which limiting conditions play in the scope of laws (as I have said, laws hold only in certain general situations, and then only *ceteris paribus*); the part theories assume in nomological explanations; and so forth. (For a more detailed account of nomological explanation, see Hempel, 1965).) But these refinements are not necessary to appreciate the function laws play in the deductive-nomological conception of scientific explanation, which is all that is required for present purposes.

In nomological explanations a structural identity exists between explanation and prediction. In the case of explanation, an event e is known to have occurred, and the general laws and statements about its particular causes are sought; in the case of prediction, the general laws and the statements of particular causes are given, and the statement describing the particular event e not yet having occurred is deduced from them. A prediction is thus simply the obverse of a nomological explanation. (This of course does not mean that they are identical: they differ with respect to the scientists' information, explanation dealing with events known to have occurred, prediction with events not known to have occurred. But the important point is that according to nomologicalism *unless an explanation could have functioned as a prediction it is not acceptable as an explanation.*)

The functional equivalence between explanation and prediction underlies the sciences' capacity to empirically test explanations. The hypothesis that c explains e is testable precisely because this explanation rests on the general law "If C, then E." Such a general law makes the prediction that whenever C occurs E will result; given this, scientists can produce C themselves and observe whether E invariably occurs. If it does, then the general law is acceptable as the basis for explaining e; if it does not, then some other hypothesis is needed. Predictability is thus crucial not only for explanation but also for the experiments by which such explanations are tested.

The symmetry between nomological explanation and prediction reveals the peculiarly unhistorical nature of nomological science. An event e occurs at a particular historical moment, but this event is explained only when it is subsumed under a law which contains no essential time markers, when, that is, it is seen as part of a timeless regularity. Laws don't contain specific times or places in them; they pick out invariably recurring patterns which apply universally to any and all datable entities which potentially instantiate them. Consequently, a fundamental difference exists between nomological science with its timeless laws and history with its inevitably timed events. According to nomologicalism, true explanation occurs only when historical accounts (which explain particular datable events described as such by relating them to other datable events described as such) are replaced by scientific explanations (in which particular events are seen as instances of certain perfectly general patterns). This might be put by saying that according to nomologicalism the c and e of historical explanations must be replaced by the C and E of scientific explanations.

According to the nomological ideal, to be genuinely scientific social science needs to discover general laws and on this basis to make empirically ascertainable predictions about certain types of human behavior. Thus nomologicalism directs psychologists to discover "laws of psychological development" or "laws of thought"; or economists to uncover the "laws of the market" or the "laws of capitalism"; or sociologists to find "laws of small group interaction." As long as social scientific explanations are not based on these or similar laws nomologicalists argue they will be deficient on two grounds: first, they will not adequately explain because they will not show how a particular social occurrence was part of some deeper social pattern; second, they will not be able to make predictions, and so will not be able to figure in experiments to determine if they are warranted by the evidence. According to nomologicalism a social science without laws is explanatorily deficient and empirically untestable. It is thus no science at all.

8.2 Laws in Social Science

Can the events and objects of the social sciences be treated in the same nomological way as the events and objects of the natural sciences? Some have argued that they cannot, citing their intentional character as rendering them unfit for nomological treatment. It will be useful to examine the strengths and weaknesses of this *Argument from Intentionality*. I will begin by presenting the Argument in its strongest form, and then offer some criticisms of it.

As we saw in chapters 5 and 6, many of the objects of social science are intentional phenomena (and even those which are not, like economic depressions, take place against a background of intentional phenomena).

159

This means that their identity is a function of their meaning (so that, for example, an act is an act of praying because of the intentions it expresses, or an institution is a bank because of the ideas of its depositors, employees, and the general public).

Because social phenomena are meaningful, social scientists characterize their objects of study in virtue of their meaning, not in terms of their physical properties which can be described in purely physico-spatial terms. Thus, anthropologists want to explain why the members of a tribe are *dancing*, not why their feet are *moving*; political scientists study citizens' *voting*, not why the arms of certain bodies are *rising*; and intellectual historians characterize texts not in terms of their physical properties but in terms of what they say. Intentional phenomena are meaningful, and social science willy-nilly operates in a world of significance.

A key fact about intentional phenomena is that they are subject to constant change because of conceptual innovations a group's members may introduce and/or come to accept. As conceptual developments occur, new sorts of meaning are made possible and so new sorts of intentional thought and activity. Of course, these conceptual innovations assume a bewildering number of types and forms (indeed, the ways innovation occurs and produces changes are themselves subject to innovation). And rates of innovation may vary widely. But all societies, even the most closed and isolated, are subject to developments of thought occasioned by alterations in what must be done to survive and prosper, by shifting relationships within the group itself, by contact with foreign groups, and by the widespread tendency of humans to ask further and further questions about their world.

The crucial point for the Argument from Intentionality lies in the unpredictability of conceptual innovation. To predict a conceptual innovation would require that predictors be able to say of what this innovation consisted, and this would mean that predictors would themselves already have to be in possession of it. In order to accomplish this task predictors themselves would have to make all the creative leaps which go to make up the innovation. In order to have predicted in 1850 the emergence of the economic theory found in Keynes's 1936 *The General Theory of Employment, Interest, and Money* economists would already have to have formulated at least the rough outlines of the theory themselves.

Especially for innovations which themselves depend upon a host of other innovations, or for innovations which involve fundamental alterations in basic concepts, prediction is decidedly unachievable. To have predicted in 1500 the emergence of capitalism would have required the predictor to have been in possession of concepts which themselves depended on developments in such wide areas of thought – from the very abstract ("commodity") to the more concrete ("contract"), from the theoretical ("private property") to the more practical ("wage labor") – that such a prediction is unthinkable.

Note that this unpredictability is not confined to human *thought*. Given the constitutive role thought plays in intentional activities and relationships, changes in thought mean changes in these activities and relations themselves. The practical impossibility of predicting conceptual innovation thus means that social scientists will not be able to predict novel social forms which result from such innovation. Social institutions and practices, as well as the beliefs and desires of members of particular social groups, are continually in a state of flux which will always appear indeterminate to those studying them because their changes result from innovations that are themselves unpredictable.

Consider the profound changes in the government's relationship to, and responsibilities toward, the economy resulting from the conceptual changes ushered in by Keynes's 1936 work. Prior to this period governments in liberal polities were not expected to manage the economy, nor to bring about full employment. Once the ideas of Keynes and his followers became a part of political and economic life, governmental institutions, relationships, and activities changed in crucially important ways. Political scientists in 1860 interested in studying the relationship between the liberal state and the economy, but unable to predict the conceptual innovations made by Keynes et al., would be unable to foretell the ways in which this relationship would fundamentally alter as a result of these innovations. The usefulness of their work would thus be confined to a period prior to Keynes, and would be inapplicable afterwards.

Or consider Marx's "iron laws of capitalism" formulated around 1860. Marx thought he had uncovered the basic laws which govern a capitalist economy; on this basis he made a number of daring predictions (for example, the inevitable pauperization of the working class). But this attempt was *bound* to fail just because capitalist systems are constantly evolving in part as a result of conceptual innovation. Marx could never have known of the theoretical innovations of Keynes and others, innovations which fundamentally altered the institutions and practices about which Marx was trying to theorize. Such unpredictable changes made Marx's so-called laws just that, *so-called* laws which applied, if at all, only to a specific historical period of capitalism. They could be nothing else, given the intentional nature of the objects with which he was dealing, and the intentionalist vocabulary by means of which he described these objects. (In this Marx was no different from any other social scientist.)

The example of Marx suggests a particularly important sort of conceptual innovation, that associated with critical theory (which we discussed in chapter 6.4). Critical theories isolate causal conditions in social life whose force depends on the ignorance of a certain group as to the nature of their collective existence and what is frustrating them. The point of critical theory is to enlighten this group about these causal conditions and the ways in which they are oppressive so that, being enlightened, this group can alter these conditions and thereby transform their lives. By such transformative action this group would falsify the original theory because its life will now have assumed a new character as a result of the efficacy of the original theory. A critical social theory anticipates its own demise.

What bearing does this have on the question of the nomological character of social scientific explanations? According to the Argument from Intentionality, just this. In order to produce acceptable general laws, concepts which refer to objects in some steady state, or which change in some apprehensibly regular manner, must be employed. If an object or event cannot be described in a way that reveals it to be part of a regularly recurring sequence of events, then there is no way to determine whether a hypothesis is universal or sufficiently confirmable to be a general law. But to be general laws properly so called, causal generalizations must be so confirmable. Thus, general laws are not possible in sciences devoted to such phenomena.

Consider an analogy suggested by Alasdair MacIntyre (1972). Imagine geologists studying rocks which rapidly changed their shapes, sizes, colors, and chemical composition in a manner which eluded geologists' predictive capacities. Retrospectively these geologists might be able to understand why a class of rocks assumed the form it did, but prospectively they would be unable know what form the members of this class will take. Their problem is that their rocks will not stay still enough, or evolve in a sufficiently regular fashion, so that they can be identified as part of a typical pattern. If the objects to which the terms "rocks of type A" and "rocks of type B" refer are forever shifting in unforeseeable ways, geologists could not formulate general laws employing these terms because there would be no way to ascertain whether the purported general law held and if so over what range of phenomena.

According to the Argument from Intentionality, the imaginary case of the geologists is the real situation of social scientists bent on explaining intentional phenomena. To describe their objects of study, social scientists employ terms such as "the political realm" and "the economy"; but these refer to objects which ceaselessly shift as a result of conceptual innovation. The result is that any general law which used such terms would be unconfirmable. In order to produce a general law, regular outcomes resulting from certain specifiable factors must be ascertainable in a wide variety of cases; but if the factors and the outcomes are constantly changing in unpredictable ways, sufficiently confirmatory instances cannot be forthcoming.

Note how this conclusion limits the range of social scientific generalization. If people in different groups are radically different from one another as a result of the (unpredictably changing) intentions which underlie them, then only generalizations about certain classes of people historically situated in a specific cultural and social milieu can be made. Moreover, as this milieu changes over time, so also will the generalizations about the people in it. The result is a science which consists of historically bound, and therefore very limited, generalizations: generalizations historically and culturally situated, good only for a particular place or time. This is the main conclusion of the Argument from Intentionality.

This Argument is supposed to show that intentional phenomena can not be explained nomologically, and that the social sciences cannot be nomological sciences. But does the Argument from Intentionality actually show this?

A crucial fact for answering this question is that science does not explain events as such, but only events *described in a particular way*. Only when an event is described is there something to explain; and since events can be described in any number of different ways, which description is used to characterize it will importantly determine what constitutes its explanation. For example, assume that on 12 July 1984 Ronald Reagan deposited $500 into the First Savings Bank of Washington. This event might be described as "Ronald Reagan deposited $500 into his Washington account"; an explanation of this event *so described* calls for information about Reagan's intentions. But this same event can also be described as "a depositor put money into a bank"; an explanation of this event *described in this way* requires more general information about depositors and banks. This event can also be described in purely physical terms (such as "a brain state caused a certain mammal to move in particular ways"); in this case the explanation of the event *so described* demands details about the physical condition of the president (perhaps his brain states, and so on). The same event can be described by means of particular designatory terms (such as "Ronald Reagan"), while others might employ general designatory terms (such as "depositor"); some descriptions will employ intentionalistic terms which characterize entities in terms of their meaning ("deposited"), while others will employ nonintentionalistic terms which portray entities in purely physical terms ("brain state").

What is to be explained is not an event in itself, but an event characterized in a certain manner. But this means that one cannot assume – as the Argument from Intentionality does – that intentionalistic phenomena must be described in intentionalistic terms. Phenomena characterized in virtue of their meaning can be re-characterized in purely physical terms. The Argument from Intention purports to demonstrate that intentionalistic phenomena cannot figure in general laws, but it in fact does not show this. All it shows is that intentional phenomena *described by means of intentionalistic terms* (like "belief," "action," "institution") are unsuitable candidates for nomological treatment. This does *not* preclude the possibility that these same phenomena be re-described nonintentionalistically and in this way be rendered possible candidates for scientific laws.

Nomological explanations require that phenomena be described by means of very general terms before they can figure in scientific laws. Only when events are described in ways which omit what is distinctively particular about them and which instead pick out what they have in common with other events can they be seen as members of the same class and so as possible instances of some constantly recurring pattern. This is as true of non-human events as human ones. Mt Pinatubo erupts; the Little Engine That Could begins to chug; the pressure in Mario Andretti's tires begins to rise. Described by means of these particular designatory terms these events seem to have little in common. Only when they are re-described by means of more general designatory terms (perhaps first as "a volcano erupts, "a steam engine produces power," and "tire pressure increases," and then by means of even more general terms like "gas," "confined space," "temperature", and "pressure") will their similarity as instances of Boyle's law become apparent.

The lesson from the Argument from Intentionality is simply that if human doings and products are described by means of an intentionalistic vocabulary which individuates and characterizes them in virtue of their meaning then they will not be fit subjects for nomological treatment. But far from showing that human doings and products cannot be treated nomologically, the Argument ironically suggests a way such treatment might be possible: do not use intentionalistic terms to describe human events and objects, but re-describe them nonintentionalistically so that their homogeneity with respect to causes and effects will be capturable by means of general laws. Examples of this strategy in the history of social science are the approaches of operant conditioning theory, cognitive simulation, and sociobiology.

Consider sociobiology. (In this I am following the important work of Rosenberg (1980). Note that I use sociobiology for illustrative purposes only, with no commitment one way or the other as to the ultimate cognitive merits of this approach.) Sociobiology argues that the lowest level predicate by which animate entities can be characterized in order to figure in biological laws is that of "species," not that of any particular species (such as "homo sapiens" or "canis familiaris"), or any particular type of species (like "mammal" or "reptile"). That is, no generalization about the behavior of beavers or mammals or even the occupants of the earth will be a general law properly so-called as long as these animals are described by means of the particular terms "beaver," "mammal," or "occupant of the earth." These terms refer to entities in virtue of their spatio-temporal particularity – their location on earth, for instance – whereas genuine laws must prescind from such particular designation. The notion of "species" does precisely this: it refers to *any* biological line of descent or lineage. Thus, the theory of natural selection which articulates the laws governing the evolution of species applies to all species including those which might be found on planets other than earth. (This, of course, does not mean that terms like "beaver" or "mammal" have no role to play in sociobiology; it means only that these terms will not figure in its general laws.)

An example of a sociobiological law governing all species is the following from the theory of natural selection: "If x is a homogeneous subclass of species S and is superior in fitness to the other members of the species, then the proportion of x in the species will increase." Notice here no mention of any particular species, nor the use of any intentional vocabulary. This law governs all species – including the species "homo sapiens." (Note that this law would be a mere tautology if "fitness" were defined as "more likely to reproduce successfully." Then the "law" would say merely that the subclasses which are superior in their ability to reproduce successfully are likely to reproduce successfully. This isn't a law at all, but a claim which is true by virtue of the definition of its terms. In sociobiology "fitness" is thus defined independently of this ability, and so its results are possible laws which purport to reveal something about the world, not mere definitional truths which disclose only something about the meanings of the words sociobiologists use.)

Sociobiology is an example of a general conceptual strategy: when the stock of concepts available to describe events proves inadequate to the scientific task of picking out entities and events in a way that makes them suitable for nomological treatment, re-conceive the basis for one's descriptive vocabulary and invent another basis which will prove adequate to the task. This is exactly what happened in physics and in biology; there appears to be no principled impediment for its happening in the study of human beings.

Of course if such a strategy is followed human beings may not be social scientifically described by means of concepts currently employed in the social sciences (including "human being" if sociobiology is correct, and including "intention" and its cognates if the Argument from Intentionality is correct). This would involve some loss: human behavior and relations would come to be described so generally and so without meaning that what seems integral to them would be abstracted out of their description. But this happens in physics or biology as well. In physics Mt Pinatubo no longer is characterized as a particular mountain located in the Philippines northwest of Manila, but instead becomes a container of gas – and in this way becomes indistinct from other containers of gas as different as steam engines and tires. Described as "a container of gas" Mt Pinatubo loses its distinctiveness as a particular mountain. But this loss produces a gain as well, for now the eruption of the mountain can be seen as an instance of Boyle's Law and therefore explicable, whereas as long as it continued to be described by means of the particular designatory term "Mount Pinatubo" its eruption would remain scientifically inexplicable. The same is true of human behavior: if it is described non-intentionalistically some important aspects of it (even what seems distinctive about it) will be omitted; but so describing it may make it suitable for figuring in general laws, and so render it no longer scientifically mysterious.

To summarize: all the Argument from Intentionality shows is that a social science which employs an intentionalistic vocabulary is not likely to develop general laws, and so cannot provide nomological explanations. But this does not show that nomologicalism is unacceptable as a philosophy of social science. To become nomological social science must reconceive its basic conceptual commitments, substituting a non-intentionalistic framework for its current intentionalistic one. In this way the laws governing human behavior can at least possibly be discovered.

8.3   The Inadequacy of Nomological Explanations

According to nomologicalism, social science must seek the right level of description for the phenomena it wishes to study before it can be successful. If a suitably general non-intentionalistic level of description can be developed, genuine laws of human behavior can then be discovered, and social science can at last become truly scientific. Let's assume for the sake of argument that scientific explanations must ultimately be nomological and that, say, sociobiological laws which encompass human doings and products are ascertained. Does this mean that nomologicalism is correct, that social science can abandon intentionalistic descriptions and be satisfied with its non-intentionalistic general laws and deductive-nomological explanations? I think not. Nomological explanation may be insufficient for social scientific purposes. Let me elaborate the three grounds on which this diagnosis of the inadequacy of nomologicalism rests.

In the first place note that social scientists may well be interested in the unique and datable events which make up the human record *as unique and datable events*. A political scientist may be curious about the behavior of the Nazi party in Germany as the particular party it was and not merely as an instance of the behavior of political parties in general. Even political scientists interested in political parties in general often limit their interest to certain historically specific settings (say, modern industrial economies). Historical sociology (a prime example of which is Max Weber's *Protestant- ism and the Spirit of Capitalism* because it focuses on a historically unique economic form) and ethnographic anthropology (a prime example of which is Evans Pritchard's *The Nuer* because it concerns a single tribe in Africa) are social scientific approaches in which the object of study is an histori- cally specific individual entity *understood in its specificity*.

Moreover, and even less surprising, social scientists legitimately may wish to inquire about intentional phenomena *as intentional phenomena*. It may well be that such phenomena can be studied by means of the non- intentionalistic vocabulary of operant conditioning theory or sociobiology, but this involves a kind of description that does not capture what social scientists may want to know about. Thus, the success of certain economic groups may instantiate some law of natural selection, but anthropologists may want to know about the thoughts and feelings that went into the actions and relations of these groups, and may want to know about them in terms of their intentional content. Sociobiology cannot in this case replace anthropology even if it is immensely successful in its own terms precisely because these terms do not capture what is of interest about human phenomena to anthropologists and those non-anthropologists who are part of their audience.

This interest in the particular as particular and the intentional as intentional is reinforced by a second reason why even a successful nomological social science would need to be supplemented. Human doings and products are peculiarly nonhomogeneous and peculiarly open. They are peculiarly nonhomogeneous because their similarity in terms of their meaning is compatible with dramatic physical differences (think of all the ways of signalling – including in some circumstances making no movement at all!). They are peculiarly open because they can be extended in highly creative ways: what constitutes a particular sort of intentional phenomenon can radically change as a result of conceptual innovation.

Think, for example, of fitness as it applies to human societies. It is often said that in human history physical evolution has been superseded by cultural evolution. This means that what constitutes fitness for humans depends much more on the power of cultural imperatives than on bodily characteristics. Moreover, what constitutes success, and what imperatives will likely lead to success, will vary immensely from one cultural setting to another. In part because of conceptual innovations in communication, medicine, and political organization, the abilities apt for success have changed dramatically from one cultural setting to another.

To appreciate the particular ways fitness is achieved in human settings some reference to cultural meanings will thus be required. From the laws of natural selection we may know that a group of people succeeded because it was more fit than another, but this will not in itself explain why this success took the particular form it did. In order to understand this, the cultural imperatives in question must be described in intentional terms. Anthropologists interested in the specifics of historical evolution thus will need to understand the demands and opportunities of particular cultures. Here intentional behavior described in intentional terms must supplement sociobiology for a full appreciation of human evolution.

A third reason why nomological explanations may be insufficient is that large-scale changes which take place over a long period of time in human history may not by governed by a single law, even though each of the particular steps along the way are governed by its own general law. In this case, to explain the entire movement from beginning to end would require something more than a nomological explanation. Let me explain. (This argument is from Danto (1985, chapter 11.)

Assume an historical process in which some entity x (say, the Roman Empire) underwent a two-staged sequence of change from a to b, and from b to c. Schematically this can be represented in this way: x was a at time t; but h occurred at time t + 1 and because of this x became b; but then j occurred at time t + 2 and because of this x became c. Assume further that each stage is covered by a general law: the first stage by (1) "for any X, if H then B," and the second stage by (2) "For any X, if J then C." But it does *not* follow from these assumptions that the entire process from a to c is covered by a single general law. Why? Because the occurrence of J in the second law is not necessarily linked to the occurrence of either B or H in the first law. The whole process would be covered by a single law only if b or h triggered j; then the general law (3) "For any X, if H then B and if B then J and if J then C" would cover the entire process. The point here is *not* that such a single general law is impossible or incoherent, but that *the existence of such a law does not follow from the existence of two general laws each of which covers a single stage in the process of x-changing from a to c.*

A single general law covering a complex historical process is called an *historical law*. (3) above is thus an historical law. The notion of historical law finds its home in the Idea of Universal History (in postmodernist parlance, this Idea is called a "metanarrative"). According to this Idea the ensemble of human history comprises a single story in which a single subject – for example, humanity (Kant) or Spirit (Hegel) or species-being (Marx) – undergoes a process of development. The unfolding of the plot of this Universal History is meant to follow an "internal logic" precisely because this process is thought to be governed by some historical law. Thus, for example, for Marx human history is the story of development through various modes of production – from slave to feudal to capitalist to communist; he claimed this development follows a necessary path because it embodies an historical law which dictates that one stage in the sequence will inevitably lead forward to the next stage.

The Idea of Universal History has much less grip on historians and philosophers today than it did two hundred years ago. We are far more aware of the complexities and contingencies which mark human history. We see more clearly than did Condorcet or Schiller or Saint Simon or Kant or Hegel or Marx the difficulties involved in formulating an acceptable historical law.

For the purpose of assessing nomologicalism, the most important point is that an historical process may not be covered by a single historical law even though each of its stages is. In such a case nomological explanation needs to be complemented by a history in which the movement of x from a to c unfolds as a sequence of stages which are only contingently linked. Such an explanation would be essentially historical in character, consisting of a story which took the following form: x was a at t; but then at t + 1 h occurred, and so x became b (this change is governed by general law (1)); but at t + 2 j occurred (this is a contingent occurrence), and because j occurred x became c (this change is governed by general law (2)). Since in this case the process of change from a to c is not itself governed by an historical law, the explanation of this process must assume a non-nomological, essentially narrative, form.

To sum up: Nomological explanation is not sufficient in itself. Social scientists may legitimately be interested in phenomena in terms of their uniqueness and/or their intentionality; and/or they may wish to understand why the general regularities discovered by nomological social science take the form they do; and/or they might seek to understand a long-term historical process which is not itself governable by an historical law. In these cases nomological explanation must be supplemented by forms of explanation other than the nomological. To one of these we shall now turn.

8.4   Historicism

For the past two hundred years historicism has been the chief antagonist of nomologicalism. As I said at the outset, by *historicism* I mean the view that the identity of social entities or events lies in their history such that to understand them is to grasp their historical development. According to historicism as I use the term, to understand a nation or a person or an institution is to discover the process by which it became what it is. (Note that the term "historicism" is used in ways different from my use, though mine is the most common. In particular, my meaning is *not* that of Karl Popper in his well-known book *The Poverty of Historicism* (1957).)

The clearest example of historicist explanations are those in narrative histories. When Thucydides describes the progress of the Peloponnesian War, or E. H. Carr the steps by which the Bolsheviks seized power during the Russian revolution, they show how various actions and events led forward one to another toward a particular end. The significance of each action is understood in terms of its role in an unfolding drama. In these and countless other cases, particular acts are related to other particular acts not as instances of a certain general law, but in their particularity as each pushes forward a continuing line of transformation.

This type of explanation is broadly genetic in character. *Genetic explanations* present the explanandum event e as the final stage in a sequence of events which produced it. Accordingly, they explain e by describing the successive stages by which e came to be e. In a genetic explanation the stages are not just chronologically arranged; each stage must be shown to lead to the next culminating in the event in question. Genetic explanations are explanatory in that they set out the sequence of events through which some earlier entity or system has been transformed into a later one. Put schematically, e is explained as the outcome of a process in which in certain circumstances a led to b which led to c which led to d which led to e. Notice here the phrase "in the circumstances." There is no implication that a always leads to b, or that a to e is part of a lawful pattern; only given the particular conditions which obtained at the time did a lead to b, and so on. Thus, genetic explanations are schematized by means of small letters: it is the rich particularity of each event temporally situated in the historically specific process a to b to c to d to e which explains e, not a, b, c, d, or e being an instance of some broad class of event A, B, C, D, or E.

Thus, in explaining the outbreak of World War I historians might recount the story which begins with the assassination of Archduke Ferdinand (call this a); the response to a by Austria of declaring war on Serbia (b); the response to b by Russia of declaring war on Austria (c); the response of Germany to c by declaring war on Russia (d); and so on until all the major nations were at war with one another (e). Here there is no claim that b will always follow a, that a nation will respond to an assassination of its leader by declaring war on the country of its perpetrator. Only in the particular historical circumstances did such a response occur because of the unique historical situation of the antagonists.

170

Genetic explanations assume a broadly narrative form. That is, they tell a story with a beginning point (a), a middle (a to b, b to c, c to d), and an end (e). The story indicates the connections between the various events as they push toward a particular point. Narratives link events into a sequence of interconnected episodes, interconnected in that they each individually and all collectively go toward producing a particular end point. This is indeed how they explain the occurrence of this end point, as the result of a process which culminates with the occurrence of e. (Thus, the outbreak of World War I (e) is genetically explained by means of the narrative in which a leads to b (the assassination leads to Austria declaring war on Serbia) which leads to c and so on which finally leads to e (the outbreak of the War).)

Historicism derives its appeal in part from the intentional character of human activity and arrangements which we discussed in section 8.1. Human activities and relationships rest on a unique configuration of ideas, concepts, motives, beliefs, and perceptions such that they differ substantially from one another. Historicists claim it is misleading at best to believe that as nations Austria of the Hapsburg Empire or England under a parliamentary system are sufficiently alike as "nations" that they can fit within meaningful general laws. A nation is the emergent product of its own developing culture, language, institutions, and particular citizens – the emergent product of its own historical process. To abstract from this process is precisely to obliterate what is distinctive and illuminating about a nation. Only by appreciating its distinctiveness in all its rich particularity can a nation and its behavior be understood. The same is true of individual institutions and people, their actions and relations.

Genetic explanations thus must contain a rich store of descriptive material in which the specificity of a given social entity or event is captured. If general categories or generalizations are employed they will be highly qualified and located within a particular historical time frame or setting. And the connections between the various phases of the development which comprise the genetic explanation of an event or entity will be localized to the highly specific situations which pertained at the time. As I already said, Weber's *The Protestant Ethic and the Spirit of Capitalism* is an excellent example of this; in it capitalism is explained as the historically unique outcome of the concatenation of certain historically specific developments in sixteenth-century Protestant doctrine and practice.

In so far as social scientific explanations are genetic in character these sciences are essentially retrospective rather than predictive. Because in genetic explanations generalizations hold only within particular time periods, and because their basic mode of explanation is narratival and so essentially backward-looking, they reveal which particular factors led to what particular changes in the past or the immediate present, but they are unsuitable for predictions of what will happen. In contrast to nomologicalism which insists that as explainable social entities and events must be predictable, according to historicism social entities and events are retrospectively intelligible but prospectively indeterminate.

8.5   The Inadequacy of Genetic Explanations

According to historicism genetic explanations are sufficient unto themselves. By showing phenomena to be the result of a particular line of development, they are adequately explained; nothing more is required. Is this so?

Note in the first place that genetic explanations are causal in nature. Event a produces b which spawns c which leads to d which engenders e: But "produces," "spawns," "leads to," and "engenders" are all causal verbs; they clearly indicate that the connection between the various stages of the sequence in a genetic explanation is more than one of temporality but is also one of causality. In short, the genetic explanation of e consists in providing the causal etiology of e.

The causal nature of genetic explanations has an important bearing on the question of their adequacy. Since Mill the standard account of causality has been in terms of the language of necessary and sufficient conditions. This is the way most social scientists construe the term. (See Further Reading for other accounts of causality.) According to the Millian account, if c is the cause of e this means either c is a sufficient condition of e and/or that c is a necessary condition of e. But relations of necessary and/or sufficient conditionship clearly rest on a general law: both types of relation assert that *whenever* a certain type of event occurs or fails to occur another type of event will occur or fail to occur. In the case of sufficient conditionship, the general law is of the form "If C, then E"; in the case of necessary conditionship, "If no C, then no E." An ascription of causality construed in terms of necessary and sufficient conditionship thus implicitly involves reference not only to some particular conditions c but also to a general law which asserts an invariable, functional relationship between one class of events C (the independent variable) and another class of events E (the dependent variable).

Given a Millian construal of causality, it follows that genetic explanations in which particular causal relations are asserted *implicitly rest upon some general laws*. If historians claim that the assassination of Archduke Ferdinand caused the outbreak of World War I this causal claim rests on some unspecified general law. Again, the sociological claim that extreme inequality in land distribution leads to political instability may be understood to hold only in certain historically specific situations; nevertheless, the causal relationship asserted implies that some general law is at work.

However, a glaring fact calls this Millian nomological analysis of causality into question. Social scientists *do* presently provide many satisfactory causal explanations of everything from voting patterns to revolutions to changes in suicide rates but no general laws properly so-called linking the variables in these explanations currently exist. Social scientists are far more confident in their singular causal explanations than in any putative law of human behavior which links the terms of these explanations together. Doesn't this show that genetic explanations are sufficient unto themselves, that they do not require general laws for their backing?

But note that the Millian thesis is *not* that for every causal explanation a general law under which it is subsumable is ready to hand; indeed, the thesis does *not* entail even that the terms or the form of the relevant general law be stable. The thesis claims merely that there is a general law under which the events invoked in a causal explanation, including those in genetic explanations, fall. Thus it is perfectly consistent to claim that smoking causes lung cancer, to believe that such a claim rests on a general law which links events currently described as "smoking" and "lung cancer," and yet admit that at this moment no such law is known and indeed that the terms of the relevant law aren't known either.

Indeed, a biochemist might even consistently believe that these laws will *not be formulated in the same terms as those of the singular causal explanation* (in this case, will not employ such crude terms like "smoking" or "cancer"). Thus, an historian may confidently assert that soil erosion led to the decline of agricultural production in the American Southwest, or an agronomist may confidently defend the causal claim that soil erosion generally leads to a decline in agricultural production, even though both believe it impossible to link these events by means of a law which uses such a gross term as "soil erosion." They may well believe that the event which they now describe as soil erosion will have to be redescribed in terms of a radically different vocabulary – from chemistry, for instance – before the appropriate law could be formulated.

To borrow a crucial distinction from Davidson (1970), causal explanations may be either heteronomic or homonomic. *Homonomic* explanations are those whose underlying law is of the same vocabulary and form as the explanations themselves. *Heteronomic* explanations are those whose supporting law is only statable in terms fundamentally different from that of the explanation. Given the arguments above about the special features of intentional descriptions of intentional phenomena, it ought to be clear that their explanations are heteronomic: the laws which support them require

173

recourse to another sort of vocabulary altogether (in the examples, recourse to the non-intentionalistic terms of sociobiology).

Thus, that currently acceptable genetic explanations are not coverable by known general laws, or even by laws whose terms and form are known, does not imply that such explanations do not implicitly rest on some laws. Indeed, because genetic explanations consist in picking out the causal process in which one event leads to another and so on, the events which figure in historical explanations must be covered by general laws at some (unspecified) level of general description (at least in so far as causality is understood in Millian terms). The progress of social science (perhaps reconceived in the manner of sociobiology) in fact consists in part in the development of such laws. As these laws come on line, some of the genetic explanations currently believed will be strengthened, but others will be modified or called into question. Thus, far from genetic explanations being antithetical to scientific law, they require it.

Of course, reiterating a point from section 8.3, this does not mean that for every genetic explanation of a complex process a single historical general law exists which covers every stage of the process. A genetic explanation of e as the causal result of the sequence a to b, b to c, c to d, and d to e rests on general laws which govern the movement from one phase to the next, but it does *not* thereby follow that the entire process from a to e instantiates a general law. Genetic explanations are *supplementable* by nomological explanations, but are not necessarily *replaceable* by them.

Moreover, even if genetic explanations are supplementable by general laws it does not follow that social science must await such laws to provide useful satisfactory explanations. The heteronomic explanations of social science do not require laws to provide insights into the causal relations of the human world, any more than medicine must await certain biochemical laws before it can assert that smoking causes cancer.

8.6   Summing Up

This chapter has shown that the traditional antagonism between nomologicalism and historicism (with all its attendant oppositions) is ill-conceived. Each position is one-sided in itself, and requires the other as a supplement in order to achieve a satisfactory account of understanding human beings. Far from being mutually exclusive, both are required to do justice to the richness of social inquiry. In social science there is room – indeed a need – for *both* nomological and genetic forms of explanation.

Thus historicist genetic explanations, though providing insightful explanations of human phenomena, rest on and call for the development of genuine general laws. Though genetic explanations focus on specific inter-actions of historically bounded individuals organized into a sequence, they are causal in nature and, given a Millian construal of causality, ultimately depend upon promissory scientific laws in which to embed their particular connections. (This is not to say that these laws must be framed in terms of the same vocabulary as that employed in a particular genetic explanation; as we have seen, the explanations of the social sciences intentionalistically formulated are heteronomic in character. Nor is it to say that on their own genetic explanations are uninformative or useless.)

But the general laws of social science are likely to be so abstract that they will omit a great deal of what social scientists will rightly want to know about human phenomena. Typically certain sorts of social science will be concerned with the historically unique as historically unique – will investigate the emergence of capitalism in the seventeenth century, for example, or the Nuer tribe, or the relationship between inmate behavior and the design of modern-day asylums, or the effect of certain voting systems on parliamentary power in industrial societies.

Moreover, because social scientific laws will undoubtedly be formulated in non-intentionalistic terms (say, in the language of sociobiology) it will be impossible simply by means of them to explain the particular mecha-nisms by means of which these laws are instantiated in human life. As a result, social science will undoubtedly turn to intentional descriptions and explanations to understand the details of the laws and how they function.

Furthermore, some processes in human history, particularly ones of long duration and rich complexity, may not be coverable by a general historical law even though each stage in this process is. Lacking historical laws social sciences must turn to history and genetic explanation as a way of explain-ing the course of these processes.

The broad view of this chapter has been that nomological explanations and genetic explanations are part of one general endeavor to explain human activity and the products of this activity. Each provides what the other lacks; only together can they offer a complete picture of what we as humans do and are.

So, to return to the question of this chapter, is our (scientific) under-standing of others essentially historical? Yes and No. The social sciences will always have a historical dimension to them, offering genetic explana-tions of intentional and historically unique phenomena. But this will not be their only dimension; they will also rightly continue to search for the laws which govern human phenomena (though such phenomena will undoubtedly not be described as specifically human – that is, inten-tionalistically – in order to be capturable in such laws). The search for laws will continue because genetic explanations ultimately require them in order to be complete, and because the causal explanations which science seeks are ultimately general in character. Thus the social sciences are both essentially historical *and* not essentially historical.

Moreover, this answer itself provides the basis for an answer to the deep multicultural question, are people in different cultures fundamentally the same or fundamentally different? The answer is: both. Looked at from the abstract perspective of what is perfectly general about humans (or species), people are the same. But viewed from the concrete perspective of what is distinctive about particular humans, they are quite different. Difference and similarity need not be antithetical, any more than nomologicalism and historicism are.

Further Reading

The position in this chapter is heavily indebted to Rosenberg (1980), Davidson (1967 and 1970), and Danto (1985). I have also benefited from extensive discussions with Lee McIntyre and from his unpublished Ph.D. thesis on this topic; see also McIntyre (1993 and 1996).

For an excellent collection of essays on the topics of law and explanation, see Martin and McIntyre (1994, part II). For a sophisticated analysis of the issues discussed in this chapter, see Henderson (1993), chapters 6–8.

For nomologicalism, see Hempel (1965) and the essays in part II of Martin and MacIntyre (1994). For the Argument from Intentionality, see Fay (1983).

For the Idea of Universal History, see Mink (1987), essay #9. For a criticism of this Idea, see Lyotard (1984).

For historicism, see Reill (1975), Troeltsch (1957), Meinecke (1972), Mannheim (1956), and Mandelbaum (1938).

For sociobiology, see Wilson (1978), Ruse (1979), and Rosenberg (1980).

For an account of narrative as a kind of explanation, see Roth (1988; 1989; and 1991).

The literature on causality is enormous. The view presented in this chapter follows Davidson (1967). This view is broadly Humean (see Hume, 1739). This is the dominant view in the history of modern philosophy, one that Mill (1843) developed. For a recent presentation and exploration of this view from the perspective of scientific explanation, see Hempel (1965, especially pp. 348–51).

An important alternative construal of causality is that which understands causes as recipes for the production of outcomes. In the words of one of its most articulate spokespersons: "The notion of causation is essentially connected with the manipulative techniques for producing results" (Gasking, 1955, p. 483). This view has a distinguished pedigree in the history of philosophy, extending back to Bacon through Reid and Collingwood to von Wright. See von Wright (1971, chapter 2) for a sophisticated account of this construal, and the bibliography cited in the footnotes to this chapter.

Another important account of causality alternative to that of Hume and Mill is that of causal realism. According to causal realism, the cause of an event e is some underlying mechanism which in suitable conditions produces e. Underlying mechanisms have natural powers whose exercise is causally responsible for particular outcomes. The search for causes is thus the search for such mechanisms, not the search for general laws. In this way causal realism denies that causality is nomological. For causal realism, see Harré (1970); Harré and Secord (1972); Bhaskar (1978); and Keat and Urrey (1975). For a criticism of causal realism as surreptitiously smuggling general laws back in on another level, see Miller (1972) and Fay (1983).

9

Do We Live Stories or Just Tell Them?

9.1   Narrative Realism

All the world's a stage
And all the men and women merely players.
They have their exits and their entrances,
And one man in his time plays many parts,
His acts being seven ages.

(As You Like It)

In these famous lines Jaques gives voice to an idea that most of us have had when reflecting on our own or others' lives, namely, that human lives are enacted stories. True, our lives often seem a welter of unrelated events; but at particular times we get the sense that we or others are part of a drama whose plot we can dimly perceive, a plot that provides an underlying unity and meaning to our or others' experiences, relations, and activities. On this view, both self-knowledge and the knowledge of others consist in apprehending this underlying plot and making it explicit.

Is Jaques correct? That is, are our lives in fact stories in which we are the central characters? Or, more broadly, does our culture enact some inherent narrative pattern? Or is Jaques incorrect: are the stories we or others tell instead mere constructions which we make up after the fact in order to render our lives and cultures meaningful? Do we perform in the stories we or others relate about us, or are they instead simply tales we or others spin to lend some semblance of order to lives in themselves without inherent order? Are our stories *in* our lives to be extracted from them, or are they only *about* our lives such that they are imposed on them? In short, are the stories of our lives lived or merely told?

These questions arise in part out of the multicultural experience of

178

difference. What is the relationship between me the storyteller and you the other about whom I tell a story as a way of comprehending your thoughts and deeds? When I come to tell the story of someone else who is quite different from me as a way of understanding that person, am I looking for something which is a property of that person's life – its dramatic structure or plot? Or am I inventing a pattern which is significant for me given who I am but which may not be significant for the person I am trying to understand in part because it is not contained in that person's life? Am I trying to discover something which is already there, or to create something which isn't? The possibility of genuine understanding of others, and of what such understanding consists, ride on the answers to these questions.

These questions are also crucial for clarifying the notions of agency and culture which we explored in chapters 2 and 3, notions critically important for the idea of multiculturalism. In those chapters we discovered that culture is an ongoing process, not a static entity; and we also learned that agents are agents only when situated within such a process. But cultures are in part comprised of stories by means of which members weave webs of significance, webs which make sense of the past and inform future choices. As we shall see in this chapter, agents are story-telling animals in part because only by setting their acts into a narrative context can these acts take place. The question of this chapter – what is the nature of the stories we tell about our own and others' lives? – is thus central for understanding multiculturalism.

Let's begin with the doctrine which gives philosophical expression to Jaques's idea that we are all actors in an unfolding plot: narrative realism. *Narrative realism* claims that narrative structures exist *in* the human world itself and not just in the stories people tell *about* this world. Human lives are already formed into stories before historians or biographers – or indeed, the persons living these lives – attempt to tell these stories. Because narrative structures inhere in particular lives the job of historians is to mirror this already existing structure. True stories are found, not constructed.

An analogy might make narrative realism clearer. The DNA molecule seems to have a particular structure independent of any attempt to understand it. The job of molecular biologists thus appears to be the discovery of an already existing pattern, not the creation of a pattern to be imposed on material itself formless. The DNA molecule is double-helical in form, and this is why Crick and Watson's double helix model is acceptable. According to narrative realism the same is true for historians and biographers: their task is to tell stories whose beginnings, middles, and endings mirror the actual beginnings, middles, and endings of the events being narrated. The narrative structure is already *in* the material, and good histories and biographies reproduce this pre-existing structure.

We have already encountered one quite ambitious version of narrative realism: the idea of Universal History. (Recall that it claims that all of human history is the unfolding of a single story waiting to be told by some universal historian like Saint Simon, Hegel, or Marx.) But this ambitious version – which we have already rejected – is not the only version of narrative realism. A more modest version claims that the lives of individuals (including individuals organized in groups) incarnate particular narrative patterns of events. As Alasdair MacIntyre put it in his widely-heralded book *After Virtue*, human history is comprised of "enacted dramatic narratives in which the characters are also the authors" (MacIntyre, 1981, p. 200).

The historical realist's idea is roughly this: just as with molecules and planetary systems there are natural joints and patterns in human lives. The "natural joints" of human lives are their natural beginnings, middles, and endings. Recall that for Jaques there are seven such natural parts of the "strange, eventful history" which is a human life. On a larger scale, historians do not *decide* that World War I began in August 1914, or that it ended in November 1918, or that it progressed through definite identifiable phases. The order of World War I is first and foremost in the war itself, and only afterwards in the minds and books of historians who have been fortunate enough to grasp this order. As MacIntyre put it:

> And to someone who says that in life there are no endings, or that final partings take place only in stories, one is tempted to reply, "But have you never heard of death?" Homer did not have to tell the tale of Hector before Andromache could lament unfulfilled hope and final parting. There are countless Hectors and countless Andromaches whose lives embodied the form of their Homeric namesakes, but who never came to the attention of any poet . . . There is a crucial sense in which the principate of Augustus, or the taking of the oath at the tennis court, or the decision to construct an atomic bomb at Los Alamos constitute beginnings; the peace of 404 BC, the abolition of the Scottish Parliament and the battle of Waterloo constitute endings; while there are many events which are both endings and beginnings. (pp. 197–8)

Human lives set their own contexts: birth is the beginning, death the ending, and in between there are natural climaxes, denouements, and so on.

But at least in this simple form, is narrative realism very convincing? In what sense must the narrative of peoples' lives end with their physical death? Mightn't death be merely a stage of existence, those who die living in another realm and perhaps continuing to produce effects in this world as ghosts or specters? Many people throughout history have believed this – have believed it about Jesus, for example. Moreover, even if people don't live on in any ordinary sense of "live," might not their story continue beyond the grave? Does the story of Socrates cease with his drinking of the hemlock? Does the story of Lincoln end with him in Ford's theater?

Further, is it clear that the story of a human life must begin with birth? Hindus telling the story of their life will commence long before they assumed the re-incarnated form they now possesses, just as Plato's story of the slave boy in the *Meno* begins prior to his birth. Wordsworth, conceiving his life as a gradual fall from rapture, wrote:

> The Soul that rises with us, our life's Star,
> Hath had elsewhere its setting
> And cometh from afar:
> Not in entire forgetfulness
> And not in utter nakedness,
> But trailing clouds of glory do we come
> From God, who is our home:
> Heaven lies about us in our infancy!
>
> *("Intimations Ode")*

Even prescinding from those stories which see humans as having a prior existence, people are born into the world as embodied, situated creatures with definite needs, dispositions, and social relations. In order to portray the impact of this situatedness a biographer might plausibly begin a person's story prior to his or her birth – with parents, with the formation of the family, with the creation of the social order, with intellectual forebears, and so on. When asked to tell their own story Cheyenne Indians most often begin, "my grandparents . . ."

The way the different Gospels recount the beginnings of the story of Jesus Christ is fascinating in this regard. Mark begins the story with Jesus' baptism by John the Baptist at which moment God supposedly picked Jesus out and made him the Chosen One. No birth stories are to be found in Mark because for Mark nothing about Jesus is special until his baptism. Not so, according to Matthew and Luke. These gospels tell the traditional nativity story because for these writers Jesus' birth was miraculous and fulfilled the ancient prophecies. For Matthew and Luke the story of Jesus Christ begins with his birth (or indeed his conception) not his baptism. In the gospel of John once again no birth story is told; the book of John begins, "In the beginning was the Word, and the Word was with God, and the Word was God." According to John, Jesus was the Christ from the beginning of time. Note the progression here: from Jesus' baptism (when he was around thirty), to his conception, to the beginning of time. Is it obvious that the story of Jesus Christ "really" begins with his birth, that Matthew and Luke are correct and Mark and John are wrong?

Given these considerations a narrative realist might wish to recast the claim that there is a natural beginning (birth) and natural ending (death) into the more modest assertion that each life is structured into a narrative sequence and that certain episodes will figure prominently in it. The main point of narrative realism is that there really are starting points, endings, and climaxes *in* human affairs. Perhaps it is naive to think that these correspond directly with physical births and deaths, though that these usually will be significant in whatever story is unfolding seems undeniable.

At a certain point the love affair begins and at another it is over (though the participants may not have realized it at the time); the same is true of a battle or a presidential campaign or an economic boom. That something integral to the 19th century died during World War I – that World War I marks the end of the 19th century and the beginning of the 20th – does not seem to be the product of some historian's imagination. When Robert Graves entitled his memoir *Goodbye To All That* he seemed to express a truth about the nature of the War itself and what it meant, not a personal opinion or an arbitrary point by which to demarcate a fundamental historical change. Of course historians may argue about the precise date such a shift occurred, but according to historical realism this debate is *not* about where to impose a date on a welter of events themselves meaningless, but to uncover the break as it was in these events themselves.

What is true about large-scale events such as wars, depressions, migrations, and the rise and fall of empires, realists also believe is true of individuals, their particular actions and their lives taken as wholes. Realists claim that the identity of a particular act derives from the intention it expresses, and that an intention is what it is by virtue of the historical setting into which the agent places it. (Thus, for example, my act of opening the window is an act of cooling because I place it in a narrative context: the window was closed and so I got hot; but if I open the window I will be cooler in the future.) Moreover, each of our lives consists in refashioning the continuous narrative we tell ourselves about ourselves, adjusting it and our behavior as we go along. The basic plot of our lives, of which we are in part the author, is precisely the trajectory of this ongoing narrative line. Consequently, the job of the biographer is to discover this already existing line and to show how our individual choices and acts both embody and develop it. Precisely because our lives are already narratively shaped by our intentions we can ask, which biography is true? As MacIntyre put it when discussing the life of Thomas Becket:

182

Consider the question of what genre the life of Thomas Beckett belongs, a question which has to be asked and answered before we can decide how it is to be written . . . In some of the medieval versions, Thomas's career is presented in terms of canons of medieval hagiography. In the Icelandic *Thomas Saga* he is presented as a saga hero. In Dom David Knowles's modern biography the story is a tragedy, the tragic relationship of Thomas and Henry II, each of whom satisfies Aristotle's demand that the hero be a great man with a fatal flaw. Now it clearly makes sense to ask who is right, if anyone: the monk William of Canterbury, the author of the saga, or the Cambridge Regius Professor Emeritus? The answer appears to be clearly the last. The true genre of the life is neither hagiography nor saga but tragedy. (p. 198)

Given this analysis, the question about narrative realism devolves into the question of whether the intentional nature of individual actions or whole human lives or collective undertakings is such that they actually embody a particular narrative line, and consequently whether the attempt to render these actions intelligible must consist in trying to uncover this pre-existing narrative line. (Note here the similarity with the intentionalist theory of meaning we examined in chapter 7.) As agents, do our acts both individually and collectively necessarily play a role in a particular story which is our lives?

To answer this question let's explore some episodes from an excellent book of historical biography, Phyllis Rose's *Parallel Lives: Five Victorian Marriages* (Rose, 1983). This book consists of portraits of five marriages of literary figures in the nineteenth century – those of Thomas Carlyle, John Stuart Mill, John Ruskin, Charles Dickens, and George Eliot. To examine the historical realist position I will focus on two particular cases in this book: Carlyle's autobiographical account of his own marriage, and Rose's treatment of Froude's biography of Carlyle. In each of these cases Rose the biographer perforce introduces elements which go beyond the lived intentions of the people involved – elements the addition of which will highlight the fundamental difference between living and the story of that living. These differences will reveal the ways narrative realism is one-sided and partial. (In section 9.3 I will return to the important truth in realism.)

Jane Welsh and Thomas Carlyle had been married for forty years when Jane died suddenly in 1866. It was then that Thomas discovered, along with her letters and journals, a diary Jane had begun in 1855 in which she detailed the misery of her marriage occasioned by Thomas's neglect of her and by his attention to Lady Harriet Ashburton. Rose claims that this diary was intended by Jane as an act of revenge against Thomas, a written statement of how he had wronged her to be read after her death to produce a deep sense of guilt in him.

It worked. When Thomas read the diary he was genuinely shocked; he came to revise entirely his understanding of his relationship with Jane. Rose quotes from Froude's biography of Carlyle: "'He never properly understood until her death how much she had suffered, and how much he had to answer for'" (p. 255). Rose herself writes:

> Carlyle saw the story of her life as she had laid it out for him in her letters and journals to be found after her death, a story of great promise, great gifts, great advantages sacrificed for a man who ultimately neglected her, and he swallowed the story hook, line, and sinker. (p. 254)

Indeed, Carlyle published a book, *Reminiscences*, in which he portrayed their relationship in just these narrative terms.

The significance of the Carlyle case is that it clearly reveals an element in Carlyle's story which was not a part of his intentions, conscious or otherwise. This element is the *causal outcomes* of his acts.

As Rose says (p. 250), while Jane was alive Thomas did not intend to cause his wife the deep suffering he in fact did cause, nor was he aware that he was doing so. Ignorant of the causal outcomes of his behavior for his wife, especially his behavior with Lady Harriet, he thought of his relationship with Jane in relatively positive terms. But when he read in her diary of the consequences of his actions, how they produced anguish in her, he came to describe his behavior and his relationship in radically different terms.

This is as it should be. For stories are comprised not just of actions and their intentions, but also of the *results* of these acts and intentions. In fact, so important in a story are these outcomes that actions are often redescribed in terms which portray them as causes of these outcomes. Hitler, intending to gain *lebensraum* for the so-called Aryans, ordered his armies into Russia; on the basis of Hitler's intentions this act could thus be described as "a move for living space." But this act ultimately led to Hitler's demise because it brought Russia into the war, opening up another front with which Hitler's armies ultimately could not contend; in light of this eventual outcome, the act of invasion has now been redescribed by one of his biographers as "the beginning of Hitler's downfall" (though this is not a description which could have been given of the act at the time of its occurrence just because its outcomes were not evident at that time). Note that if the invasion had produced another causal result – say, the conquering of Russia – it might well have been redescribed as "the beginning of the thousand-year Reich."

What is true of individual acts is also true of entire episodes: their nature is deeply affected by causal outcomes. Someone drops a handkerchief, another picks it up; the parties begin to talk; perhaps there is an immediate attraction, perhaps even a formed intention to see one another again. But into what story do these acts fit? At the moment of meeting it cannot be the story of their affair because at this point the affair has not occurred and it is not clear that such a relationship will in fact materialize. Only because of later events, the effects of their meeting, can and will the meeting be seen, and be redescribed retrospectively, as the start of the affair. Similarly with the affair itself: is it the beginning of a marriage? The first step in one or both of the parties' eventual misery? Or . . . ? We shall have to await the outcome of the affair in order to be able to say.

So important are causal outcomes that descriptions of events apt for fitting them into stories centrally employ what Arthur Danto (1985) called "narrative sentences." In narrative sentences an earlier event or object is described in terms of later events or objects. Thus, for example: "*Lyrical Ballads* initiated the romantic movement in English poetry"; or "In 1755 Leopold Mozart, the father of the greatest composer of the eighteenth century, . . ."; or "The shot fired at Concord began the American War of Independence." Terms like "anticipated," "caused," "predicted," "instigated," "predated," and "influenced," as well as certain referring devices ("the person who [was to do something in the future] . . ."), typically occur in narrative sentences. In these sentences an event or object acquires new properties by standing in a new relation with events or objects which came after them. (In 1755 Wolfgang had not yet been born; at the time when the shot was fired at Concord no one could have known that a war of independence was to take place.) In all of them the original entity is described in terms which it could not have been described at its occurrence because the description refers to events or objects which hadn't occurred at that time.

The importance of causal outcomes and narrative sentences for stories is not accidental. Stories tell what happened next as a result of something's occurring, and what happened after that. To see this consider the following collection of sentences: "X intended a and did y; X intended b and did z; X intended c and did q." This isn't a story at all because it doesn't indicate the causal connections between the various events. Compare this pseudo-story with the following real story: "X intended a and did y; y produced z, and this led X to intend b and to do q." The causal outcomes of actions (here, z) provide at least part of the connective tissue in virtue of which events are linked together to form a story. Thus, descriptions of y such as "the cause of z" will abound in narrative accounts of X.

Carlyle's revision of the narrative of his marriage is understandable only because learning of significant causal outcomes of his acts necessarily led him to redescribe those acts, thereby fitting them into a different story.

What is true for Carlyle is also true for Rose herself: knowing that Jane's diary produced in Thomas the intended outcome of guilt, Rose quite properly can redescribe Jane's diary as an instrument of revenge. This is not a description Jane herself could have given because she could not have known what effect her diary would actually have (it might have left Thomas unmoved). The story of Jane's diary is as much a function of its effects as of its causes.

Because the identity of an act or a life is a function of its causal outcomes a fundamental indeterminacy characterizes their description. Since the causal repercussions of any act or life can continue indefinitely into the future even after the participants have died, and since the nature of the story told about this act or life will be deeply affected by these repercussions, the narrative of a life can never be settled. There is no one "definitive story" to be told about a life. Thus, no life can be a story "in itself" because the stories of lives are not self-contained: as new causal outcomes resulting from that life emerge, new stories can and will be told about it.

But causal outcomes are not the only element left out of the narrative realist account of narratives. Another element – what I shall call *significance* – is just as important. The importance of significance can be demonstrated by turning to another case from Rose's book, her treatment of Froude's classic biography of Carlyle.

Froude's work was published in 1884. In it he depicted the horror of the Carlyles' marriage by placing it within a particular sort of narrative; Rose characterizes it this way:

> It is a magnificent, compassionate work, portraying a genius whose very strength and breadth of thought unfit him for the small negotiations of daily life. Because his vision is essentially tragic, Froude does not *blame* Carlyle for making his wife wretched any more than one would blame Othello for mistreating Desdemona. Nevertheless, his work is structured on an ironic (and implicitly critical) principle: Carlyle sees to the heart of society but not into the mind of his partner for life. He is a great man, a great thinker, but a pathetic human being. He hurts Jane without knowing it, and he is lonely and wretched at the same time. Froude basically adopts Jane's view of the marriage as suggested by the 1855–56 diary – an heiress debased to a servant and neglected in her middle age for a more glamorous woman, her serious illnesses not understood or sufficiently sympathized with. And I have no doubt that that is how Carlyle, seeking punishment and expiation, would have wanted the story told. (p. 257)

But Rose wishes to question this biographical story organized around the idea of "the tragic ironies of greatness." Informed by modern feminism Rose believes the story of the Carlyles' marriage ought not to be told in terms of the personal characteristics of the principals involved, but rather in terms of the possibilities of traditional marriage itself. Rose denies that the Carlyles' was a particularly wretched marriage. Of course it was marked by deep disappointments and conflicts, but then she thinks any long-term intimate union will be so marked. As Rose summarizes:

> To say that they (the Carlyles) clashed in many ways and in so many ways disappointed each other is to say no more than that they were married, and for a long time. They acted out the possibilities of the form. (p. 259)

For Froude the Carlyles' marriage is a story of the tragic irony of the great man who grasps life in the large but who cannot understand or abide its particular embodiments. For Rose the Carlyles' marriage is a story of two people caught in the web of the institution of traditional marriage. In Froude's story the peculiar qualities of Thomas and Jane are important features. In Rose's story they are secondary; fundamental are the possibilities and limits of traditional marriage itself. Froude can tell his story of the Carlyles independently of the story of other marriages; Rose cannot, for she believes that to understand the Carlyles' marriage requires that one see it as an instance of a recurring type. This is why Rose describes the Carlyles' relationship in the context of four other marriages. As she says in the Postlude:

> My aim throughout this book has not been to show that Dickens or Ruskin or Carlyle were "bad" husbands, but to present them as examples of behavior generated inevitably by the peculiar privileges and stresses of traditional marriage. (p. 269)

How to account for the difference between Froude and Rose? It is not because Rose discovered "new facts" (she herself explicitly says this on p. 17). That is to say, this is *not* like the first case in which different narratives are constructed on the basis of learning new causal outcomes of actions. Nor is this a case in which different authors express different critical judgments about an agreed-upon story. It is the stories themselves, and not judgments about them, which are different. How, then, can the two biographers with the same facts tell two different stories about the same marriage?

A biography cannot just consist of a recounting of intentions, acts, and their effects. The reason is simple: there are an infinite number of these in any human life. Carlyle spoke on 5 August 1857 at 10:01 a.m.; when he did he moved a number of air molecules around him, in turn causing the plants in the room to sway ever so slightly, prompting motes of dust to fall to the carpet, producing . . . However, none of these events are part of any biography of Carlyle, nor are they likely to be (though in principle they could be), precisely because none of these events appears to have any significance for anyone in Carlyle's life or for Carlyle himself or for anyone

187

who came after him. In biographies not just intentions, acts, and effects are important, but *significant* ones. The story of the Carlyles' marriage as told by Rose is importantly different from that of Froude precisely because Rose interprets the significance of the events in question differently from Froude.

How is significance to be understood here? Biographers attempt to reveal the nature of a person's life as they see it by showing how it falls into some recognizable pattern (Froude's "the tragic ironies of greatness," Rose's "victims of patriarchal marriage"). To do this they must pick out, from among the countless events in a life, those which when properly combined reveal the sort of life it was. Depending on what the biographer takes to be the basic plot of the life, different events will be described differently, figure more or less prominently or not at all, and so forth. Thus for Froude the fact that Carlyle was an historian of genius was of primary significance, whereas for Rose it is only secondarily so. Significance, therefore, can be defined in terms of the capacity to advance an emerging narrative pattern.

No "basic structure" inheres in the life of Carlyle or anyone else. Countless facts, themselves the result of interpretations, can be arranged in any number of different ways to form a coherent configuration which makes a life intelligible. These interpretations, these arrangements, these judgments of intelligibility all involve the active participation of biographers as they attempt to elaborate the story of a life. Writing a story is not, therefore, the activity the mimetic theory of narrative realism would have it. The subject's life does not impress its structure on a passive observer like an object leaving its impression on hot wax, or like an object being reflected in a mirror – to invoke two metaphors dear to the history of narrative realist thought. Writing a biography requires the biographer to extract from the myriad of details of a person's life those which cohere into a recognizably intelligible shape. That is, biography involves the creative imagination of the biographer as well as the intentions of the biographee.

Nowhere is it more important to acknowledge the importance of the active role of the biographer than in the notion of intelligibility itself. As we saw in chapter 5.4, intelligibility is not a given, fixed notion. What is and what is not an intelligible order is not only a function of the life led but also a function of who is interpreting that life. Intelligibility is always intelligibility *for someone*, i.e., it is *relative to some interpreter(s)*. The relation-ship between biographer and the life of the biographee is like the relation-ship between translator and that which is to be translated. What is the correct translation of "Comme il faut"? The question is nonsensical until it is clear who the translation is for, into what language it is to be translated.

188

Similarly, the meaning of a life is meaningful only if it speaks to a particular audience. Translation and biography are inherently relative activities. (This is a repetition of points made in chapter 7.2 in expounding Gadamerian hermeneutics.)

It follows that the intelligibility of a life will be different for different interpreters as they, with their own understandings, attempt to translate that life into terms which speak to them. Definitive biographies exist no more than do definitive translations: each age, each cultural group, constituted by its own commitments, beliefs, values, and so on, must confront the past anew, attempting to make it accessible to that age and group in its present configuration. Stories of lives led involve a continual mediation of past lives by present concerns, such that as the present changes so also will the shapes of the stories told about these past lives.

Indeed, the relation is more complex than this. For the way in which a generation understands the past is in part a function of what it takes itself to be, but how it understands itself is in part a function of what it takes the past to be. The relation between the past, the present, and their interpretation is not simple or unidirectional; rather, it is dialectical. Biographers bring to their subjects their own preoccupations and commitments which include, among other things, a sense of the past; at the same time, biographers, if they are sympathetic and self-conscious, will find themselves changing in the process of appropriating other lives, strengthened in certain of their beliefs and attitudes, weakened in others. It is one of the enduring merits of Rose's book that she is so explicit about this:

> Although I began the book with no thesis to prove, merely with a feminist skepticism about marriage, a taste for the higher gossip, a distaste for the rhetoric of romantic love, and a desire to look at marriages as imaginative projections and arrangements of power, I ended up with a bewildered respect for the durability of the pair, in all its variations. Perhaps predictably, I became more convinced than ever about the sterility, for men as well as women, of the patriarchal ideal of marriage and more skeptical about the chances of any particular marriage to escape its influence. (p. 17)

The plot of the marriage of the Carlyles is not – nor can it be, given that plots involve assigning significance to facts in terms of the shape of the whole – a property of the marriage which exists independently of anyone's attempting to write this plot. The story of the marriage involves the construction of a narrative revelatory for a particular audience as to the nature of this marriage; thus the kind of story told will partly be relative to the plotmaker and his or her listeners. No wonder, then, that the narrative of Jane's and Thomas's life together should be so different when told by Froude in nineteenth-century Victorian society and Phyllis Rose in twentieth-century American society. Biographies involve the intersection of two lives, that of the person being written about and that of the person doing the writing. The title of Rose's book – *Parallel Lives* – refers not only to the lives of the Mills, the Carlyles, the Ruskins, and so on, but also to them on the one side and Rose on the other. Perhaps, however, the relation of Rose to her subjects, as with the relation of all biographers to their subjects, would have been better captured by the appellation "intersecting lives."

9.2   Narrative Constructivism

Rose's biographies show the ways that narrative realism is inadequate: it omits the role of causal outcomes in the stories of a life; and it neglects the importance of significance. These inadequacies might lead one to a competing account of the relation between stories and lives, namely, narrative constructivism. Unfortunately, we shall discover that narrative constructivism is just as one-sided as narrative realism.

Narrative constructivism claims that historians impose narrative structures on a formless flow of events. As one of its most articulate advocates, Louis Mink, put it:

> Stories are not lived but told. Life has no beginnings, middles, or ends; there are meetings, but the start of an affair belongs to the story we tell ourselves later, and there are partings but final partings only in the story. There are hopes, plans, battles, and ideas, but only in retrospective stories are hopes unfulfilled, plans miscarried, battles decisive, and ideas seminal. Only in the story is it America which Columbus discovers and only in the story is the kingdom lost for want of a nail. (Mink, 1987, p. 60)

For narrative constructivists the view that human lives are stories is backwards: narratives are products of art as historians and biographers attempt to make sense of life, not products in life itself. The lives of people are composed of mere sequences of events which require a biographer later to impose on this sequence a narrative structure to render them intelligible. Narratives are constructed, not discovered, are creations after the fact when one can assign – from one's own perspective – particular roles in particular stories to the various events and relationships of persons' lives.

However, a look at another case in Rose's book will reveal the way narrative constructivism is itself one-sided. The case is that of the ending of the marriage between Charles Dickens and Catherine Hogarth. In 1857, a year before he separated from Catherine, and with a deepening sense of unhappiness made all the more so by a growing attachment to the young actress Ellen Ternan, Dickens wrote a letter to a Miss Coutts about his domestic misery. In it he claimed:

> I believe my marriage has been for years and years as miserable a one as ever was made. I believe that no two people were ever created with such an impossibility of interest, sympathy, confidence, sentiment, tender union of any kind between them, as there is between my wife and me. (Rose, 1983, p. 180)

This is the first recorded statement of a version of his marriage that Dickens was to tell repeatedly both before and after his final separation from his wife in 1858. At first this statement might seem merely a rationalization for the act of separation, something added later to the act to make it palatable to the public about which Dickens cared so much. But this would be to underestimate its role in Dickens' life. As Rose says, this story of a marriage between people fundamentally incompatible "expresses the myth of Dickens' marriage as he chose to present it, as he probably believed it, in its final form" (Rose, p. 186). The point here is that Dickens was not just telling this story to others; *he was telling it to himself.* Only because he had come to believe his marriage was with someone with whom he was irreversibly incompatible could he undertake to end it. Put in the terms of this chapter, Dickens' performance of the intentional act of marital separation was in part a function of his coming to reconceive the story of his marriage.

This episode shows the way narratives are *in* life and not just *about* it. As intentional agents, we live *within* ongoing stories which we must constantly tell ourselves as a condition for being able to perform any intentional actions whatsoever. This is the true insight of narrative realism which narrative constructivism overlooks.

Why should this be so? Begin with the commonplace: intentional actions are both teleological (because directed toward an end) and motivated. An intentional action involves doing x for the sake of y (I pull the top lever (x) to vote for the Conservative candidate (y); I move my feet in time with the music (x) to express my sense of joy (y)). Moreover, intentional acts are performed for a reason: I'm dissatisfied with liberal policies, and so vote conservative as a way of effecting a change in government; I feel an exuberance and superfluity of emotion and want to express it by dancing up a storm.

Behind the obvious fact that intentional acts are directed toward an end and are done for a reason is a feature which is not so obvious: their temporal character. As teleological, actions necessarily look toward the future, at some possible state of affairs that the act is supposed to bring about. As motivated by reasons, actions necessarily look backward to the past, to

191

one's situation and how one got there. The moment of acting is precisely the coming together of the agent's sense of his or her past history, present situation, and future possibilities.

But note that this temporal dimension has a narrative structure: a beginning (the past), a middle (the present), and an end (the future). As David Carr (whose ideas I am mining here) has so aptly put it:

> We are constantly striving with more or less success to occupy the storyteller's position with respect to our own actions . . . Such narrative activity . . . has a practical function in life (as) a constitutive part of action, and not just as an embellishment, commentary, or other incidental accompaniment . . .
>
> The actions and sufferings of life can be viewed as a process of telling ourselves stories, listening to those stories, and acting them out or living them through . . . To be an agent or subject of experience is to make the constant attempt to surmount time in exactly the way the storyteller does. It is the attempt to dominate the flow of events by gathering them together in the forward-backward grasp of the narrative act. (Carr, 1986, pp. 61–2)

The stories agents tell themselves about themselves are not mere appendages imposed on activity after the fact. Activity is itself already narratively structured, such that stories are integral to the performance of every act. Acts are therefore enactments of some narrative.

Agency itself may well be fundamentally narratival. Recall from chapter 3 that the capacity to act is an achievement which requires a great deal of learning. Infants are not agents, and toddlers are so only in a limited sense. Adults too can have more or less power of agency. Part of learning how to be an agent appears to consist in acquiring a time sense in which past, present, and future are related as in a narrative. This time sense allows an agent to grasp a situation in terms of its possibilities and provides the agent with the guidance needed to decide how to behave in one way or another. Only when a person can experience the present moment as connected to the past and as pointing to a future can that person act.

Psychosis can be conceived as the failure of agency deriving from the inability to connect past, present, and future into a meaningful narrative scheme. Even neurosis may be understood as a failure of one's narrative imagination and a resulting impairment of one's powers of agency. Some recent accounts of psychoanalysis (see Schafer (1978) and Spence (1982)) have interpreted therapy directed at neurosis as a process in which elements of a patient's life experienced as disconnected and unwanted come to be re-integrated as the patient re-interprets them into a different self-narrative. On this view, therapy is the process whereby patients come to view aspects of their lives heretofore separate from them by means of a new story which reveals the ways these aspects are indeed integral. That is, therapy is the process of patients re-narrativizing important elements of their lives and in this way becoming more capable agents. In so far as this account is accurate it shows the crucial connection between agency and narratives. Here agency is possible precisely in so far as an agent's experience can be narratively organized.

What is true of individual agents is also true of ongoing activity undertaken by two or more individuals. Continual interaction requires the participants to construe their activity in such a way that it is responsive to the activity of others. Rose puts this well when characterizing marriage:

> . . . every marriage is a narrative construct – or two marriage constructs. In unhappy marriages, for example, I see two versions of reality rather than two people in conflict. I see a struggle for imaginative dominance going on. Happy marriages seem to me to be those in which the two partners agree on the scenario they are enacting . . . Every marriage seems to me a subjectivist fiction with two points of view often deeply in conflict, sometimes fortuitously congruent. (p. 7)

The marriages Rose examines are narratival in nature in that their continual existence derives from being situated within an ongoing narrative which renders the interchanges between husband and wife intelligible. Or, more accurately, from being situated within ongoing narrative*s*, since the partners may differ as to how they emplot its various activities and relations. In an important sense, a marriage just *is* in part the field of narrative possibilities construed by its partners.

Marriage is nothing special in this regard. *Any* ongoing practice will have precisely the same form. Thus, the practices of scientists or legislators or members of a university or a church, all will be narratively shaped in the sense that their participants perforce must engage in telling themselves and each other stories about the nature of their interrelations as a way of continuing to be members. Stories are thus not just *about* practices, but are *of* them. (Note that this introduces another way the social sciences are historical besides that discussed in chapter 8. As ongoing practices they are in part comprised of continually revised and reconstructed narrative interpretations of the history of the discipline and its possibilities.)

Of course – to return to a point already made in chapter 3 – this mutually shared process of narrative self-definition should not be characterized as if it were without struggle or deep disagreement. Acts belong not to a single narrative line but to a contested narrative field in which various narrative possibilities compete with one another for dominance. The importance of power and disagreement should not be ignored in the role which narrative plays in human social life any more than it should be overlooked in the discussion of human culture.

Narrative constructivism, by insisting on the purely constructed character of the narratives agents tell themselves about themselves and others, is one-sided. It fails to do justice to the fact that the ongoing activities of agents both individually and collectively already embody narratives. It thus fails to account for the fact that intentional agents employ narrative forms to display the intelligibility of their actions. Narrative constructivism fails to see the ways that life and story are of a piece.

9.3   Narrativism

A proper view of the relation of narrative and life needs to capture what is correct about realism (that narrative form is not accidental, nor a mere representational device; and that our identities as agents embody narratives) without including what is erroneous about it (that each person's life just *is* a single enacted narrative of which the agent is the partial author and the biographer a mere reporter). Moreover, it needs to do justice to the insights of narrative constructivism (that the narrative account of any life is continually and infinitely revisable) without making its mistakes (that narratives and the form of narrative are mere creations imposed on material which is non-narratival). *Narrativism* tries to be such a view, one that steers a middle course between narrative realism and narrative constructivism, hoping to capture what is worthwhile in both.

To see the narrativist position, consider one last case from Rose, that of the marriage of John Stuart Mill and Harriet Taylor; or rather, the self-deception inherent in their marriage. Rose summarizes the relationship between Mill and Taylor in this way:

> John Mill, brought up an atheist, trained to distrust any authority outside himself, a man who scorned in every way the notion of one person surrendering his will to another, nevertheless felt as one of the profoundest needs of his emotional life the need to do precisely that – to surrender his will. In imagining that being what some would call henpecked constituted a utopian marriage of equals, he created a delusion which he and his wife could happily share. He invented a role for her which she liked both in theory (she liked the idea of equality) and in practice (she liked the feel of mastery). Her subject was willing. Mill's mind approved equality but his soul craved domination. He atoned for the subjugation of women by the voluntary, even enthusiastic, subjection of one man and portrayed the result as a model marriage of equals. (p. 140)

Rose makes clear that in the Mills' marriage at least two narratives were running concurrently: the narrative in which John and Harriet believed their marriage had a part, a narrative of equality; and the narrative of the relationship of John and Harriet as told by Rose, a narrative of domina-

194

tion–subjugation overlain with an ideology of equality. Call the first narrative the "lived narrative," and the second narrative the "told narrative." Of interest is the relation between these two narratives.

Crucial is that the lived narrative was not epiphenomenal to the marriage itself. John Stuart and Harriet came together and related as they did only because they both subscribed to a narrative in which they were living a relationship of equality. The self-deception contained in this narrative was a condition for the kind of relationship they actually had in which Harriet dominated John: their belief that they were relating as equals is what allowed them to relate as master and slave. Thus the marriage was a complex of at least two narratives which were contradictory but which were inextricably intertwined.

The Mills' self-deception was not unusual. In depicting the Carlyles' courtship and Ruskin's excuses for not having sexual relations with Effie, Rose deftly and sympathetically uncovers the functional role which self-deceptive self-accounts often play in relationships ("functional" because the self-deceptive narratives keep the relationships going; without them the relationships would be – in some cases were – shattered). The lived narrative played a fundamental role in what these people actually did: narratively deceiving and acting were ineluctably bound together.

But the stories we think we are living and the stories we or others come to see ourselves to have been living are not necessarily the same. With hindsight we or others may come to reassess the nature of the narrative we thought we were living and thereby to redescribe the activities in which we were engaged. Indeed, this is precisely what hindsight is, seeing significance which becomes manifest after the fact. Thus, there is nothing surprising in Rose characterizing the Mills' marriage in terms of a told narrative of domination quite at variance with the Mills' own lived narrative of equality. (Perhaps the Mills themselves could have come to so characterize their marriage if they had been more reflective.)

This can be put schematically. At time (t) an agent (a) does (x) and in so doing enacts a lived narrative (ln) in which (x) is placed in a temporal whole in order for (x) to be an (x). But at time (t + n) the agent (a) or later biographers (b), aware of the consequences of (x) and/or operating within a different conceptual paradigm than (a), can come to see (x) as integral to another narrative (told narrative (tn)) at odds with the lived narrative. Lived narratives take the form "I am doing (x) as a part of (ln)"; told narratives have the form "(a) did (x) thinking it was part of (ln) though it was really part of (tn)." Indeed, as in the case of the Mills, the relation between the lived narrative and the told narrative may be even more complex than this: the told narrative may be of the form, "(a) (in this case the Mills) did (x) (married) thinking it was part of (ln) (a union of equals) and because of this thinking were able to do (x) as a part of (tn) (a union of unequals) though they were unaware of this."

The case of the Mills shows quite clearly both the way that narratives are *in* human activity and yet can also be *about* this activity in a way that goes beyond the lived narrative of the agents. There is nothing special about this case. Indeed, what is true of an individual couple can be true of an entire group of people, and what is true of a micro-event such as a marriage can also be true of a macro-event such as a war. Thus, for example, at the time of World War I the participants necessarily told themselves that their activities were part of a particular larger story; indeed, it is only because they did so tell themselves that they could be engaged in the activity of waging this war in the way they were. But later historians, or the participants themselves with later hindsight and reflection, may come to retell the story of this war, may refit it into a narrative of quite a different sort from that of the original participants. World War I was an embodied narrative while it being fought. But the nature of this narrative may change as the consequences of the War become evident, and as our understanding of its nature alters. It is thus no accident that the history of World War I is a continually revisable project that can go on indefinitely (just as the Peloponnesian Wars continue to challenge historians to produce ever fresh narrative accounts of them even though they've been over for twenty-four hundred years).

The insistence on the dual character of narrative – both its lived and its told character – distinguishes narrativism from both narrative realism (which insists on its lived but denies its told character) and narrative constructivism (which insists on its told but denies its lived character).

9.4 Summing Up

Reflecting on what she has learned as a biographer Phyllis Rose makes the following observation:

> At certain moments the need to decide upon the story of our own lives becomes particularly pressing – when we choose a mate, for example, or embark upon a career. Decisions like that make sense, retrospectively, of the past and project a meaning onto the future, knit past and future together, and create, suspended between the two, the present. Questions we have all asked of ourselves such as, Why am I doing this? or even the more basic What am I doing? suggest the way in which living forces us to look for and forces us to find a design within the primal stew of data which is our daily experience. There is a kind of arranging and telling and

choosing of detail – of narration, in short – which we must do so that one day will prepare for the next day, one week prepare for the next week. (pp. 5–6)

In this way she claims we are all "fitful novelists." We do not impose a narrative form onto our lives: in the first place the experiences of agency are inescapably narratival in form; and in the second place, our acts are acts only in so far as we see them as embodying some narrative. It is not as if some material exists which is not structured narratively and upon which we impose some alien order from the outside. The order we come to impute to a life or lives is of the same form as the order which already inheres in the actions whose sense we are trying to ascertain.

But it does not follow from this that an intentional action embodies a single narrative, or that there is One True Story to be told about any life or historical event. Later biographers place an agent's acts within temporal contexts of meaning as do the agents themselves; but these contexts need not be the same, and so the stories they tell need not be the same either. Those who come later have the benefit of knowing some of the causal results of particular activities, results which will cast new light on the nature of the acts in question. Moreover, new paradigms of thought may also emerge which depict human life in a new way; influenced by these new paradigms biographers and historians may become sensitive to dimensions of life which the agents themselves or other biographers and historians completely ignored or disvalued. The result will be narratives of a highly novel character.

Moreover, this process of retelling can continue indefinitely just because the causal outcomes of actions will continue indefinitely, and because new perspectives on human affairs will materialize to inform new ways of reorganizing the stories we tell about the past. There is no such thing as a biography or a history which is definitive in the sense that it is the last word that can be said about a subject. Fresh stories about the past – even the past of quite long ago (as the history of paleoanthropology demonstrates) – are an ever-present possibility as new perspectives emerge and new outcomes of past deeds and conditions become evident.

Are stories lived or merely told? The best response to this question is to attack the false dichotomy it presumes: *either* lived *or* told. Stories are lived because human activity is inherently narratival in character and form: in acting we "knit the past and the future together." But stories are also told in that with hindsight we can appreciate narrative patterns which we could not appreciate at the time of acting. We tell stories *in* acting and we continue to tell stories afterwards *about* the actions we have performed. To coin new words to express this complex view, we might say that our lives are enstoried and our stories are enlived.

197

Further Reading

The thrust of this chapter owes a great deal to Carr (1986). See also Olafson (1979).

For a discussion of narrative and its requirements see Danto (1985), especially chapters 8, 9, and 11; and the essays in Mitchell (ed.) (1981).

For historical realism, see MacIntyre (1981), especially chapter 15; and Veyne (1990).

For historical constructivism, see White (1973 and 1987); Mink (1987); and Kermode (1968). Ricoeur (1984) gives a good overview of the philosophical issues involved, in the end opting for a sophisticated constructivist position.

For narrativism see Carr (1986) and the essays collected in Sarbin (1986) and Lee (1994). For the idea of narratives as crucial for ongoing practices, see Rouse (1996). For the relation between selfhood, agency, and time, see Lloyd (1993). For narrative's role in psychoanalytic conceptions of identity, see Schafer (1978; 1981), Spence (1982), and Roth (1991).

10

Can We Understand Others
Objectively?

10.1 Objectivism

The history of social science is filled with works apparently scientific but in fact utterly ideological. Entire disciplines – for instance, phrenology and eugenics – have been constructed to further a political agenda; today they have been largely discredited because their basic concepts, methods, and results were contaminated by their political commitments. The patina of science was but a cover for a more sinister if covert operation. Even theories in standard disciplines have been exploited as Trojan horses by which an ideology has been made to seem palatable or even necessary by appearing scientifically warranted. The use and abuse of IQ testing in psychology; much soviet historiography; creationism in paleo-anthropology; racist sociologies of African-American experience; and ethnographies of native peoples written by imperialist apologists are but a few of the many instances in which propagandistic social science promoted certain values even though in so doing it forsook the truth as it could best be determined.

Some thinkers, when confronted by cases such as these, have refused to be critical. They declare that the true is nothing more than that which is politically expedient, and on this basis deny the distinction between science and propaganda. Soviet social scientists, for example, often declared the true to be that which fosters the interests of the working class as determined by the communist party. Some postmodernists have argued in the same vein; thus Hayden White (1987, p. 80) somewhat unguardedly wrote of a Zionist view of the Holocaust that "its truth as a historical interpretation consists precisely in its effectiveness in justifying a whole range of Israeli policies . . ." Other postmodernists have declared the bankruptcy of the distinction between truth and power, and have consequently undermined the distinction between propaganda and science. Thus Michel Foucault loudly proclaimed that mainstream social science is a weapon in the arsenal of administrators bent on "normalizing" their subjects and in this way pacifying them; for Foucault what is called "truth" is just one means by which power is constituted and dispersed throughout a society.

Most mainstream social scientists dismiss this line of thought as specious and dangerous. They point to the many abuses attendant upon the failure to distinguish what is true from what is valued or power-engendering (from the Catholic Church's condemnation of Galileo to the lies promulgated by Chinese Communists about Mao and the "Great Leap Forward"). They also indict the intellectual shoddiness betokened by the failure to distinguish "true" from "desired." Most practicing social scientists are keenly aware that the social sciences are particularly vulnerable to misuse as propaganda. These sciences address important questions of direct concern to social and political agents bent on using the backing of science to buttress their plans and values. For this reason, social scientists generally are keen to find a bulwark against their efforts degenerating into mere propaganda.

Objectivity has traditionally been this bulwark. Objectivity demands that scientists refuse to be intimidated by or agents for prevailing political agendas or conventional wisdom; it also dictates that they not mask their own political and personal agendas as scientific reports about how society and the humans in it function. But how is objectivity to be understood? Historically the most important construal of objectivity has been that provided by objectivism. To delineate the meaning of objectivity as it has been most influentially understood thus requires that it be adumbrated in the context of objectivism. (Briefly, *objectivism* may be defined as the thesis that reality exists "in itself" independently of the mind and that this reality is knowable as such.)

Objectivists begin by interpreting the difference between propaganda and science in terms of the distinction between our thoughts and what our thoughts are about. When we were very young most of us believed (or operated as if we believed) that simply thinking something made it so. We supposed that the world revolved around us – for instance, that all people's actions were taken in response or directed toward us, or that our wanting something was sufficient to bring it about. But as we became more aware of the extent of the world and our insignificant role in it, of the limited character of our powers and the independence of others, we gradually learned to distinguish what we thought or hoped was the case from what was actually the case. No matter how hard we wished we couldn't bend the world (our parents or our siblings or our friends) to our purposes, nor could we depend that what we thought obtained indeed did so. Our growth out of childhood consisted in part of a process of epistemic maturation whereby we came to distinguish between our thoughts and what these thoughts were about, between our mind and reality outside our mind, between truth and falsity.

Not only did we learn to draw these distinctions, but we also came to value truth, desiring to perceive what actually is the case instead of floundering in a sea of illusion. How else can we achieve our desires except by knowing what satisfies and what thwarts them? How else to gratify our curiosity about ourselves and our world? How else to gain self-clarity, to know what and who we are as opposed to what we might think or hope (or fear) about ourselves? (Of course, we don't always honor our commitment to truth; sometimes we prefer ignorance or willful lying or unconscious self-deception. But even when we violate the demands of truth we recognize the cost in so doing (or come to this recognition in cases of unconscious deception). In this way we honor truth even in the breach.)

How to construe truth in this process? The central point is the distinction between what is in our minds and what actually obtains outside of them. It is thus quite natural to think that in those cases in which the content of our minds is at variance with external realities this content is false; and that when the contents of our minds mirror what is outside of them these contents are true. Thus we come to think of knowledge as a kind of replication in which our mind's contents (how we represent reality) exactly reproduces reality as it is independent of us.

Knowing the difference between our mind and reality outside our mind, and wishing to make our mind accord with this reality in the sense of replicating it, how should we proceed? Isn't it obvious that the biggest impediment to matching our thoughts to reality are the distortions produced by our minds themselves? Our desires, our fears, our preconceptions – these and countless other subjective elements – befog our mind's mirror, clouding our mental vision and thereby preventing us from seeing reality lucidly. Thus we need to rid ourselves of these distorting elements as best we can in order to permit the light of reality to shine directly through to us.

These distorting elements are all subjective in the sense that they derive from us, the subject. If we could eliminate them these "subjective" elements would cease to have epistemic importance and the objects of our perceptions and thoughts would come plainly into view. Our statements and theories would then accord with the objects outside our minds; our beliefs would be "objective." On this account, objectivity just is the property of thought in virtue of which it accords with what actually is the case. In this way "objectivity" is a property of our thoughts in so far as they

201

are true; thus according to objectivism "objectivity" is actually synonymous with "true." This is nicely captured in the common phrase "objectively true."

Another, subsidiary definition of objectivity derives from the importance of eliminating those subjective elements which becloud our mental perception. Since objective truth is achieved by ridding ourselves of deceptive mental elements, objectivity can also be defined as the cognitive state of lacking a priori categories and conceptions, desires, emotions, value-judgments, and the like which necessarily mislead and thereby prevent attaining objective truth.

The deceptive factors which prevent us from learning about reality as it is and not as we would like it to be can all be summarized by the term "interest" in the sense of being concerned about the outcome of something. Because we fear or want or care about x we can't examine it in a way that is likely to reveal whether x is the case or not. Only if we can make ourselves disinterested – or, failing this, force ourselves to act as if we are disinterested – can reality reveal itself to us. According to objectivism, objectivity requires disinterest and all the earmarks of disinterest: an unemotional affect; a non-committal attitude; a cool, detached, dispassionate style. In this way objectivity can also be conceived as a form of self-emptying in which elements of the self are eradicated from its cognitive activities.

The failure to rid their minds of their subjective elements makes propagandists the deceivers they are. Genuine scientists instead drain themselves, becoming blank slates upon which reality can write itself. Indeed, the "scientific method" – insistent on controlled observation, double-blind tests, impersonal reports, and impartial assessment of hypotheses – is precisely the way this self-emptying is achieved.

The epistemic orientation which emphasizes the mind mirroring reality is broadly positivist in nature. (Recall from chapter 4 that positivism insists that knowledge rests on the ability to perceive cognitively unmediated aspects of reality ("facts"), and to assess explanations of these facts by means of publicly observable, empirical tests.) Thus the objectivist account of objectivity invokes a positivist epistemology.

It also presupposes a realist ontology. *Realism* as I shall use the term is the twofold philosophical thesis that, first, a reality independent of human perception and cognition exists; and second, that this reality has its own inherent order. (Note that sometimes in the literature "realism" is used to refer to one or the other of these ideas.) Objectivism as I have construed it claims that the structure of reality exists separately from the mind and thus that objective truth exists whether cognizers know about it or not, or value it or not, or wish it were the way it is or prefer some alternative. States of the world already exist in the world itself, and knowledge consists of discovering the nature of these states. So reality must be pre-ordered in the sense that its states are there waiting for knowers to find them. On an objectivist view the basic structures of reality are uncovered, not made by human knowers; they already exist preformed in reality itself. (A useful analogy here is that of the puzzle. According to realism reality consists of a number of pieces of a puzzle arranged to form the ordered picture which is Reality. Scientists attempt to discover the pieces of this puzzle and to fit them together so as to reproduce the Reality Puzzle.)

When the pre-existing order of reality is discovered one's beliefs replicate this pre-existing order. That is, what one claims to be the case corresponds to what actually is the case. This is what makes them true: true beliefs are copies of mind-independent entities. Thus, the truth of a belief does not consist in its according with some perception or conception of the world as it appears to some particular group, but rather in its corresponding to the world as it is in itself. Indeed, such correspondence is precisely what truth is.

Ultimately, since reality is pre-ordered and the totality of its basic entities is fixed there must be One True Picture of this order. A fully objective science would consist of a Theory of Everything which exactly duplicated all the elements of this Picture in their proper order. Scientific progress occurs in so far as scientists get closer and closer to painting this One True Picture.

All of this may be clearer by means of an analogy. Consider the award-winning game Mastermind. The object of Mastermind is to determine the order of a series of four colored pegs placed into four holes by one player (the codemaker) and then covered with a shield to conceal them from another player (the codebreaker). The codebreaker attempts to duplicate the exact colors and locations of the codemaker's pegs. In order to do so the codebreaker hazards a guess as to the code's identity; the codemaker then responds with information as to how the guess is like and unlike the original order. On the basis of his or her interpretation of this information the codebreaker then puts forward another hypothesis, the codemaker responds with more information, the codebreaker postulates another arrangement of the pegs, and so on. The process of hypothesis – responsive evidence – new hypothesis based on interpreting this evidence – more responding evidence – etc. proceeds until the codebreaker's arrangement of pegs exactly matches that of the codemaker. At this point the codemaker removes the shield to reveal the original pegs, showing that the two arrangements are identical.

The relevance of Mastermind to objectivism and its underlying positivist epistemology and realist ontology ought to be obvious: it simulates the situation of scientists and the cosmos as conceived by objectivism. The cosmos consists of an unknown but knowable structure which exists independently of any scientific attempts to understand it; that is, the structure is "already there" in the cosmos. Science is the attempt to ascertain this structure through a process of hypothesis-formation and testing. In this process scientists must eliminate from themselves any distortions which might interfere with their ability to see the evidence for what it is, ultimately to perceive the basic structure. (A codebreaker may detest the colors of the pegs, or "just know" that the codemaker favors a certain color scheme, or want a particular arrangement for personal reasons, or despise the codemaker; but if the codebreaker is to win the game he or she must rid him or herself of these preferences, prejudices, and passions to let the relevant information speak directly.) A true theory is one which exactly duplicates the pre-existing structure, and when this is achieved the theory is "objective." Scientific progress is the gradual accumulation of objective theories as more and more of the basic structure is discovered.

As this analogy shows, objectivism is a complex of ideas. It includes a realist ontology; a positivist epistemology; a correspondence theory of truth and scientific progress; and an axiology of disinterest. Within this complex, objectivity is conceived as a property of the results of inquiry, namely the property of these results being true. A theory or a fact is said to be objective if it fits with reality as it is in itself. Secondarily, persons or methods are said to be objective if they eliminate the subjective elements which typically prevent achieving objective truth.

10.2   Fallibilism

We already know from chapter 4.1 that certain aspects of the objectivist picture are problematic. First, its positivist account of knowledge is no longer acceptable. Facts don't speak for themselves; nature is never encountered in an unvarnished way; experience, sensations, and other perceptions require *a priori* conceptual resources in order to occur; and the language in which we think and articulate our thoughts is inherently permeated by our conceptual commitments. Perspectivism has taught us that any theory of how the cosmos works necessarily occurs from within one conceptual scheme or other, and that consequently the deep patterns science seeks to ascertain are as much imaginative constructions as they are discoveries.

Second, we also know from chapter 6.4 that to understand intentional phenomena involves evaluating their rationality. This evaluative dimension is an inescapable part of the explanatory strategy which seeks to render intentional acts and their products intelligible. Thus the positivist ideal of

204

refraining from making evaluative judgments about events and objects to be explained must be abandoned.

The paradigmatical and evaluative nature of social science entails that the notion of becoming a blank slate has to be given up, along with the idea of knowledge as a kind of mirroring some mind-independent reality. This in turn means that the objectivist account of objectivity in which inner thought matches the outer structure of the world must be abandoned. So also must objectivism's secondary definition of objectivity as being disinterested: scientists cannot be disinterested and at the same time conduct their inquiries.

Given the incoherence of objectivity understood along objectivist lines, many have concluded that objectivity is impossible. They claim that we are all biased, locked within our own cultural and conceptual paradigms, necessarily partial and prejudiced. There can be no judging among our constructions of the world: one theory can be judged superior to another only from within a particular perspective, and one cannot get outside one's perspective to adjudge its relative merit. Our scientific theories are ultimately arbitrary constructions, mere reflections of our interests.

Does this sound familiar? It ought to: it is the relativism we discussed in chapter 4.2. There too perspectivism seemed inexorably to lead to relativism. But we saw in chapter 4.3 that this was a mistake, that perspectivism need not end up in relativism. Mightn't the same be the case here? That is, mightn't the failure of the objectivist account of objectivity not necessarily lead to the abandonment of this ideal, but to a reconceptualization of it? To see that this might be so, consider another problem with the account of objectivity as conceived by objectivism, namely, its equation of objectivity with truth. Having examined this problem an alternative conception of objectivity will become discernible.

The problem stems from the difficulty of knowing when a theory is true and when it is not. Begin with the truth of a theory. Assume that we have an hypothesis (H) which predicts that under specific conditions certain empirically observable events will occur; call these events the empirical implications (EI) of H. This means that if H is true, then EI must occur when H says they will; we can symbolize this situation by the formula "If H, then EI will occur." Now assume that EI occur as H predicts, that is, that all our empirical tests of H are consistent with H. Can we conclude from this that H is true? No we cannot. It is possible that EI are caused by something other than what H claims causes them, so that even though EI occur H is nevertheless false.

An example might help here. In economics the Crude Quantity Theory of Money and Prices asserts that the price level (P) moves in direct proportion to the money supply (M). Put in arithmetic terms, the Crude

Quantity Theory can be written $P = kM$ where k is a positive constant which stipulates the proportional relationship between P and M. This formula is meant to be an empirical hypothesis with certain empirical implications which follow from this hypothesis, for example that if the money supply is increased the level of prices will increase correspondingly. But even if these empirical results occur and the level of prices rises as predicted with an increase in the money supply, this does not show that the rise in P is caused by the rise in M: both P and M might be caused by some unknown factor.

Another way of showing this point is to examine a syllogism which captures the case under discussion:

(1)   If H is true, then the statement that EI will occur is true;
(2)   the statement that EI occur is true;
(3)   Therefore, H is true.

The problem is that this syllogism is not valid; (1) and (2) together do not entail (3). This syllogism is in fact an instance of the well known Fallacy of Affirming the Consequent, which takes the following general form:

(1)   If p then q;
(2)   q;
(3)   Therefore p

Even though p entails q and q obtains, it does not follow that p obtains: ways other than p may have produced q. Thus, though the occurrence of EI is *compatible* with H's being true, it does not *guarantee* it: H may still be false even though EI occur.

An extremely important point follows from these considerations: *we can never know for sure whether a scientific hypothesis is true even if it accords with all of our empirical observations.* Another way of saying this is that we can never *prove* a scientific theory true; "proof" is an inappropriate standard when evaluating scientific theories. (This does *not* mean that some theories may not be true and others false; it means only that we can never know for certain which of them are in fact true.)

What about the falsity of a theory? That is, if we cannot know for sure whether a theory is true, can we nevertheless know with certainty that it is false? It would seem so, for if H predicts that a certain outcome will always occur and this outcome does not occur, then it seems clear that H must be false. (Thus, if the quantity of money is increased but the price level does not rise, then the Crude Quantity Theory, which says that an increase in the quantity of money will *always* produce an increase in the price level, must be false.) Just one failure of EI to occur when H says they will appears sufficient to show H is false. There thus seems to be an asymmetry between confirmation and disconfirmation: we can apparently know for sure whether a theory is false even though we can never know for sure whether it is true. (Some philosophers, notably Karl Popper (1959; 1968), have been so impressed with this asymmetry that they have built an entire philosophy of science called *falsificationism* around it. According to falsificationism science consists of making bold empirical conjectures and then falsifying them.)

But this apparent ease of disconfirmation is a chimera. In the first place we can never be certain that EI have indeed transpired. It might appear that they have occurred when in fact they have not, or it might appear that EI did not occur when they in fact did (mistakes in measuring the level of prices are not uncommon, for instance). In the second place, that the requisite background conditions obtained is also open to question. When a test does not turn out the way a hypothesis claims it should it is always open for the scientist to argue that the test sample or the test situation were contaminated, and thus to continue to believe H even though EI did not occur as they were predicted.

Moreover, H might be modified in some way so that it continues to be substantially true even though its specific formulation comes to be regarded as false. Thus, for example, the Crude Quantity Theory states simply that $P = kM$ where k is a constant. But economists found that this simple relation did not hold except in special circumstances such as when real output remains roughly the same. Did this show that the Quantity Theory was false? No: the theory needed only to be modified somewhat, keeping its core but making it more complex so as to be consistent with empirical data. Thus the crude theory was transformed into a more sophisticated version in which $P = VM$ where V is the velocity of money (the rate at which a stock of money is turning over per year). Unlike k, V is not a constant but can vary such that the relation between P and M is no longer simple. This more sophisticated expression of the Quantity Theory is far more consistent with available data (though problems with it have led to further elaborations of the theory; for instance, more sophisticated versions include a role for the level of transactions in the economy (T), such that the Quantity Theory is expressed as $P = MV/T$).

Thus from the fact that EI do not occur as H predicts we cannot conclude with certainty that H is false as falsificationism asserts. This is not to deny that falsificationism contains an important insight, however. From the failure of EI we know that *something* is amiss, even though we may not be certain what it is. In cases of the failure of EI, therefore, the ball is in the court of the proponent of H: some further claim, some adjustment in the theory or assertion about the test conditions, must be forthcoming. But only in this limited sense is disconfirmation asymmetrical with confirmation. In general, we cannot know from disconfirming instances that H is indeed false, or in precisely what ways it is so.

A profound conclusion follows from our inability to know whether a theory is true or false. *Any theory we believe, even ones for which we have excellent reasons to believe, may be false.* This conclusion is the heart of the philosophical thesis called fallibilism. According to *fallibilism*, nothing about the world can be known for certain; certainty is not something which science can provide us. This is not because science is currently flawed, a weakness correctable by better equipment, better tests, or better hypotheses. It is an inherent feature of the epistemology of science and scientific reasoning itself: no amount or quality of empirical confirmation or disconfirmation is sufficient to guarantee ascertainable truth or falsity.

It follows from fallibilism that we should never be arrogant or imperious about even our most cherished warranted beliefs: any of them may be false. Indeed, the weight of evidence may soon shift against any of our treasured theories and we may come to abandon them (though the evidence can never demonstrate falsity with certainty!). The history of science in fact shows this. Many of the most prized theories of the past – Newtonian physics; Ptolemaic astronomy; the humor theory of disease; mercantilist economic theory – have come to appear so untrue that virtually no one believes them today. Nor should we be smug in this: in a hundred years people will undoubtedly look back at many of our most esteemed scientific accomplishments with amusement at the quaintness of our views ("Can you imagine that they believed in the germ theory of disease? In the quantity theory of money? In the theory of the unconscious?"). It may even transpire that theories we have confidently rejected may reappear in somewhat altered forms scientifically stronger than ever.

Note that fallibilism is consistent with the belief that an independent structure inheres in the cosmos. Fallibilism insists simply that humans are epistemologically limited, so that they can never be sure whether they have in fact replicated this structure in their scientific theories. In itself it does not deny that such a structure exists. Put briefly: fallibilism is not inconsistent with realism.

However, can realism remain persuasive once a fallibilist approach is adopted? If one can never know whether one has achieved the One True Picture of the cosmos, then on what grounds can one assert that what such a Picture would represent – an independently existing basic structure – exists? Rather like the way the "thing-in-itself" (noumenon) began to seem otiose in Kantian philosophy once one claimed with Kant that all we can ever know about things is how they appear to us ("things-as-they-appear" or phenomena), so also the idea of a pre-formed world independent of human cognition might begin to lose its plausibility once the idea of ever knowingly putting together all the pieces of the Reality Puzzle is abandoned.

Consider again the game of Mastermind. Fallibilism renders the objectivist analogy between science and this game nugatory. If fallibilism is correct, scientists – unlike the players of Mastermind – must determine for themselves what the basic materials of the cosmic game are. In Mastermind players know beforehand that pegs, colors, and holes are the building blocks of their little cosmos; but in science what the cosmos is made of is itself a question which scientists must answer in terms of the conceptual resources available to them. Moreover, unlike codebreakers in Mastermind, scientists cannot be sure of the nature of the order of the cosmos. What constitutes an order is a question for scientists but not for codebreakers (who know that it consists of an arrangement of colored pegs): is it a mathematical formula? a nomological explanation? a genetic historical narrative? Moreover, even if scientists were to determine for themselves the basic materials and order of the cosmic game, nothing in science is analogous to the removal of the shield in Mastermind in which players can look and see directly just whether and how the arrangement of the original pegs matches that of the codebreaker. According to fallibilism the epistemic standing of any hypothesis is never entirely clear. Indeed, on fallibilistic grounds scientists cannot even be certain that a mastercode of any sort actually exists waiting to be discovered: codebreakers in Mastermind are assured that one does by the rules of the game known to all the players, but scientists can at best only hypothesize that such a mastercode inheres in the cosmos, and such an hypothesis may well be false.

Construe science as a fallibilist game and note how its directions would differ from those of Mastermind: (1) given is a raft of materials whose differentiation and nature you must ascertain for yourselves; (2) determine a unifying order in these materials, but do so without any assurance that any pre-existing order exists in them, or any clarity as to what this order might consist; (3) represent this order, but determine for yourselves what representation means; (4) test the various proposed orders so represented, but determine for yourselves what constitutes an adequate test; (5) play indefinitely, never knowing whether you have discovered a unifying order, or whether indeed such an order exists.

How does thinking of science in this fallibilist way call realism into question? In such a game the notion of a pre-ordered cosmos is completely otiose: it cannot be known; nothing can be said about it with any assurance; and it has no role in the actual playing of the game. In a fallibilist game the notion of an independently existing pre-formed structure of cosmic order loses its point.

To reinforce this loss, consider another analogy intended to illuminate the nature of science conceived along fallibilist lines, namely, that between science and cartography; also note the differences between cartography and Mastermind. In cartography mapmakers attempt to delineate certain aspects of a terrain (this terrain needn't be physical: maps of the history of ideas are every bit as much maps as those of the coastline of Maine). Cartographers devise modes of representation and projection by which to represent these aspects. But though mapmaking and Mastermind involve making sense out of data, they differ in important ways. In the first place, the aspects of the terrain the cartographers will map are not simply given; rather, their interests and the uses to which their maps are to be put dictate the focus of their endeavors. The same area can yield topographical maps, population maps, road maps, vegetation maps, maps showing the distribution of wealth, religious affiliation, and all manner of other traits. Second, what mode of representation is employed is a function of conventions of representation, what is to be represented and for what purposes, and where and how the mapmakers look at the terrain – at what level, so to speak, they perceive it. Maps of the earth from the perspective of the moon diverge substantially from those made from the earth itself; maps of the earth using the Mercator projection differ dramatically from those employing the Gall–Peters projection; two-dimensional maps from three-dimensional maps; and so on. In this mapmakers contrast sharply with codebreakers in Mastermind whose form of representation is dictated by the game itself. Third, unlike the little world of Mastermind in which the elements and their relations exist independently of the players, in cartography there are no contours of the terrain as such existing independently of any mode of representing them. The terrain is an entity in part constituted by some form of representation. (Thus, if a cartographer wishes to map the coastline of North America, what is to be mapped has to be selected out and conceived as an entity by the mapmaker. That the coastline constitutes a distinct entity in part results from the cartographer's discrimination. Coastlines could fail ever to be so distinguished, and maps of coastlines might never exist.)

In cartography there is no "One Best Map" of any particular terrain. For any terrain an indefinite number of useful maps is possible, each depending on the aspect of the terrain highlighted as an entity, the mode of its representation itself contingent on the uses to which the map will be put, and on the perspective from which the map is drawn. Unlike Mastermind, in mapmaking no sense exists to the notion that the terrain is *already mapped*, such that the job of cartographers is to *discover a pre-existing map*. Mapmakers are not trying to work their way toward the One True Map which is embodied in the world waiting to be uncovered. For mapmakers the idea of a pre-mapped world has no role to play and hence no meaning.

Note that it does *not* follow from this that no distinction can be drawn between good and bad maps (useful as opposed to useless; accurate as opposed to inaccurate; clarifying as opposed to confusing), or that any map is as good as any other. Mapmaking is not a wholly imaginative activity; it is constrained by facts as they can be best ascertained, and by the demands of the practice of mapmaking in both the construction and use of maps. The specter of epistemological nihilism which objectivists fear will result from giving up objectivism with its positivist epistemology and realist ontology has no particular foothold here. Maps may be better or worse (more reliable, more explanatory, more detailed, more inclusive, more serviceable) without requiring One True Map to serve as a template against which maps can be evaluated. The construction and evaluation of maps proceeds just fine without such a template.

The role of the codebreaker in Mastermind is to uncover the inherent structure which exists "in itself" in the pre-ordered colored pegs. But the role of the mapmaker is to convert a world encountered in experience into an intelligible world. In Mastermind one can ask, does the hypothesis match the order which is "already there" (put there by a codemaker). In cartography conceptual presuppositions help to define what order is, and hypotheses are adjudged in terms of their rational acceptability (itself determined by ongoing epistemic practices and larger social endeavors of which these are a part). In Mastermind, intelligibility is a property of some independently existing subject matter; in mapmaking intelligibility is a matter of comparing various hypotheses in terms of their ability to enlighten and empower.

If you think of science as analogous to mapmaking rather than Mastermind – which fallibilism encourages you to do – then objectivism and its underlying realism will lose their force over you. Objectivism asserts that Ultimate Reality is structured and formed "in itself," in much the way colored pegs in Mastermind are. In so doing objectivism encourages the belief that only One True Picture exists which corresponds with this preformed Ultimate Reality. (This in turn encourages the notion that a Master Codemaker has created this already-ordered Reality. Objectivism is a continuation in other terms of one influential reading of the Judeo-Christian view of the world.) Fallibilism calls this entire view into question. It suggests that all we have is ourselves scratching around trying to make our experience and our world as comprehensible to ourselves as we can, given the profound epistemic limitations under which we operate. It suggests that the various orders we come up with are in part a product of our own perspectives, imaginations, and needs, not something dictated to us by Reality Itself. To fallibilism, there isn't any One True Map of Ultimate Reality or the earth or cosmic history or human social life, a Map supposedly embedded in these things. There are only maps we construct to make sense of the welter of our experience of the world and ourselves in it, and only us to judge whether these maps are worthwhile or not.

10.3   Critical Intersubjectivity

What does all of this show regarding the notion of objectivity? Simply this: given fallibilism, an acceptable account of objectivity cannot tie it directly to the notion of truth since the idea of "objective truth" depends on a number of positions – realism, positivism, and disinterestedness – that render it unacceptable. Objectivity cannot be a quality of thoughts in virtue of which they mirror what is the case independently of these thoughts. Thus "objective" cannot mean "objectively true" if objectivity is to remain an ideal.

If objectivity does not characterize the *outcome* of research, what else might it characterize? Fallibilism suggests an alternative account of objectivity, one which construes objectivity not as a property of the results of inquiry but as a property of *the process of inquiry itself*. To fallibilists the *method* of scientific analysis, not its conclusions, is what is or is not objective. Required for a reconstructed construal of objectivity is a shift from substantive to procedural adequacy.

What makes a process of inquiry objective? In a word, that it be *fair* in the sense that its procedures and the judgments it underwrites be responsive to the evidence as best it can be determined, and responsive to other possible interpretations of this evidence. To be objective, an investigation must require its practitioners to seek out facts which appear relevant to the case, to follow the lead of these facts even if it goes against accepted preconceptions or commitments, to put their explanations up against other explanations to show that theirs are superior, and to be willing to revise or abandon their conclusions if later work warrants it.

Such an investigation is "objective" not in the sense that its results mirror the objective world, but in the sense that its practitioners in their epistemic activity transcend their narrow subjective attachments and preconceptions. Objective inquiry is one in which inquirers must forsake wishful thinking, discard agreeable interpretations when they cannot stand up to scrutiny, bracket their own perspectives in order to enter sympathetically into the perspectives of rivals, and critically examine the perspective which comes most easily to them. Objectivity thus construed is a process of de-parochialization in which investigators transcend the congenial, the personal, and the conventional. Objectivity does not consist of emptiness or disinterestedness, as objectivism would have it; rather, it is the property of being detached from one's own commitments sufficiently to subject them to examination, of being sufficiently open to the possible merits of other viewpoints.

Conceived in this way the objectivity of inquiry consists of its being a social process of ongoing criticism. It is a *social* process because objectivity requires responses to the theories and investigations of others, and the readiness to revise on the basis of their criticism. Objective inquiries consist of processes of comparison. Indeed, the need to involve others is stronger than this. According to fallibilism we can never be certain that we are right; all we can hope for is that our beliefs are better than the alternatives. Consequently, objective inquiries must insure collisions between rival perspectives. Their practitioners must positively seek out other possible opinions and actively solicit the reactions of others to warrant their claims that theirs is the most plausible alternative going.

Moreover, an inquiry can be objective only in the sense that it be an ongoing *process* of inquiry. No particular investigation or the conclusions it yields can in itself be objective. Fallibilism shows that no method or judgment can be certain, can be known to be true (or false); all methods and judgments can only be provisional. Fallibilism necessitates an attitude of distance towards any conclusion. Thus, objectivity requires that investigators be willing to respond to *future* discoveries, analyses, or criticisms as much as to those in existence at the time of the original investigation.

Objectivity conceived in this way is best termed *critical intersubjectivity*. It is intersubjective because it consists of an ongoing dialogue among rival inquirers each of whom attempts to understand the others in a manner genuinely open to the possibility that their views may have merits (indeed, more merits than one's own). It is critical because it involves the systematic examination of rival accounts and methods in a careful, probing, and open-minded way. Objectivity is thus a feature of co-operative conversations bent on collectively exploring the worth of various theories and modes of inquiry from a detached (but not necessarily disinterested) perspective.

Note that objectivity understood as critical intersubjectivity does not require that investigators abandon any and all preconceptions in the way objectivism does. The questions inquirers ask, the methods they employ to answer them, the concepts in terms of which they think about them, and

213

the standards they use to judge their conclusions all require prior conceptual commitments. But the outcome of an investigation need not be determined by its preconceptions; preconceptions can be heuristic devices as well as straitjackets which predetermine the results. Preconceptions can be provisional and revisable as well as fixed and unalterable; and they can derive from a process of open-minded response to evidence as well as being unfounded and unsubstantiated. To have preconceptions is too easily equated with being biased or prejudiced. This is a mistake: biases and prejudices are particular sorts of preconception – ones which are judgmental before the investigation begins, which are close-minded and immune to revision. But not all preconceptions are of this sort. Objectivity conceived as critical intersubjectivity requires that cognizers employ cogent arguments based on evidence that has been carefully sifted for bias.

Observe that nothing in this requires that the views which result from a critically intersubjective process in fact be true. Indeed, according to fallibilism a theory or claim can result from an objective investigation and yet not be true. A proposition may be asserted on the basis of available relevant procedures for obtaining and weighing evidence, but this is no guarantee that the proposition is true. As fallibilism shows, there are no guarantees in attempting to ascertain the truth. Thus, Marxist economics appears to be false as a theory of the capitalist economy, but any reading of *Capital* will show that Marx was vehemently objective in the manner in which he argued for his conclusions (he cited extensive evidence in support of his theory; he took into account rival theories, and responded to their actual and possible criticisms; he proposed public tests by means of which to assess his theories; and so on). Objectivity does not imply truth.

Objectivity does not betoken agreement either. Some philosophers have claimed that an objective conclusion is one which "warrants acceptance by all who seriously investigate" (Walsh, 1960, p. 96). But this is a mistake. Investigators can proceed with their analyses in an objective manner and yet arrive at different conclusions. Indeed, they may never agree, even though they continue to behave in an objective fashion. Evidence does not always speak with such clarity that it supports only one conclusion. Indeed, as fallibilism suggests, theories which do command assent at one period may well be rejected at a later time only to be resurrected at a still later time in a slightly different version. Moreover, at any one time the evidence may be interpreted in many objectively acceptable ways, may support even quite antagonistic theories. No method, no matter how cogent and responsive to evidence and criticism, can insure answers which any rational knower must accept.

But because we cannot be certain about what is the case, or because we may continue to disagree even though proceeding in a critically intersubjective manner, is no warrant for the relativist claim that any theory is as good as any other. Fallibilism need not lead to skepticism about the scientific enterprise. Because any theory *might* be acceptable does not mean that any theory *is*, or that the evidence for any theory is equally as good as the evidence for any other. Because judgments do not yield certainty is no reason to think that all judgments are arbitrary. "Anything is possible" does not mean "everything has to be taken seriously"; nor does it mean "there is no basis for judging one theory better than another."

Judges, engineers, clinicians, critics, and detectives must interpret the evidence as best they can determine it, take into account alternative interpretations, and judge that one situation obtains rather than another. In so doing they need not pretend that they are infallible; that all of their peers who are not stupid, ignorant, or malicious will necessarily agree with them; or that they may not be shown at a later date to have been mistaken. Nevertheless, their judgments can be objective in the requisite sense, based on a critical use of the evidence as their practice can best define it. Their assessments can be honest, well argued, considered, responsive to the data and to the criticisms of others. If they are not, we castigate those who made them, and seek others who can behave in a fairer and more mature manner. (Just imagine how you act when, in seeking advice about your health or your money, you encounter a doctor or a financial planner who does not act in an objective manner: here the claim that every judgment is "biased" and therefore "merely subjective" suddenly seems purely rhetorical.)

There is no reason why social scientists can't be objective in exactly this same fallibilist sense. Indeed, don't most social scientists act this way most of the time (even when some of them are denying that they are being objective!)? Though they work within traditions of discourse which provide them with the conceptual resources needed to carry on their work, these traditions are not closed, static, immune to both internal and external criticism. Normally, social scientists yield to the better argument even when it goes against their preconceptions or their value commitments. Normally, social scientists seek evidence for their conclusions, submit their work to outside evaluators, respond to criticism, and in general attempt to be fair in the conduct of their work.

None of this should be taken for granted (as the importance of propaganda and ideology in human history shows). To behave objectively in this fallibilist manner, and to institutionalize norms which seek to insure objective research, is an enormous achievement of inestimable value. One of the merits of construing objectivity along fallibilist lines as critical intersubjectivity is that this achievement can thereby be illuminated.

10.4   Accountability

One dimension of objectivity understood as critical intersubjectivity requires special mention. This dimension is what might be called *accountability*. Accountable social scientific inquiry is one which takes into account both its cognitive commitments and its positionality. Let me explain each of these.

According to objectivism objectivity consists in looking at the world from a god's-eye point of view in which all of the viewer's interests and presuppositions are eliminated and the world is seen directly as it is. Another way of putting this is that the objectivist ideal envisions the disappearance of the author who in effect becomes a recording device upon which Reality is written. The problem with this picture is its epistemological incoherence. All inquiry is inevitably perspectival, and its results inherently partial and interested. All knowledge claims are necessarily embedded within a specific way of engaging the world. It follows that objectivity cannot be the elimination of all cognitive and moral presuppositions; far from opening the eyes of potential cognizers such an elimination would in fact render them blind, unable to see anything at all.

Fallibilism abandons the ideal of a god's eye point of view. It reconceives objectivity not as the escape from cognitive commitments and lenses, but instead in part as the critical recognition of them. Note that critical recognition does not just mean making one's epistemological presuppositions as clear and evident as possible; such recognition further requires a reflective, self-critical engagement with one's particular cognitive commitments and presuppositions. For fallibilists objectivity requires that knowers not only acknowledge the contingent limits of their theoretical and ethnographic practices, but also criticisms of them and responses to these criticisms.

Moreover, critical recognition must pervade a scientific inquiry throughout and not just be confined to its starting point. Sometimes those who urge that the presuppositions of an inquiry be made explicit are content to do so only in the preface to a work, with no mention or awareness of how these presuppositions operate in the body of the work. Such shunting to the preface is inadequate precisely because the entirety of an inquiry is shot through with its conceptual and evaluative premises. Thus critical recognition must show itself in the work itself and not just in its preamble.

Such critical recognition ought to take place in at least three main areas. In the first place, the basic conceptual commitments of a particular conceptual scheme provide the material in virtue of which phenomena are observed, categorized, characterized, and interpreted. These commitments are therefore a decisive factor in the actual work of description and explanation which comprises the main body of social scientific analysis. Objective social science is one in which the role these basic commitments play is made evident.

Second, objective investigators must be self-consciously critical of their conception of evidence. Thus, how according to a particular conceptual scheme certain phenomena come to count as evidence, what they are evidence for, and what assumptions lie behind these evidential relations must be examined and defended. In so doing researchers must make clear just how their conceptions of evidence have shaped their inquiry and its results.

Third, objectivity requires that investigators be self-consciously critical of their standards of significance. Different conceptual schemes have different notions of what is interesting, important, or epistemically productive. These notions of significance are crucial not just in the choice of topics to be investigated and the range of phenomena deemed worthy to be studied; they also figure directly in the kinds of description these phenomena receive and the explanations sought to render them intelligible. Significance is thus not just a factor that merely precedes an inquiry, aiming it in a certain direction; rather it structures the entire enterprise of description and explanation itself.

To say that objectivity requires that investigators critically engage their own intellectual and evaluative presuppositions does not mean that this is their only or prime activity. Some recent attempts inspired by "postmodernism" to be self-consciously critical have been carried to such an extreme that social science comes to be a form of biography in which social theorists reveal a great deal about themselves but almost nothing about those they are studying. Some current ethnographies have degenerated into narcissistic forms of self-display in the name of being "epistemologically self-conscious." But to have commitments does not mean one is trapped in a hall of mirrors in which one can only see aspects of oneself, nor does the obligation to make explicit these commitments mean that this is the extent of social inquiry. Objectivity does require epistemological self-consciousness but is not limited to such self-consciousness. In the last analysis the worth of social science is what it tells us about those under study, not just what it reveals about the social scientist.

Critical recognition is one key aspect of accountability but it is not the whole of it. Objectivity demands not just that investigators be accountable in the sense of recognizing their intellectual and political commitments. It also requires that they take into account the ways their investigations are socially positioned. All investigations are situated within a network of social relationships comprised of other investigators, various audiences, and the subjects of research. Here the issues are who gets to speak, who is acknowledged as an authority and why, whose concerns are responded to, who has access to the material, and how these authorizations both constrain and enable various forms of social relation and behavior.

Self-aware social analyses consequently must include within themselves answers to the questions, what does this social analysis do? To whom is it expressed and why? To whom in what language is it available? What narrative or other reportorial conventions does it follow? Who is permitted or enabled to respond in what name and with what effect? In answering these questions investigators must be particularly mindful of the ways any analysis involves the use of power in which investigators define and delimit the identity of those under study by venturing to speak for them.

Traditionally social science has assumed the voice of the impersonal, omniscient third person. By adopting this rhetorical form, the social scientist reports on how things are as if these reports derived from an anonymous, detached, utterly neutral investigator. This form can thus be misleading because it suggests a neutrality in endeavors which are inherently interrelated to others in very specific ways. Specific observers positioned in a particular way view specific situations from a particular point of view with certain kinds of effects. As such, they may grasp important dimensions of a society or culture or the acts and relations of intentional agents. But in operating this way they invite at least implicit responses from others with different perspectives, including those being reported about. Responses to a situation are made from a particular position *vis-à-vis* others who are themselves positioned in particular ways.

Objectivity demands that this positionality not only be acknowledged but that the voices of excluded others somehow find their way into social scientific reports and analyses. Some social scientists have indeed experimented with varying degrees of success with literary forms more suitable for rendering the voices of potential interlocutors more explicit (use of the first person; inclusion of direct words of the subjects being studied; writing bilingually; and so forth). Some of these attempts at acknowledging positionality show how their observations and explanations are in fact forms of social interaction marked by important power differentials by making this an explicit aspect of their analysis. Other attempts bring the voices of others (especially those under study) right into the text itself so that these voices do not remain silent.

These experiments are interesting attempts at instantiating the ideal of objectivity in the full work of describing and explaining social phenomena. But two caveats are in order here. First, sometimes the inclusion of many different voices produces not a kaleidoscope in which the different positions of the various agents are revealed but instead an incoherent jumble of voices and perspectives producing not dialogue but babble. Objectivity does not require giving up coherence.

In the second place, third-person analyses have the distinct advantage of inviting critical response from others (since they presume to speak for everyone), whereas first- and second-person accounts can have the effect of insulating themselves from the criticism of others. They forestall criticism by in effect saying "this is how I see things" with the implication that if others see them differently then this is no cause for dispute or further examination (rather in the way that "I prefer chocolate" closes down any discussion about the merits of various flavors). However, the heart of objectivity understood as critical intersubjectivity is the social process of ongoing criticism. Any literary form which precludes or discourages this process cannot promote objectivity in the requisite sense.

With these provisos in mind it still is the case that objectivity requires that social analyses self-consciously acknowledge their positions relative to other investigators, their audiences, and the subjects of their investigations. Such an acknowledgment is a further way social science is accountable, in this case to those with whom and to whom it is related.

Thus objective social science is accountable in at least two senses. In the first place it is *accountable for* its intellectual and evaluative commitments. This accountability is satisfied when social scientific works make explicit and critically engage with the conceptual presuppositions with which they operate and their alternatives. In the second place, objective social science is *accountable to* those it is writing for and about. This accountability is satisfied when social analyses acknowledge their positionality *vis-à-vis* other investigators, their audiences, and those under study, and when these other voices are given some active role to play in social analyses themselves.

10.5 Summing Up

The question of objectivity has particular force in a multicultural setting. This setting supports the idea that there are different ways to conceive the cosmos, that not all these differences are in theory eradicable, and that therefore disagreement is an intrinsic epistemic feature of human society. This idea in turn undermines the objectivist notion that at least in principle a single One True Picture of the cosmos exists and that we can ascertain Reality As It Is In Itself. Given this, the ideal of objectivity conceived along objectivist lines cannot be acceptable. All thinking occurs within a conceptual scheme of one sort or another, and thus the idea of cognizing without preconception or without interest is incoherent. Multiculturalism supports perspectivism; this is all to the good. But from this point multiculturalists often take a further, more questionable, step. Lacking any other conception of objectivity besides that of objectivism, and imbued with perspectivism, they embrace the relativist conclusion that all thinking is merely the expression of interest or power or group membership. In a multicultural age if one is wedded to an objectivist construal of objectivity the relativist position that we can never get beyond our own prejudices emerges as the only tough-minded one. In this way multiculturalism thus seems drawn to the view that underneath all its trappings social science is no more than prejudice and thus ultimately mere propaganda.

In this way a disappointed objectivism turns into its supposed opposite of relativism. But in fact objectivism and relativism are not true opposites; indeed, they exist on the same spectrum albeit at opposite ends. Both assume that objectivity requires unmediated access to the world, the only difference between them being that objectivists believe this access attainable at least in theory, while relativists deny this access attainable even in theory. Objectivism and relativism are simply opposite sides of the very same coin.

The proper response to the choice between objectivism and relativism is to deny that they are the only alternatives by showing that their common assumptions are problematic. This is precisely what fallibilism combined with perspectivism does: it provides a conception of knowledge that does not depend on the notion that science must be able to mirror Reality Itself, and that it must eliminate all perspectival elements to do so. On this basis, fallibilism rejects the definition of objectivity as meaning "objectively true"; instead it re-conceives objectivity to mean "critically intersubjective," and it provides a clear sense of how this intersubjectivity can be achieved through fair-minded social criticism and accountability. Thus, even though we cannot achieve "objective truth" as objectivism conceives it, we needn't conclude that all attempts at knowledge are biased or the mere expression of interest or power. Relativism results from an uncritical use of an outmoded notion of objectivity derived from the same axis of thought as that of objectivism.

The answer we've arrived at – objectivity understood as critical intersubjectivity – harmonizes with a theme of multicultural philosophy of social science: the theme of interaction and appropriation. Neither scientific communities nor cultures themselves are enclosed entities internally fixed and externally walled off from one another. Instead, they require critical appropriation by their members to continue, and they are essentially permeable. Multiculturalism should make evident the ways human living involves listening and learning from others through exchanges, clashes, borrowing, bending, altering, responding, and even stealing.

Critical intersubjectivity enshrines this into a principle. It demands that cognizers be open to others, engage them, seek out and hearken to their observations, discoveries, and criticisms. Thus, multiculturalism understood in these terms conduces not to the enclosed little worlds of relativism but to the interactive forum of fallibilism.

So, can we objectively understand others? No, if objectivity is interpreted in an objectivist fashion to mean "as they are in themselves." But Yes if objectivity is interpreted in a fallibilist way to mean "in an openminded, responsive to evidence, accountable, criticism-seeking manner."

Further Reading

For an excellent overview of the material discussed in this chapter, though approached from a different perspective, see Bernstein (1983) and Longino (1990).

For a good historical account of objectivism and its critics as it pertains to history, see Novick (1988). The essays in Martin and McIntyre (1994), part VII are a good collection devoted to the topic of objectivity in the social sciences.

For relativist criticisms of objectivism, see Rorty (1979; 1982; 1991), White (1973; 1987), and Fish (1980). For criticisms of both relativism and objectivism, see Scheffler (1982) and Laudan (1990). For a deep analysis of objectivity understood as a "view from nowhere" see Nagel (1986).

On the social and political dangers of relativism, see Bloom (1987).

For an excellent overview of the large technical literature on realism and truth, see Devitt (1991). For realism and criticisms of it, see Putnam (1981; 1992). In these works Putnam develops a distinction between metaphysical realism and internal realism. (The former is what I have been calling realism in this chapter.)

One source of fallibilism comes from the pragmatism of John Dewey (1925; 1929). Another derives from the falsificationism of Karl Popper (1948; 1959; 1968). Quine (1960), especially chapters 2 and 8, provides a number of important ideas useful for fallibilism, notably the underdetermination of theory by evidence and the indeterminacy of translation.

For critical intersubjectivity, see Haskell (1990) and Bevir (1994). Critical intersubjectivity is related to what Sen (1992) calls "positional objectivity."

For feminist reconceptions of objectivity (which argue for a position similar to that of section 10.4), see Longino (1990); Harding (1986) and (1991, especially chapter 6); and Haraway (1991).

My discussion of accountability is indebted to Rouse (forthcoming) and Rosaldo (1989, especially part III). For further discussions of accountability and issues related to it, see the important edited volume by Clifford and Marcus (1986). Also Ashmore (1989); Woolgar (1988); Woolgar (ed.) (1988); and Harding (1991).

Cultural anthropologists have discussed what I call "accountability to" since at least the

221

early 1970s; see, for instance, Fabian's (1971) "methodology of dialectical dialogue," a "dialectical interaction between the researcher and his or her subjects." Three important works in this regard are the edited volume of Clifford and Marcus (1986) cited above; Dumont (1978); and Marcus and Fischer (1986).

A brilliant discussion of cartography is Monmonier (1995).

11

Conclusion: What's to be Learned from a Multicultural Philosophy of Social Science?

11.1 Beyond Pernicious Dualisms

A dualistic way of thinking predominates in the philosophy of social science. That is, questions are conceived in terms of *either* one option *or* another and then one of them is defended as the correct one. This has indeed been the case in the debates examined in this book. The questions posed in the chapter titles invite a "yes" or "no" response, and the major positions in the field have opted for one or the other of these responses.

One of the main lessons of our analyses has been to call this dualistic way of thinking into question. Time and again we have seen that options posing as competing alternatives are not in fact in necessary opposition; that positions masking as complete answers are only partial and one-sided, requiring their supposed opposite for completion; or that questions which invite a choice between two possibilities are better answered by questioning their presuppositions and thereby undermining them rather than answering them in their own terms. Throughout the book a plea to avoid pernicious dualisms has been a constant motif.

Consider the following dichotomies we have encountered in the preceding chapters:

Some (Pernicious) Dualisms

Self	vs.	Other
Atomism	vs.	Holism
Our Culture	vs.	Their Culture
Sameness	vs.	Difference
Agency	vs.	Social System
Autonomy	vs.	Tradition
Insider	vs.	Outsider

Self-knowledge	vs.	Knowledge of others
Observer	vs.	The Observed
Understanding them in our terms	vs.	Understanding them them in their terms
Understanding Others	vs.	Criticizing Others
Present	vs	Past
Meaning	vs.	Cause
Relativism	vs.	Objectivism
Subjectivity	vs.	Objectivity
Tell Stories	vs.	Live stories

These dualisms are not all of the same sort, nor do they fall into neat categories themselves. But if our reflections have been cogent these dichotomies and the dualistic mode of thinking which underlie them are simplistic. Dualism sets up a confrontation between two entities and forces one to choose in terms of this opposition: either this side or that side. It does not allow for the possibility that each of the terms of the "opposition" in fact requires and draws upon its supposed opposite. Consequently it does not allow for the option of adopting both sides, of seeing them in terms of "both/and" rather than "either/or."

Our analyses have employed a dialectical mode of thinking. In a *dialectical* approach, differences are not conceived as absolute, and consequently the relation between them is not one of utter antagonism. Indeed, on a dialectical view, alternatives, while genuinely competing, only appear to completely "other" to each other. They are in fact deeply interconnected, and the confrontation between them reveals how these differences can be comprehended and transcended (transcended not in the sense of being obliterated but in the sense of being held in tension within a larger framework). Competing alternatives originally thought to have exhausted the possibilities can then be replaced with a wider viewpoint which recognizes the worth in the original positions but which goes beyond them.

Thus, in chapters 2 and 3 atomism and holism appeared as two antithetical approaches to the study of society, atomism insisting that the basic elements of social analysis are individuals, holism countering that the basic elements are society and culture. But both of these views are not only one-sided but need insights from each other to produce an adequate view. Atomism correctly insists that societies are comprised of individuals, and that individuals are unique agents; but atomism also neglects the fact (insisted by holism) that individuals need others to be what they are. Holism correctly highlights the ways culture and society enable and constrain, but it goes too far in this, neglecting agency, reifying culture and

224

society into things which directly imprint their members rather than processes of enculturation and socialization, which are processes of active appropriation. Thus to the question, does our culture and society make us what we are?, the proper response is to subvert the presupposition of this question, namely, that *either* we make our culture and society *or* they make us. We *both* make our culture and society and they in turn make us.

In chapter 6 the opposition between interpretivism (which claims that others must be comprehended in their own terms) and anti-interpretivism (which claims that others must be comprehended in the terms of social science) also bespeaks a false dualism. Here the dualism rests on a false dichotomy between meaning and cause. Philosophers have often argued that understanding meaningful phenomena consists of grasping their sense not explaining their causes, and that consequently social science should consist of interpretations not causal theories. But this argument is one-sided: interpretation is necessary but not sufficient for the explanation of intentional phenomena. Ascertaining the identity of intentional phenomena characterized as such does require uncovering the meaning these phenomena have for those experiencing, performing, or producing them. But social science also needs to ascertain the conditions which produced these meaning-laden processes and products, and to accomplish this it must develop causal theories which go beyond the terms of those it studies. Moreover, social science also needs to discover the competencies in virtue of which agents can form intentions and perform intentionally. Competence theories also transcend the terms of those being analyzed. The result is that social science will *both* comprehend others in their own terms *and* in the terms of social science.

We also saw in chapters 5 and 6 that the opposition between understanding others and criticizing them is often a false one. Typically, to understand is one thing, to evaluate is another. Since social science is concerned to understand others and not to judge them, philosophers have often claimed that assessments of the merits of others' thoughts, actions, or relations has no place in scientific analysis. But this is simplistic. In the first place, the explanation of intentional actions and their products will assume a different form depending on whether they are rational or not. Intentional actions adjudged irrational must be explained in terms of principles other than those of ordinary rational connection, and they must include some account of how these non-standard principles operate. (An example of this is Freud's theory of the unconscious and the peculiar principles which govern its "primary processes," such as displacement and condensation, by means of which thought and action are connected.) Because the explanation of rational actions and products differs from the explanation of irrational ones, social scientists cannot refrain from assessing whether an action is rational or not.

In the second place, certain forms of thought, though underwriting ongoing practices and relations, are systematically illusory. Indeed, these practices and relations are possible only because of the illusory character of the thought which engenders them, so that to understand them social scientists must unravel the ways agents are systematically unclear to themselves. (As we saw in chapter 6, an example of this from Marx is the religious practices associated with a Christian God and what he claimed to be the alienation inherent in the belief in such a God.) Here such notions common in critical social theory as manifest and latent content, false consciousness, ideology, repression, sublimation, and hegemony play a substantial role in the explanation of social phenomena. These notions as well as many others all involve critique in the sense that their use rests on a criticism of the social practices and intentional states of certain groups of people. Here again assessment is a crucial and unavoidable element in social scientific explanation.

Another false dichotomy is that between nomological and genetic explanation. On the basis of these supposedly mutually exclusive choices, historicists (those who have claimed that the explanation of intentional phenomena must be genetic in character) have argued that the social scientists are fundamentally historical. On the other hand, nomologicalists (those who have argued that the explanation of social phenomena is no different from that of natural phenomena, namely, nomological in form) have asserted that the social sciences are no more historical than physics or chemistry. But as we saw in chapter 8, nomological and genetic explanations are incomplete in themselves; indeed, they require the other in order to provide a full explanation of social phenomena. Thus the social sciences need *both* nomological *and* genetic explanations, not one *or* the other. And thus such sciences are historical in one important sense, but not so in another.

In chapter 9 the apparently exhaustive and mutually antagonistic alternative of narrative realism and narrative constructionism was shown to rest on certain assumptions which if transcended yielded another view – narrativism – which keeps elements of both but in a higher synthesis. The question is not whether we live stories *or* whether we merely tell them. To conceive of the matter in this way sets up a false choice, thereby preventing us from seeing that we *both* live and tell stories, and in precisely what ways we do.

The dichotomy between the past and the present is another one which has bedeviled social thought. But as we saw in chapter 7 and chapter 9

226

when discussing the meaning of intentional phenomena, the past and the present interpenetrate one another. As Faulkner so well put it: "The past never was; it is." The present is the continuation of the past, and the past lives on in the present. Moreover, what we take to be the nature of the past is in part a function of what we take to be the present. The past and the present, far from being separate time periods, commingle and define themselves in part in terms of the other.

Or again, in chapter 10 the options between objectivism and relativism, despite their apparent mutual incompatibility, were shown to presuppose a broadly positivist epistemology and realist ontology which conceive knowers as mirrors of an independently structured Reality. In that chapter we attacked these positivist and realist presuppositions, and in the process opened up the possibility for another way of conceiving of knowledge, namely, fallibilism. Fallibilism, in turn, suggests another conception of objectivity – critical intersubjectivity – a conception which attempts to do justice to the insights of both objectivism and relativism.

In all these cases we have replaced a dualistic with a dialectical view. This is much easier to accomplish if a *processural* conception of identity replaces a substantivist conception. In chapter 2 the notion of self as only externally related to others, as over and against them, was undermined when it was conceived as a temporal flow unified relationally rather than a thing unified substantively. Also in chapter 2, when ethnography was seen not to be the portrayal of independently existing social interactions but the result of an interactive process between the ethnographer and the social agents themselves, the dichotomy between the observer and the observed was rendered nugatory. In chapter 3 the dichotomy between culture and individual lost its grip when culture was thought of as an ongoing process of interaction rather than an entity which shaped its participants, a welter of heated conversations rather than a template or a text. In chapter 7, when an interpretation was conceived as a moment in an ongoing process in which ever fresh meaning-potentials are actualized for particular audiences in particular settings rather than as a finished product which captures an already existing meaning, then the antagonism between "interpretation in their terms" and "interpretation in our terms" broke down. And in chapter 10, when objectivity was understood as a process of intersubjective dialogue following fallibilistic principles rather than being in touch with Reality As It Is In Itself then the ground which supports the opposition between relativism and objectivism washed away.

Self, culture, interpretation, objectivity – even though these are all quite different sorts of entities, we tend to think of them as things rather than as processes and therefore to see them in opposition to other things

227

which supposedly confront them. But think of them as verbs rather than nouns, as ongoing activities rather than as fixed entities, and at least one of the major sources of the tendency to conceive them in dualistic competition with their supposed opposite will lose its force.

11.2   Interactionism

Nowhere has the dualism in the philosophy of social science been more critical than discussions of the relation between self and other, and the related topic of the relation between sameness and difference. In chapter 2 we saw that atomism, reinforced by the solipsism of chapter 1, pictures the relationship between self and other as one of radical distinction (figure 11.1):

Figure 11.1

To this picture the holism of chapter 3 and the relativism of chapter 4 can be added, enriching atomism by explaining why self and other should be conceived as separate: since both self and the world in which it lives are a function of the cultural paradigm and society which shapes them, each self-world must be distinct. The result is a more elaborate picture of the opposition between self and other (figure 11.2):

Figure 11.2

But solipsism, atomism, holism, and relativism are all deeply problematic. They overstate difference and understate what is shared and similar; they overstate the power of the group and understate the power of agency; and they overlook possibilities of interaction. We all live in the same world (though we do so differently); the identity of the self is bound up with its relations to others; and selves necessarily share certain fundamental capacities and dispositions not least of which is the capacity to act. Factoring in these considerations, a less separatist portrayal of the relation of self and other begins to emerge (figure 11.3):

Figure 11.3

However, even figure 11.3 is misleading. Understanding others (especially via the critically intersubjective procedures of social science) is
deeply interrelated with understanding ourselves. Changes in our understanding of others lead to changes in our self-understanding, and changes
in our self-understanding lead to changes in our understanding of others.
Moreover, because forms of social life are in part constituted by self-
understandings, changes in self-understandings ultimately mean alterations in the way we live. Figure 11.3 is too static; it fails to capture
the dynamic quality of the relation of self-understanding and other-
understanding and thus of self and other, and consequently the processual,
animated nature of personal identity.

A little reflection will help point the way to improve figure 11.3. Begin
with a basic category of multicultural analysis, that of identity and difference. Notice the "and": identity and difference are not antagonistic categories. They are mutually necessary for each other, dialectically interrelated
both epistemologically and ontologically.

Epistemologically all understanding is comparative: there is no *self*-
understanding if no *other* understanding. Only through interaction with
others do I learn what is distinctive and characteristic about myself.
This is why travelling in a foreign country or reading biographies of
others is so *self*-revealing. For instance, you might think of yourself as
"weird" in some way because you think no one else feels or acts as you.
(Note that this initial judgment is essentially comparative; we are social
from the start.) But then you discover others have felt or done what you do.
This discovery can release you from the feeling of being peculiar or ab-
normal, thereby transforming your experience. The same is true in reverse.
We've all had the experience of thinking that what we do or value or
condemn is the norm, and then being shocked to discover that this isn't so:
do you mean to say the classical Greeks practiced sodomy? This discovery
changes our perception of who we are by removing our sense of moral
certitude.

Identity and difference are also interrelated ontologically. To be an x is
precisely not to be a y or z. What makes you an x – a Muslim, say, or a
white male, or a heterosexual – is that you are not something else (a
Catholic or a black woman or a homosexual). In this way your identity is
shaped by your relations to entities from which you differ. A classic

example of this is the identity of those in post-colonial societies. These tend to stress that which does not derive from the colonizers – the indigenous, the local, the traditional. But in this the colonizer obviously remains an ever-present negative influence. Even the designation "post-colonial" expresses the essentially relative nature of the identity of newly emerging societies.

Because of the interrelation of identity and difference an ineradicable tension between the self of the social scientist and the other of those under study will pervade any social inquiry sensitive to cultural and social difference. This shows itself in a number of ways in multicultural social analysis:

(1) As shown in chapter 6, in understanding others social scientists must try to understand them in their own terms; but they must also use categories which go beyond those employed by those being examined.

(2) As revealed in chapter 2, the interviews, participant observations, and other ethnographic techniques by which social scientists observe others are social interactions which precipitate out certain forms of behavior. In this way social scientists are not mere observers of totally independent objects, but active shapers of that which they study.

(3) As demonstrated in chapter 7, the same is true even when no physical interaction occurs between interpreter and interpreted. Meaning itself is dyadic either because the meaning of an intentional act, text, relation, or product is in part actualized in the process of interpretation itself (when "meaning" means "significance for"), or because the rendering of others' intentions requires translating them into the interpreter's terms (when "meaning" means "the intentions with which"). Social scientific interpreters are thus actively engaged in that which they study even when what they study occurred long ago.

(4) Also in chapter 7, in discussing the hermeneutic circle, we learned that the relation of social scientists and those under analysis is dynamic and continuing. A new understanding of others changes social scientific conceptions; but every change in these conceptions produces changes in the way others are interpreted, triggering new forms of understanding. This interactive process is ongoing, a continual round of ramifying changes in comprehension.

Given this, social science must be "reflexive." That is, social scientists must be aware of who and what they are, what they bring to social analysis, how they are seen by those they study, what behavior their presence precipitates (including provoking self-consciousness) and in this way altering, heightening, or dampening certain forms of emotion, relation, or

Conclusion

activity. Social scientists must be aware of the reverberations they create in others (and themselves), and be so in a way described in chapter 10 as "accountable."

The relation between social scientist and those under scrutiny is thus dialectical. As we saw in chapter 3, the same is true for cultures themselves. Human history involves a constant process of interaction and exchange, of isolated groups coming into contact with one another, fighting, borrowing, altering, changing and being changed. Not encapsulation but exposure to others through trade, transfers of technology, cultural interchange, skirmishes, and even wars is at the heart of human societies and their history. Human history is in part the story of ever-evolving forms of intermingling among strangers who through often enforced association become partners or enemies or some new hybrid. Even in long-term conflicts marked by hatred and threat traditional enemies become part of each others' identities at least negatively. The ancient conflicts between Jews and Muslims in the Middle East show this dramatically.

Far from being static, enclosed, coherent entities, cultures are crossroads in which critical skills and resources are traded, stolen, improved upon, passed along to others. Human history is as noisy as a bazaar as different ways of life clash and their participants argue, pilfer, plagiarize, subordinate, enslave, but always interact with and alter each other. This is why so much can be learned by focusing on the liminal, on borderlands, on the clashes of groups and ideologies forced together to mingle and to confront.

The notion of a "pure culture" in which some integral, isolated whole forms itself out of itself and resists the influences of others is an utter myth. All cultures result from encounters with others in which attractive or threatening novelties are taken in, digested, and made part of the culture even as they are subtly transformed, or are resisted in a way that hardens certain activities and practices which were originally "natural" and spontaneously performed but are now self-consciously undertaken. Cultures are better conceived as interactive zones of activity than as individual things.

This does not mean that the history of cultural interaction should be understood simply as a process of cultural diffusion in which new ideas are communicated from one group to another. The spread of ideas, techniques, and forms of organization always involves power between groups differentially placed. Cultural interaction is not like an ideal student study group; it includes threats, manipulation, and coercion as much as rational analysis and reflection. But nor is cultural interaction just a process of domination in which the stronger enslave the weaker (either directly through external imposition, or indirectly by managing the minds of the dominated by controlling access to the stream of ideas available to them (so-called

231

"hegemony")). Attempts at imposition invariably provoke resistance. As explained in chapter 3, following rules is never automatic; it requires adaptation and interpretation which opens up a space for controversy and defiance. Cultural and social interaction involves complex patterns of appropriation and negotiation among groups which differ as to their power, and the study of this interaction requires sensitivity to the interplay among intricate processes of imposition, resistance, conflict, and adaptation over time.

What occurs between cultures and societies is also to be found within single cultures or societies. As we saw in chapter 3, cultures are never simple, consistent entities. The schemes of meaning which organize social life are not fixed texts but are more like heated conversations in which rival interpretations and conceptions compete in an ongoing process of cultural formation. Societies, too, are comprised of conflicting processes of structuration in which individuals and groups with different resources and skills seek to fashion lives satisfying to them. The result is that differences within a society or a group are often as great as differences between them, and intrasocial relations are characterized by complicated patterns of arbitration and appropriation.

Even single individuals are not coherent monads separated from others. As we saw in chapter 2, the self is not a thing but a process, and not an inner process of isolated self-creation and self-direction but an interactive process in which relations with others are crucial. Selves are selves only in and through interactions with others. And just as these interactions are often conflictual, unclear, or very much of the moment, so also selves are changeable, multivocal, full of ambivalences, self-conflict, and self-alienation.

Given all this, a more dynamic and interactive picture of the relation of self and other is required than that of figure 11.3:

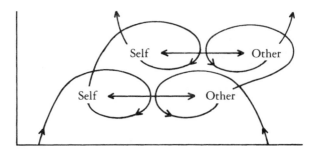

Figure 11.4

232

Figure 11.4 attempts to portray the essentially dialogical and essentially dynamic character of self and other through time in which the interaction among selves and others shapes the ongoing processes which are their identity.

Conceptions of social and individual identity are not of merely academic interest. Indeed, they are crucial for the multicultural politics of our time. Members of minority groups have often conceived their lives as a choice between assimilationism and separatism (notice the dualism here). For example, this way of thinking dominated nineteenth-century discussions of how Jews should relate to the dominant Christian cultures of Europe; it also continues to provide the terms for debates as to how African-Americans should relate to white society. According to this scheme the choices for minorities are those of sameness (in which they attempt to become indistinguishable from the majority), or difference (in which they attempt to preserve and perpetuate what distinguishes them as a minority). Thus assimilationist Jews in Europe were eager to shed their Jewish particularity in which differences in speech, clothing, kinds of employment, manners, food, and so forth would be obliterated; separatist Jews, on the other hand, argued that they must preserve their distinctive practices as a way of maintaining their identity derived from their unique historical heritage. According to the dichotomy presented to them the issue was either for the self and other to become identical, differences disappearing (the "melting pot"), or for them to remain segregated, differences hardened and reinforced (the "mixed salad"). Note that both alternatives assume a static, merely oppositional conception of the relation of self and other.

But there is a third alternative: interactionism. *Interactionism* is both a view of human history and culture, and an ethic recommending a certain attitude and response to multicultural exchange. As a view of human history and culture interactionism conceives of the relation of the self and other dialectically; it denies that "at bottom" the self and the other are essentially distinct and fixed, or that a particular identity means utter difference from that which it is not. Instead it insists that the identity of the self is intimately bound up with the identity of the other (and vice-versa), that self and other are constantly in flux, and that they are both similar as well as different. (Figure 11.4 is the way interactionism conceives the relation between self and other.) Consequently interactionism focuses on the points of contact between different groups, especially on those bridgeheads which serve as the basis for exchange. ("Exchange" should not be understood as always a pleasant and willing sharing; provocations, threats, and resistances are all forms of exchange which involve being forced to evaluate and sometimes to abandon or to alter old ways.)

As an ethic interactionism urges us to search not *beyond* cultural and social differences but *within* them for new forms of identity. Interactionists believe that cultural and social exchange does not nor should not necessarily result either in obliteration of difference (as in assimilationism) or its continuation (as in separatism), but to self-challenge, learning, and consequent growth. (Continuing the food metaphor, a good symbol of interactionism is the stir fry in which various ingredients change their individual flavors and textures in the process of being cooked together, but which continue to be recognizably different entities.)

Interactionism doesn't envision the transcendence of difference (something it thinks is impossible in any case). Nor does it envision the safeguarding of the "essential" or the "pure." Instead it envisions and encourages a dynamic commingling in which parties constantly change. In this differences aren't overcome nor are they simply maintained; instead they are recognized, scrutinized, situated, challenged, and perhaps transformed. In encounters between selves and others, between similarity and difference, the choice is not to adopt one or the other, but to hold them in dynamic tension.

One must be careful here. Intercultural contact is not always benign; indeed, it can sometimes be devastating. Consider the Native Americans of North America and their "interchange" with white settlers from Europe. Here cultural contact occurred in the context of a brutal fight over land and resources in which the whites held great superiority in military power, the Native Americans were susceptible to new diseases, and in which ways of life were incompatible. The result was not a "stir fry" but a slaughter of millions and a cultural, economic, and political impoverishment for those who remained. (Of course, history is littered with these sorts of "exchanges.")

But even here the value of interactionism is confirmed, albeit ironically. The principal lesson of the ethic of interactionism is: engage, learn from, adapt – or perish. Intercultural contact – usually in the context of profound differences of power – is going to occur no matter what the participants wish. (As we have seen, even closing borders behind "iron curtains" and the like fails to keep the "enemy" outside.) The question is how to conceive of this contact and how best to respond to it.

Interactionism as a view of human history concentrates on contact among different groups and individuals, and the mutations which result. It identifies as a central task for social science to uncover precisely how earlier webs of ideas and practices internalize, adapt, exploit, or re-see what was once alien and perhaps more powerful. Interactionism as an ethic urges people to engage differences in ways that explore possibilities for productive and positive learning from each other. People can learn *about* others and *from* others, thereby not only learning about them and themselves but

234

also opening up new possibilities for themselves and others in the processes of engagement.

11.3 Recruitability and Engagement

How does social science understood in the terms we have been using contribute to the idea and the ideal of interactionism?

Historically the usefulness of social science has been conceived in terms of social control. Comte's famous epigram puts this conception succinctly: "From Science comes Prevision; from Prevision comes Control." We've already examined the basis for this conception in chapter 8. Science paradigmatically has been taken to be nomological in that it seeks to discover general laws of the form "If X, then Y" or "if no X, then no Y." Knowing that X-type events relate to Y-type events in these ways opens the possibility of producing or preventing Y-type events: initiate x (an increase in the basic interest rate, for example), and y will occur (a decline in the level of aggregate demand); or prevent x (do not increase the money supply and hold its velocity and the level of transactions constant), and y will not occur (a rise in prices).

Unfortunately, if what we've said in chapter 8 holds water, predictions in the social sciences are so highly circumscribed that they provide only a limited basis for social control. Social scientific generalizations expressed in intentional terms – and these comprise the vast majority of social science – hold good only within narrow cultural horizons. Those generalizations expressed in non-intentional terms (like those in sociobiology), while possibly general laws, are either so abstract or refer to elements beyond the control of social engineers so as to be of restricted use for the purposes of social management.

Historically, successful interventions underwritten by social scientific knowledge have been confined to sharply delineated time periods. This has been true even of economics, the most highly productive social science in developing causal generalizations. Economic forecasting and policy recommendations based on econometric models of a whole economy or of sectors within it have been effective but only in a highly qualified sense: they work only within limited time-frames. The longer the time period the more people's beliefs and calculations change – in part as a result of internalizing what economic planners are up to – and the more their behavior changes as a result. The upshot is that economic predictions and policies become less and less effective. In this and other areas the dream of Comte has proven to be unrealizable.

This is not to deny the worth of predictions, even if they are rough and ready and temporally situated. But the limited value of such knowledge raises the question of other uses of social science. Fortunately, a multicultural philosophy of social science conceives usefulness in ways other than knowing how to control and manipulate. Three in particular stand out.

The first and most obvious is improving possibilities for communication. By revealing what others are doing and feeling, that is, by revealing the rules and assumptions upon which they think and act, social science makes it possible for people to engage in dialogue. Such a science helps to clarify the vocabulary and the grammar of social and psychological lives originally merely mysterious or misunderstood, and therefore essentially mute. By revealing the point of apparently strange practices, by translating the language of so-called deviants, by uncovering the concerns, hopes, and fears of those in different classes, religions, genders, or racial groups, social science can unearth the reasons for apparently odd behavior and in this way render it intelligible and thus something about which people can talk.

Moreover, significant in this is not just the ability to communicate with others heretofore silent. Learning new concepts by which to grasp the sense of others' behavior and mental lives affords new means of self-comprehension. In learning about others people necessarily learn about themselves – at least what is distinctive about their lives, and sometimes the ways they are related to groups of people they thought radically different; in these ways they may come to redefine themselves. A second use of social science is thus to increase self-knowledge. (This brings us full circle from chapter 1, in which solipsism assumed that it takes one to know one because only we know ourselves. We now see that this thesis is completely impoverishing and stultifying.)

A third use of social science is the enlargement of moral imagination. Social science can extend the reach of reason-explanations to areas of human behavior and feeling where it had previously seemed sense could not be found. (Freud is as obvious example of this, but anthropology is full of such instances.) In this way what constitutes rational or intelligible behavior is extended beyond the familiar. Moreover, others may have discovered questions you haven't even posed, or have developed ideas to answer these questions which haven't occurred to you, or have seen the point in practices and relations which have heretofore eluded you, or have constructed schemes of meaning which reveal aspects of yourself and the world closed to you. In these and other ways encountering others can enrich the possibilities for our own lives.

These three uses of social scientific knowledge emphasized by a multicultural philosophy of social science can be summarized by means of

236

a concept developed by Robert Kegan to discuss human development, namely, recruitability. *Recruitability* refers both to the capacity to elicit another's regard in you and your capacity to become invested in the lives of others. Recruitability varies substantially among people. Babies have an inborn ability to evoke others' interest in them, but they lose the naturalness of this ability as their bodies mature and they no longer are "cute"; moreover, they have virtually no interest in the lives of those around them (in part because they don't distinguish between what is and what is not themselves). Some adults are inept at eliciting the interest of others, and others (sociopaths and narcissists in particular) are not interested in others except as extensions of their own desires. Kegan claims that developing both aspects of recruitability – the ability to elicit others' regard and to have regard for others – is fundamental to human development, necessary to achieving mature relationships between oneself and what is not oneself.

Kegan also claims that recruitability is a power that can be developed through education in which our capacity to see ourselves as distinct but related to others who are different is heightened. This ability to see others as both distinct and yet related is precisely what is fostered by social science. By learning about the ways others are like and unlike us, and we are like and unlike them, about the nature of lives organized along different but relevant lines to those of our own, we increase the possibility of becoming engaged by others. In learning their vulnerabilities and their strengths as they confront the human exigencies of birth, death, work, sex, the search for ultimacy, and so on – indeed, in learning the different ways they conceive of vulnerability and strength – we are opened up to them. At the same time we learn how to appeal to them, how to trigger their interest in us.

Recruitability actualizes all three of the uses highlighted by a multicultural philosophy of social science: an enhanced ability to listen and to respond to others; a deepened appreciation of the ways others contribute to our own self-knowledge; and an enlargement of our moral imaginations. By activating the desire and ability to recognize and be drawn into the states and doings of others, as well as the ability to evoke in others the desire to recognize and be drawn into our own states and doings, social science can contribute to our development as mature human beings who both recognize our own distinctiveness from and our interrelatedness to others, eager to mutually share with others in the struggle and joy of living.

A multicultural philosophy of social science also highlights values often not associated with science. Traditionally the philosophy of social science has accented those values implicit in nomological theorizing: clarity, order, control, similarity, and generality. These *are* values, but they are not the only ones. Multicultural philosophy of social science should attune us to other values which have often been ignored when discussing social science: ambiguity, tension, change, difference, and particularity.

These sometimes neglected values of multiculturalism are nicely captured in Gloria Anzaldua's notion of *mestizaje consciousness*. *Mestizaje consciousness* is that way of being typical of those living in what she calls borderlands – places in which people of different cultures perforce rub against one another, intermingle, and interbreed:

> The new *mestiza* (person of mixed ancestry) copes by developing a tolerance for contradiction, a tolerance for ambiguity. She learns to be Indian in Mexican culture; to be Mexican from an Anglo point of view. She learns to juggle cultures. She has a plural personality, she operates in a pluralistic mode – nothing is thrust out, the good the bad and the ugly, nothing rejected, nothing abandoned. Not only does she survive contradictions, she turns the ambivalence into something else. (Anzaldua, 1987, p. 79)

Mestizaje consciousness is not mere cultural bricolage in which various cultural elements are adopted as bric-a-brac to ornament one's personality. Instead it involves an ongoing practice of cultural negotiation in which multiple, often opposing, ideas and ways of being are addressed, appropriated, and negotiated in the course of which both they and their appropriators are transformed. Social science not only provides means by which to engage in this process of negotiation, but should instill an appreciation of the pleasures and benefits from living in a polyglot world rich with opportunities for growth and mutual learning.

Of course we must not be Pollyannish here. The gains from social science are not won without cost. In the first place, social scientific explanations are often unsettling, especially if to explain means to unmask. Participants discover the nature and limits of what they have unselfconsciously been doing, and in this way are often rendered too self-conscious, too aware of alternatives, too unsure of their activities and relations to continue them with the ease and self-assurance they once had. Social scientific knowledge forces people to live with a sense of the ultimate contingency of their arrangements, of options they now have to consider, of ways of living that need to be defended and rationalized rather than just performed. All of this confuses and disorients.

Learning about others and oneself can also produce tension and fear as much as openness and willingness to explore alternatives as a way to growth. All of us are threatened by what is different or strange, and all of us are perturbed by challenges to what we consider essential to who and what we are. Anxiety and defensiveness can result from social science;

indeed, sometimes these may lead people to become more rigid rather than less. The growth achieved as a result of an increase in self-knowledge and knowledge of others is achieved only by bearing the costs of these feelings. (Of course, one of the most important areas of research for social science in a multicultural world is exploring the ways humans can positively respond to knowledge of, and interaction with, those who are different.)

To close this discussion of the use and value of social science understood from the multicultural – and hence interactionist, if I am right – perspective, I should note that the emphasis on mutual learning which I take to be central to multiculturalism has not always been prevalent in the writings of multiculturalists themselves. Instead, they have often conceived the multicultural perspective as the "respect for difference" and they have defined this respect as the "acceptance of every culture's various practices." Cashed out in this way respect for difference does not include or esteem mutual interchange and education.

But respect understood as unconditional mutual acceptance is a bad idea. I don't respect a student by accepting everything he or she says; students don't respect me by mimicking me. Respect demands that we hold others to the intellectual and moral standards we apply to ourselves and our friends. Excusing others from demands of intellectual rigor and honesty or moral sensitivity and wisdom on the grounds that everyone is entitled to his or her opinion no matter how ill-formed or ungrounded, or – worse – on the grounds that others need not or cannot live up to these demands, is to treat them with contempt. We honor others by challenging them when we think they are wrong, and by thoughtfully taking their criticisms of us. To do so is to take them seriously; to do any less is to dismiss them as unworthy of serious consideration, which is to say, to treat them with disrespect.

Respect means the willingness to listen, openness to the possibility of learning from, responsiveness, criticizing when necessary. Respect means to engage with intelligence, sensitivity, and openmindedness. So if respect is to be the chief value of multiculturalism then it cannot simply mean acceptance; rather, it must mean the refusal to judge peremptorily, to quickly classify by means of already determined categories, to consign to some category of Otherness by which to keep others at arm's length and thereby contain and dismiss them. Respect does not mean that everything they do is "fine for them" or beyond the pale of critical judgment.

Emphasis on the acceptance of difference is meant to express and encourage tolerance. Sometimes it succeeds in this. But sometimes it can have the opposite effect. Valorized differences can harden into Difference.

Those different from us in particular ways can quickly become an "Other" quite unlike us. This is the beginning of the downward slide which starts with "they don't think the way we do," moves on to "they don't feel pain or love the way we do," graduates to "they behave more like animals," and concludes with "they are monkeys, pigs, vermin." The first step toward hatred is the dehumanization of those who are strange, odd, unlike us; and the first step toward dehumanization is the insistence on absolute and irreconcilable difference. In this way an insistence on difference can lead to intolerance. Balkanization *is* a genuine danger of multiculturalism.

Respect conceived as the mere acceptance of difference stymies interaction, dialogue, and mutual learning. It enjoins us to appreciate others but not to engage them in mutual critical reflection. The end product of multiculturalism misinterpreted as mere acceptance can thus be isolation ("We're us and They're them"). This is not respect but neglect.

In a double irony, sometimes the emphasis on difference is a result of scapegoating in which we project parts of ourselves we abhor onto others who are black (when we are white), foreign (when we are American), female (when we are male), devils (when we are upright). In this case it is not really *their* difference to which we are responding but to differences *within ourselves* which we cannot accommodate and with which we deal by denying their source in us by seeing others through the hated category we despise. Here the emphasis on difference has the vehemence it does because it stems from ourselves. In this case the insistence on difference is not a way of seeing others but a way of mis-seeing them (in fact is a case of actively *not* seeing them and of seeing ourselves in a self-deceptive way). Here the emphasis on difference is not a mark of respect for others but a mark of disrespect for (aspects of) ourselves.

Because of these problems with the concepts of respect and acceptance multiculturalism is better defined by means of the concept of *engagement*. Engagement suggests that mere acceptance of differences is insufficient. Social science sensitive to the demands of living in a multicultural world is devoted to understanding the nature of these differences; it seeks to learn *why* people differ and *how* these differences sprang up over time and in what manner they *relate* to us. Attempting to explain differences is one way to begin critically appropriating cultural differences: what is the meaning of that practice? why do it this way? how does it compare with the way we do it (if we do something analogous to what they do), or why do they do this and we don't? What if they (and we) did things this way rather than that? Questions like these open up for us (and maybe for them) the possibility of recognizing that we or they may be limited or deficient in certain ways, as well as a way of appreciating our or their strengths. Asking these questions is the beginning of the process of enlargement, of learning about others and ourselves, and of growing in the process of trying to understand others.

"Recognize, appreciate, and celebrate difference" is too restrictive and too static a slogan. "Engage, question, and learn" better captures the dynamic character of social science and the synergistic character of genuine multicultural interaction.

11.4 Summing Up

Twelve theses of a multicultural philosophy of social science:

(1) *Beware of dichotomies. Avoid pernicious dualisms. Think dialectically.*

Much social thought consists of oppositional categories – self vs. other; particular vs. universal; subjectivity vs. objectivity; insider vs. outsider; civilized vs. primitive; male vs. female; homosexual vs. heterosexual; white vs. black. The same dualistic thinking mars metatheories in the philosophy of social science: atomism vs. holism; cause vs. meaning; interpretive social science vs. causal social science; historicism vs. nomologicalism; narrative constructionism vs. narrative realism. Such thinking promotes an "either – or" mentality in which one category precludes its supposed opposite. But many categories are fluid and open. Often one side of a dichotomy depends on and invokes the other – in which case the dichotomy is subverted. Frequently an entity can be in both categories; or one category gradually slides over into its supposed opposite; or binary alternatives rest on fallacious presuppositions which mistakenly restrict the range of possible choices.

(2) *Don't think of others as Other. Conceive of similarity and difference as relative terms which presuppose each other.*

It is very easy to exaggerate the differences between self and others, between us and them, between members and non-members. But sameness and difference require each other. We are the persons we are in virtue of our relations with others; indeed, all personal identity is essentially dialogical in character. There is no self-understanding without other-understanding, and the extent of our self-consciousness is limited by the extent of our knowledge of others. To identify others as different requires that we also identify the ways we are similar.

(3) *Transcend the false choice between universalism and particularism, assimilation and separation. Instead of trying to overcome differences or hardening*

them, interact with those who differ by means of these differences with an eye toward ongoing mutual learning and growth.

A misleading dichotomy: the particular (understood to mean the ways people differ) and "the" universal (understood to mean what is common to all people (the "simply human")). Conceived in this way, the alternatives appear to be assimilationism (in which differences are obliterated and the universally human is instantiated) or separatism (in which differences are emphasized and maintained and the particular is highlighted). But this is a false choice. On the one hand, "the" universal only exists in and through particulars, "the human" only in particular human beings. On the other hand, a particular is never simply a particular, utterly different from other particulars; particulars express what is human in individual ways, though no single particular exhausts the meaning of "the human."

The notion of "the" universal reifies what is fluid and changeable. "The" universal exists in an open and changing set of particular embodiments each of which expands its content and range. Thus talk of "the" universal is misleading. Put another way: the "simply human" is not just what is common to all humans; their differences also embody their humanity and extend "the human" in novel ways. In every action and relation humans at the same moment partake of the universal and the particular.

(4) *Think processurally, not substantively (that is, think in terms of verbs, not nouns). Include time as a fundamental element in all social entities. See movement – transformation, evolution, change – everywhere.*

Much social thought reifies activities and processes, turning them into things with fixed identities: "the" self or "this" society or culture are treated as objects with definitive boundaries and essential structures. This in turn encourages a synchronic rather than diachronic conception of social interactions and practices. But social and psychological entities are activities, not things. Consequently they are better described by means of verbs rather than nouns. We talk of human beings as if they were entities like stones, and not continuous processes of activity – forgetting that "being" is a gerund, and that it refers to an ongoing process.

(5) *Insist on the agency of those being studied.*

Expressions of cultural and social life are produced by agents and their activities, not by passive objects or nodes in a mechanical system. Members of social groups are not interchangeable units whose behavior merely fulfills certain social functions or roles in a "system." Culture doesn't stamp out those who embody it like a cookie-cutter, and society doesn't determine its members the way a furnace determines heat output. Human beings appropriate their culture, they don't reproduce it. They apply old rules to new situations and in the process change the rules; they

242

give new point to the old, and beget the new. They learn, adapt, alter, create.

(6) *Recognize that agents are agents only because they are situated within systems which simultaneously empower and limit.*

Agents are not free floating. Without their culture they would have no being and no capacity. Agents are also subject to all sorts of constraints imposed on them by others and by the systems of meaning and power within which they think and live. Culture and society both limit and enable – and sometimes enable by limiting.

(7) *Expect more light from whatever human act or product you are trying to understand.*

Interpreters wish for closure. They want to settle once and for all the meaning of actions and their products (texts, buildings, institutions, and so on) in which they are interested. Some have sought to satisfy this wish by discovering the meaning an act or its products had for those who did or made it. However, even in discovering others' intentions they must be translated into terms meaningful for interpreters, and as interpreters change so will these terms. Moreover, interpretation cannot stop with authors' intentions. The meaning of intentional entities also refers to their significance, and significance arises out the interaction between them and their interpreters. Consequently meaning itself changes over time.

(8) *Do not conceive of societies as integral monads isolated from one another, or others simply as members of a particular culture or group. Attend to borderlands in which different peoples rub up against one another and change in the process. Focus on the hybrid. Pay heed to internal stress, to resistance, to struggle, to the failure of the center to fix and control those in the periphery. And see ambiguity, ambivalence, contradiction everywhere.*

A great temptation in social science is the lure of clarity, fixity, order. Social scientists sometimes seek to discover the essence of that which they are studying, hoping thereby to comprehend it. Thus they are particularly prey to the equation of one culture = one society = one set of constitutive meanings: the notion of society as an "organic unity." But this notion is mistaken. Even the most apparently homogeneous societies are marked by important internal differences (of religion, sex, class, caste, ethnicity, and so on). Even the most isolated societies are influenced by foreign ways (especially today, impacted by the global economy and the cultural ecumene).

(9) *Acknowledge the past's role in empowering you. But recognize the ways you make the past what it is.*

The past is not past: it lives in the present, in the resources tradition provides to its bearers, in the effects which continue to ripple through time long after an event has occurred, in the minds of self-conscious creatures bent on understanding who they are by grasping where they have been, and in the genetic explanations of social scientists and historians. In this way the past changes as the present changes. Nor is the present just the present: to be an act every act anticipates a projected outcome and looks backwards to what preceded it for its motivation. The present thus contains within itself the past and the future.

(10)   *Attend to the historical and cultural embeddedness of social scientific knowledge. Expect that what we know today will be outmoded by conceptual and other changes in our own lives as well as the lives of those we study.*

Another great temptation of social science is the aspiration to universality, sameness, and repetition. Here explanatory success is conceived as the discovery of constantly recurring causal patterns, general laws fundamental to the workings of all humankind (rather like the cosmic patterns of the heavens). But generalizations about intentional phenomena so described are inescapably historical in character, and the general laws that can be discovered about human doings will inevitably be at such an abstract level that much of what social science wants to know cannot be answered by these general laws.

(11)   *Don't hide behind an illusory façade of neutrality to convince yourself or others that you are objective. Acknowledge the intellectual equipment you bring to the study of others; be aware of the ways you change those with whom you interact; and make your assessments of what others do explicit. But always do so in a way that is responsive to the evidence as best you can determine it, and accountable to those whom it is writing for and about. Seek out the criticism of others.*

The objectivity of science has typically been defined as the separation of scientists from their field of study – separation physically as not interfering with it; separation emotionally and evaluatively as being neutral with respect to its doings; and separation intellectually as being without preconceptions regarding it. But this is an outmoded conception of objectivity. No social scientific investigation can occur without deploying prior conceptual resources; all ethnography involves the interaction of observers and observed, each changing the other; and neutrality can often preclude the sorts of critical judgments necessary to understand others. Objectivity requires fairness and accountability, not neutrality; it is a way of conducting research, not a mirroring of Reality As It Is.

(12)   *Acceptance or celebration is not enough. Engage others.*

Advocates of multiculturalism frequently claim that the scientific study of others will lead to a respect of those who are different – to an appreciation of the integrity of alien ways of life, and a celebration of their difference from us. But this is too static and too distanced. In the first place, distinctions of "we" and "them" are fungible, relative, and dynamic. In the second place, everything others do is not acceptable (any more than is everything "we" do). Sometimes understanding others demands that we criticize them and/or ourselves. And what we gain from them should not be limited to mere "appreciation": in coming to understand them we open up the possibility of learning about others and ourselves, of questioning and borrowing, of connecting with them, all to the end of altering and enlarging ourselves and them.

Appreciation, agreement, consensus – none of these is the goal. Interaction and growth are the ends of social science understood from a multicultural perspective.

Further Reading

An important inspiration for this chapter is Kegan (1982).

The anti-dualist, dialectical position urged in this chapter derives from Dewey (see Dewey (1938); Bernstein (1966)), and behind Dewey, Hegel (see Hegel (1977) and Taylor (1975)). See also Bernstein (1971); Putnam (1978; 1981; and 1992, part II); and Rorty (1991). Basseches (1984) presents the psychological dimensions and requirements necessary for dialectical thinking. See also Senge (1990) for an interesting application of this to business planning. Rich (1979) offers a provocative feminist reconstruction of education and rationality along interactionist, dialectical lines.

Another source for non-dualist thinking is post-structuralism which is devoted to deconstructing binary oppositions and replacing them with open fields of "contestation." See Lyotard (1984); Derrida (1973a; 1973b; 1981); Rosenau (1992); and Seidman (1994).

For a discussion of multiculturalism, see the essays collected in Lemert (1993), especially part V, and in Goldberg (1994). See also Said (1978 and 1993), Appiah (1992), Anzaldua (1987), West (1993), Weeks (1991), and the essays collected in Fuss (ed.) (1991) and in Ferguson, Gever, Minh-ha, and West (eds) (1990).

On the dangers of multiculturalism, see Schlesinger (1992) and the fascinating Finkielkraut (1995).

For a discussion of the political meaning of difference, see Taylor (1992), Young (1990), Benhabib (1992), and Walzer (1992 and 1994).

MacIntyre (1989) discusses the border status of persons in two rival linguistic communities, the problems of translation, and possible ways for these problems to be resolved.

Interactionist approaches can be found in a number of social sciences. For an attempt to describe gender differences in moral thinking in a way which attempts both to do justice to these differences and yet to transcend them, see the classic Gilligan (1982). (Note that Gilligan's work is not always read in this way, that it is sometimes read as proposing an alternative that is wholly different from the dominant masculine way of moral thinking. I think this is a dualistic reading of non-dualistic work.) The work of the anthropologist Marshall Sahlins (1985 and 1995) is very much in line with the interactionist approach. Sahlins studies the ways conceptual schemes and social practices of one people change with a new encounter, especially the arrival of a colonial power. For an interesting use of interactionist thinking applied to the experience of the exile, and particularly composers exiled during World War II, see Goehr (forthcoming). For a deconstruction of the category "woman," see Butler (1990). The strategy pursued by Butler in which traditional categories are opened up, called into question, subverted as a way of opening up the possibility of newer forms of activity, relationship, and identity is what I envision social analysis doing when carried on within an interactionist perspective.

Bibliography

Aboulafia, Mitchell 1986. *The Mediating Self. Mead, Sartre, and Self-Determination*. New Haven, Connecticut: Yale University Press.

Alexander, J. and Seidman, S. (eds) 1990. *Culture and Society. Contemporary Debates*. Cambridge: Cambridge University Press.

Althusser, Louis 1970. *For Marx*. Translated by Ben Brewster. New York: Vintage Books, Random House.

Anscombe, G.E.M. 1957. *Intention*. Oxford: Blackwell.

Anzaldua, Gloria 1987. *Borderlands/La Frontera. The New Mestiza*. San Francisco: Spinsters/Aunt Lute.

Appiah, Kwame Anthony 1992. *In My Father's House. Africa in the Philosophy of Culture*. Oxford: Oxford University Press.

Ashmore, Malcolm 1989. *The Reflexive Thesis*. Chicago: University of Chicago Press.

Aune, Bruce 1977. *Reason and Action*. Dordrecht, Holland: D. Reidel Publishing Company.

Bailey, F.G. 1969. *Stratagems and Spoils*. Oxford: Blackwell.

Barnes, Annette 1989. *On Interpretation*. Oxford: Blackwell.

Barta, Roger 1994. *Wild Men in the Looking Glass*. Ann Arbor, Michigan: University of Michigan Press.

Barth, Frederik 1959. *Political Leadership among the Swat Pathans*. London: Athlone Press.

Basseches, Michael 1984. *Dialectical Thinking*. Norwood, New Jersey: Ablex Publishing Corporation.

Bauman, Zygmunt 1976. *Towards a Critical Sociology*. London: Routledge and Kegan Paul.

Beattie, John 1964. *Other Cultures*. New York: The Free Press.

Becker, Ernest 1973. *The Denial of Death*. New York: The Free Press.

Becker, Gary 1976. *The Economic Approach to Human Behavior*. Chicago: University of Chicago Press.

Beer, Samuel 1965. *Modern British Politics*. London: Faber and Faber.

Benhabib, Seyla 1992. *Situating the Self. Gender, Community, and Postmodernism in Contemporary Ethics*. London: Routledge.

Bernstein, Richard 1966. *John Dewey*. New York: Washington Square Press.

——1971. *Praxis and Action. Contemporary Philosophies of Human Activity*. Philadelphia: University of Pennsylvania Press.

Bernstein, Richard 1976. *The Restructuring of Social and Political Theory*. New York and London: Harcourt Brace Jovanovich.

—— 1983. *Beyond Objectivism and Relativism*. Philadelphia: University of Pennsylvania Press.

Best, Stephen and Kellner, Douglas 1991. *Postmodern Theory*. New York: The Guilford Press.

Bevir, Mark 1994. Objectivity in History. *History and Theory*, vol. 33, no. 3, pp. 328–44.

Bhabha, Homi K. 1994. *The Location of Culture*. London: Routledge.

Bhaskar, Roy 1978. *A Realist Theory of Science*, second edn. Hassocks, Sussex: Harvester Press.

Blau, Peter 1964. *Exchange and Power in Social Life*. New York: Wiley and Sons.

Bloom, Alan 1987. *The Closing of the American Mind*. New York: Simon and Schuster.

Bohman, James 1991. *New Philosophy of Social Science*. Cambridge, Mass.: MIT Press.

Borger, Robert and Cioffi, Frank 1970. *Explanation in the Behavioural Sciences*. Cambridge: Cambridge University Press.

Brown, Norman O. 1959. *Life Against Death*. Middletown, Connecticut: Wesleyan University Press.

Bryant, C.G.A. and Jarry, D. 1991. *Giddens' Theory of Structuration. A Critical Appraisal*. London: Routledge.

Burge, Tyler 1979. Individualism and the Mental. In P. French, T. Euhling, and H. Wettstein, 1979. *Studies in Epistemology*. Midwest Studies in Philosophy, vol. 4. Minneapolis: University of Minnesota Press.

—— 1986. Individualism and Psychology. *Philosophical Review*, vol. 95, no. 1, pp. 3–45.

Burke, Kenneth 1957. *The Philosophy of Literary Form*. New York: Vintage Press.

Butler, Judith 1990. *Gender Trouble. Feminism and the Subversion of Identity*. New York: Routledge.

Carr, David 1986. *Time, Narrative, and History*. Bloomington, Indiana: Indiana University Press.

Cherniak, Christopher 1986. *Minimal Rationality*. Cambridge, Mass.: MIT Press.

Chomsky, Noam 1965. *Aspects of a Theory of Syntax*. Cambridge, Mass.: MIT Press.

Clifford, James 1988. *Predicament of Culture*. Cambridge, Massachusetts: Harvard University Press.

Clifford, James and Marcus, George (ed.) 1986. *Writing Cultures. The Poetics and Politics of Ethnography*. Berkeley: University of California Press.

Collingwood, R.G. 1961 (1946). *The Idea of History*. Oxford: The Clarendon Press.

Cowell, F.R. (1962). *Cicero and the Roman Republic*. Baltimore, Maryland: Penguin Press.

Danto, Arthur C. 1973. *Analytical Philosophy of Action*. Cambridge: Cambridge University Press.

—— 1985. *Narration and Knowledge*. New York: Columbia University Press.

Davidson, Donald 1963. Actions, Reasons, and Causes. *Journal of Philosophy*, vol. 60. Reprinted in Donald Davidson, 1986. *Actions and Events*. Oxford: Oxford University Press.

—— 1967. Causal Relations. *Journal of Philosophy*, vol. 64. Reprinted in Donald Davidson, 1986. *Actions and Events*. Oxford: Oxford University Press.

—— 1970. Mental Events. In L. Foster and J. Swanson (eds), *Experience and Theory*. Amherst: University of Massachusetts Press, pp. 79–101. Reprinted in Donald Davidson, 1986. *Actions and Events*. Oxford: Oxford University Press.

—— 1973. Radical Interpretation. *Dialectica*, vol. 27. Reprinted in Donald Davidson, 1986. *Inquiries Into Truth and Interpretation*. Oxford: Oxford University Press.

—— 1974. On the Very Idea of a Conceptual Scheme. *The Proceedings and Addresses of the American Philosophical Association*, vol. 47. Reprinted in Donald Davidson, 1986. *Inquiries into Truth and Interpretation*. Oxford: Oxford University Press.

—— 1982. Paradoxes of Irrationality. In James Hopkins (ed.), *Philosophical Essays on Freud*. Cambridge: Cambridge University Press.

—— 1986a. *Inquiries Into Truth and Interpretation*. Oxford: Oxford University Press.

—— 1986b. *Actions and Events*. Oxford: Oxford University Press.

de George, R. and de George, F. (eds) 1972. *The Structuralists. From Marx to Lévi-Strauss*. Landover Hills, Maryland: Anchor Publishing Company.

Dennett, Daniel 1971. Intentional Systems. *Journal of Philosophy*, vol. 68.

—— 1991. *Consciousness Explained*. Boston: Little, Brown and Company.

Derrida, Jacques 1973a. Structure, Sign, and Play in the Discourse of the Human Sciences. Reprinted in Jacques Derrida 1973. *Writing and Difference*. Chicago: University of Chicago Press.

—— 1973b. *Speech and Phenomena*. Evanston, Ill.: Northwestern University Press.

—— 1981. *Positions*. Chicago: University of Chicago Press.

Devitt, Michael 1991. *Realism and Truth*, second edn. Oxford: Oxford University Press.

Devor, Holly 1989. *Gender Bending. Confronting the Limits of Duality*. Bloomington, Indiana: Indiana University Press.

Dewey, John 1925. *Experience and Nature*. Lasalle, Ill.: Open Court.

—— 1929. *The Quest for Certainty*. New York: G.P. Putnam's Sons (Capricorn Books).

—— 1938. *Logic: The Theory of Inquiry*. New York: Henry Holt and Company.

Doi, Takeo 1980. *The Anatomy of Dependence*. Tokyo, New York and San Francisco: Kodansha International Ltd.

Douglas, Jack 1967. *The Social Meaning of Suicide*. Princeton: Princeton University Press.

Downs, Anthony 1857. *An Economic Theory of Democracy*. New York: Harper and Row.

Dray, William 1957. *Laws and Explanation in History*. Oxford: Oxford University Press.

—— 1993. *Philosophy of History*. Englewood Cliffs, NJ: Prentice Hall.

Dreyfus, Hubert L. and Rabinow, Paul 1982. *Michel Foucault. Beyond Structuralism and Hemeneutics*. Chicago: University of Chicago Press.

Dumont, Jean Paul 1978. *The Headman and I. Ambiguity and Ambivalence in the Fieldworking Experience*. Austin: University of Texas Press.

Durkheim, Emile 1938. *The Rules of the Sociological Method*. Translated by Sarah Solovay and John Mueler. New York: The Free Press.

—— 1951. *Suicide*. Translated by J.A. Spaulding and G. Simpson, Glencoe, Ill.: The Free Press.

Eagleton, Terry 1983. *Literary Theory*. Minneapolis: University of Minnesota Press.

Easton, David 1965. *A Systems Theory of Political Life*. New York: John Wiley and Sons.

Elster, Jon (ed.) 1986. *Rational Choice*. Oxford: Blackwell Publishers.

—— 1989. *Nuts and Bolts*. Cambridge: Cambridge University Press.

Evans-Pritchard, E.E. 1940. *The Nuer.* Oxford: Oxford University Press.

Fabian, Johannes 1971. Language, History, and Anthropology. *Philosophy of the Social Sciences,* vol. 1, pp. 19–47.

Fay, Brian 1975. *Social Theory and Political Practice.* London: Allen and Unwin.

—— 1983. General Laws and Explaining Human Behavior. In D. Sabia and J. Wallulis 1983. *Changing Social Science.* Albany, New York: State University of New York Press. Reprinted in Michael Martin and Lee C. McIntyre, (eds) 1994. *Readings in the Philosophy of Social Science.* Cambridge, Mass.: MIT Press.

—— 1987. *Critical Social Science.* Oxford: Polity Press and Ithaca, New York: Cornell University Press.

Fay, Brian and Moon, J. Donald 1977. What Would an Adequate Philosophy of Social Science Look Like? *Philosophy of Social Science,* vol. 7, pp. 209–27. Reprinted in Michael Martin and Lee C. McIntyre (eds) 1994. *Readings in the Philosophy of Social Science.* Cambridge, Mass.: MIT Press.

Ferguson, R., Gever, M., Minh-ha, T., and West, C. (eds) 1990. *Out There: Marginalization and Contemporary Cultures.* Cambridge, Mass.: MIT Press.

Fingarette, Herbert 1969. *Self-Deception.* London: Routledge and Kegan Paul.

Finkielkraut, Alain 1995. *The Defeat of the Mind.* Translated by Judith Friedlander. New York: Columbia University Press.

Fish, Stanley 1980. *Is There a Text in This Class?* Cambridge, Mass.: Harvard University Press.

Foucault, Michel 1977. *Discipline and Punish.* Translated by Ann Sheridan. New York: Random House.

—— 1978. *The History of Sexuality, vol. 1.* Translated by Robert Hurley. New York: Random House.

—— 1981. *Power/Knowledge.* Edited by Colin Gordon. New York: Pantheon.

Frankfurt, Henri 1971. Freedom of the Will and the Concept of a Person. *Journal of Philosophy,* vol. 67, no. 1, pp. 5–20.

Freire, Paulo 1972. *Pedagogy of the Oppressed.* New York: Herder and Herder.

Friedman, James 1986. *Game Theory with Applications to Economics.* Oxford: Oxford University Press.

Fuss, Diana (ed.) 1991. *Inside/Out: Lesbian Theories, Gay Theories.* New York: Routledge.

Gadamer, Hans-Georg 1992 (1960). *Truth and Method.* New York: Crossroad.

Gasking, D. 1955. Causation and Recipes. *Mind,* vol. 54.

Geertz, Clifford 1972. Deep Play. Notes on the Balinese Cockfight. *Daedalus,* vol. 101, pp. 1–37. Reprinted in Clifford Geertz, 1973. *The Interpretation of Cultures.* New York: Basic Books.

—— 1973a. Thick Description. In Clifford Geertz, 1973. *The Interpretation of Cultures.* New York: Basic Books.

—— 1973b. *The Interpretation of Cultures.* New York: Basic Books.

—— 1983. *Local Knowledge.* New York: Basic Books.

Gellner, Ernest 1973. *Cause and Meaning in the Social Sciences.* London: Routledge and Kegan Paul.

Geuss, Raymond 1981. *The Idea of a Critical Theory.* Cambridge: Cambridge University Press.

Giddens, Anthony 1976. *New Rules of Sociological Method*. New York: Basic Books.

——1979. *Central Problems in Social Analysis. Action, Structure, and Contradiction in Social Analysis*. Berkeley: University of California Press.

——1991. Structuration Theory. Past, Present, and Future. In C.G.A. Bryant and D. Jary, 1991. *Giddens' Theory of Structuration: A Critical Appraisal*. London: Routledge.

——1992. *The Transformation of Intimacy*. Palo Alto, Calif.: Stanford University Press.

Gilligan, Carol 1982. *In A Different Voice*. Cambridge, Mass.: Harvard University Press.

Ginet, Carl 1990. *On Action*. Cambridge: Cambridge University Press.

Goehr, Lydia. Forthcoming. The Double Life of Music and Musicians in Exile. In R. Brinkmann and C. Wolff (eds) *Music and Migration*. Cambridge, Mass.: Harvard University Press.

Goldberg, David Theo (ed.) 1994. *Multiculturalism. A Critical Reader*. Oxford: Blackwell.

Goldman, Alvin 1970. *A Theory of Human Action*. Englewood Cliffs, NJ: Prentice Hall.

Gramsci, Antonio 1971. *Prison Notebooks*. Selected, translated, and edited by Quinton Hoare and Geoffrey Nowell Smith. New York: International Publishers.

Grandy, Richard 1973. Reference, Meaning, and Belief. *Journal of Philosophy*, vol. 70.

Grice, Paul 1957. Meaning. *Philosophical Review*, vol. 66, pp. 377–88.

Griffin, John Howard 1961. *Black Like Me*. Boston: Houghton Mifflin.

Grossberg, Lawrence (ed.) 1992. *Cultural Studies*. New York: Routledge.

Habermas, Jürgen 1971. *Knowledge and Human Interests*. Boston: Beacon Press.

——1975. *Legitimation Crises*. Boston: Beacon Press.

——1979. *Communication and the Evolution of Society*. Boston: Beacon Press.

——1988. *On the Logic of the Social Sciences*. Cambridge, Mass.: MIT Press.

Hall, Stuart (ed.) 1980. *Culture, Media, Language*. London: Hutchinson-CCCS.

Hampshire, Stuart 1970. *Thought and Action*. London: Chatto and Windus.

Haraway, Donna 1991. *Simians, Cyborgs, and Women*. New York: Routledge.

Hardin, Russell 1995. *Once For All. The Logic of Group Conflict*. Princeton: Princeton University Press.

Harding, Sandra 1986. *The Science Question in Feminism*. Ithaca, New York: Cornell University Press.

——1991. *Whose Science? Whose Knowledge?* Ithaca, New York: Cornell University Press.

Hark, Michael Ter 1994. *Beyond the Inner and the Outer: Wittgenstein's Philosophy of Psychology*. Synthese Library 214. Dordrecht: Kluwer.

Harré, Rom 1970. *The Principles of Scientific Thinking*. London: MacMillan.

Harré, Rom and Secord, Paul 1972. *The Explanation of Social Behaviour*. Oxford: Blackwell.

Haskell, Thomas 1990. Objectivity Is Not Neutrality. *History and Theory*, vol. 29, no. 2 (May), pp. 129–57.

Hegel, G.W.F. 1956 (1831). *The Philosophy of History*. Translated by J. Sibree. New York: Dover.

Hegel G.W.F. 1977 (1807). *The Phenomenology of Spirit*. Translated by A.V. Miller. Oxford: Oxford University Press.

Heidegger, Martin 1962 (1927). *Being and Time*. Translated by John Macquerrie and Edward Robinson. New York: Harper and Row.

Held, David 1980. *Introduction to Critical Theory*. Berkeley: University of California Press.

Held, David and Thompson, J.B. 1989. *Social Theory of Modern Societies. Anthony Giddens and his Critics.* Cambridge: Cambridge University Press.

Hempel, Carl 1965. *Aspects of Scientific Explanation.* New York: The Free Press.

Henderson, David K. 1993. *Interpretation and Explanation in the Human Sciences.* Albany, New York: State University of New York Press.

Hiley, David R., Bohman, James F., and Shusterman, Richard (eds) 1991. *The Interpretive Turn.* Ithaca, New York: Cornell University Press.

Hirsch, E.D. 1967. *Validity in Interpretation.* New Haven, Connecticut: Yale University Press.

Hobbes, Thomas 1839. *The English Works of Thomas Hobbes.* Edited by Thomas Molesworth. London: J. Bohn.

Hodges, H. A. 1969. *Wilhelm Dilthey. An Introduction.* London: Routledge, Kegan Paul.

Hollis, M. and Lukes, S. (eds) 1986. *Rationality and Relativism.* Cambridge, Mass.: MIT Press.

Homans, George 1967. *The Nature of Social Science.* New York: Harcourt, Brace, and World.

Hookway, Christopher and Pettit, Paul (eds) 1978. *Action and Interpretation.* Cambridge: Cambridge University Press.

Horkheimer, Max 1937. Traditional and Critical Theory. Reprinted in Max Horkheimer, 1972. *Critical Theory.* New York: Herder and Herder.

Howard, Roy J. 1982. *Three Faces of Hermeneutics.* Berkeley, Calif.: University of California Press.

Hoy, David 1982. *The Critical Circle.* Berkeley: University of California Press.

—— 1991. Is Hermeneutics Ethnocentric? in David R. Hiley, James F. Bohman, and Richard Shusterman (eds) 1991. *The Interpretive Turn.* Ithaca, New York: Cornell University Press.

Hume, David 1969 (1739). *A Treatise on Human Nature.* Reprinted from the original edition. Edited by L.A. Selby-Bigge. Oxford: Oxford University Press.

Ingils, Fred 1994. *Cultural Studies.* Oxford: Blackwell.

James, Susan 1984. *The Content of Social Explanation.* Cambridge: Cambridge University Press.

Jarvie, I.C. 1972. *Concepts and Society.* London: Routledge and Kegan Paul.

Jenks, Chris 1993. *Culture.* London: Routledge.

Johnston, Paul 1993. *Wittgenstein. Re-thinking the Inner.* London: Routledge.

Keat, Russell and Urrey, John 1975. *Social Theory as Science.* London: Routledge and Kegan Paul.

Kegan, Robert 1982. *The Evolving Self.* Cambridge, Mass.: Harvard University Press.

Keiser, Lincoln 1991. Friend By *Day, Enemy By Night. Organized Vengence in a Kohistani Community.* Fort Worth, Texas: Holt, Rinehart, and Winston.

Kenny, Anthony 1963. *Action, Emotion and Will.* London: Routledge and Kegan Paul.

Kermode, Frank 1968. *The Sense of an Ending.* Oxford: Oxford University Press.

Korner, Stephan 1970. *Categorial Frameworks.* Oxford: Blackwell.

Koselleck, Reinhardt, 1985. *Futures Past.* Cambridge, Mass.: MIT Press.

—— 1988. Critique and Crisis. Cambridge, Mass.: MIT Press.

Krausz, Michael (ed.) 1989. *Relativism. Interpretation and Confrontation*. Notre Dame, Indiana: Notre Dame University Press.

Krausz, M. and Meiland, J. (eds) 1982. *Relativism: Cognitive and Moral*. Notre Dame, Indiana: Notre Dame University Press.

Kripke, Saul 1971. Naming and Necessity. In D. Davidson and G. Harman (eds) 1971. *Semantics of Natural Language*. Dordrecht, Holland: Reidel.

—— 1982. *Wittgenstein on Rules and Private Language*. Cambridge, Mass.: Harvard University Press.

Kuhn, Thomas 1970. *The Structure of Scientific Revolutions*, second edn. Chicago: Chicago University Press.

—— 1977. Second Thoughts on Paradigms. In Thomas Kuhn 1977. *The Essential Tension*. Chicago: University of Chicago Press.

Lacan, Jacques 1977. *Jacques Lacan, Ecrits: A Selection*. Translated by Alan Sheridan. New York: W.W. Norton and Company.

Laing, R.D. 1960. *The Divided Self*. London: Tavistock Press.

Lakatos, Imre 1970. Falsification and the Methodology of Scientific Research Programmes. In I. Lakatos and A. Musgrave 1970. *Criticism and the Growth of Knowledge*. Cambridge: Cambridge University Press.

Lakatos, I. and Musgrave, A. (eds) 1970. *Criticism and the Growth of Knowledge*. Cambridge: Cambridge University Press.

Laudan, Larry 1990. *Science and Relativism*. Chicago: University of Chicago Press.

Lee, D. John (ed.) 1994. *Life Before Story. Autobiography from a Narrative Perspective*. New York: Praeger.

Lemert, Charles (ed.) 1993. *Social Theory. The Multicultural and Classic Readings*. Boulder, Colorado: Westview Press.

Lepore, Ernest (ed.) 1987. *Truth and Interpretation: Perspectives on the Philosophy of Donald Davidson*. Oxford: Blackwell.

Lévi-Strauss, Claude 1967. *Structural Anthropology*. Garden City, New York: Anchor Books.

—— 1970. *The Savage Mind*. Chicago: University of Chicago Press.

Levy-Bruhl, Lucien 1931. *La mentalité primitive* (Herbert Spencer Lecture). Oxford: Oxford University Press.

Linbloom, Charles 1990. *Inquiry and Change*. New Haven, Connecticut: Yale University Press.

Little, Dan 1991. *Varieties of Social Explanation*. Boulder, Colorado: Westview Press.

Lloyd, Genevieve 1993. *Being in Time. Selves and Narrators in Philosophy and Literature*. New York and London: Routledge.

Longino, Helen 1990. *Science as Social Knowledge. Values and Objectvity in Scientific Inquiry*. Princeton: Princeton University Press.

Louch, A.R. 1966. *Explanation and Human Action*. Oxford: Blackwell.

Luce, R. Duncan and Raiffa, Howard 1957. *Games and Decisions*. New York: Wiley.

Lukes, Steven 1970. Some Problems About Rationality. In Bryan Nilson (ed.) 1979. *Rationality*. Oxford: Blackwell.

—— 1982. Relativism in Its Place. In M. Hollis and S. Lukes (eds) 1986. *Rationality and Relativism*. Cambridge, Mass.: MIT Press.

253

Lyotard, Jean-François 1984. *The Postmodern Condition. A Report on Knowledge*. Translated by
   G. Bennington and B. Massumi. Minneapolis: University of Minnesota Press.
MacIntyre, Alasdair 1971. *Against the Self-Images of the Age*. London: Duckworth.
—— 1972. Predictability and Explanation in Social Science. *Philosophic Exchange*, vol. 1
   (Summer).
—— 1981. *After Virtue*. South Bend, Indiana: Notre Dame University Press.
—— 1989. Relativism, Power, and Philosophy. In Michael Krauz (ed.) 1989. *Relativism:
   Interpretation and Confrontation*. South Bend, Indiana: University of Notre Dame
   Press.
McIntyre, Lee 1993. "Complexity" and Social Scientific Laws. *Synthese*, vol. 97.
McIntyre, Lee 1996. *Laws and Explanation in the Social Sciences*. Boulder, Colorado:
   Westview Press.
McNeill, William H. 1995. The Changing Shape of World History. *History and Theory*, vol.
   34, no. 2.
Mahajan, Gurpreet 1992. *Explanation and Understanding in the Human Sciences*. Oxford:
   Oxford University Press.
Malinowski, Bronislaw 1944. *A Scientific Theory of Culture*. Chapel Hill: University of North
   Carolina Press.
Mandelbaum, Maurice 1938. *The Problem of Historical Knowledge*. New York: Liveright
   Publishing Company.
Mannheim, Karl 1956. Historismus. Translated by P. Kecskemeti and reprinted in *Essays
   on the Sociology of Knowledge*. London: Routledge and Kegan Paul.
Marcus, George and Fischer, Michael (eds) 1986. *Anthropology as Cultural Critique. An
   Experimental Moment in the Human Sciences*. Chicago: University of Chicago Press.
Marcuse, Herbert 1964. *One Dimensional Man*. Boston: Beacon Press.
Martin, Michael and McIntyre, Lee C. (eds) 1994. *Readings in the Philosophy of Social Science*.
   Cambridge, Mass.: MIT Press.
Marx, Karl 1845. A Contribution to the Critique of Hegel's "Philosophy of Right," An
   Introduction. In Joseph O'Malley, *Karl Marx's Critique of Hegel's "Philosophy of Right."*
   Cambridge: Cambridge University Press, 1970.
—— 1977 (1851). *The Eighteenth Brumaire*. In *Karl Marx. Selected Writings*. Edited by David
   McClellan. Oxford: Oxford University Press.
Masterman, Margaret 1970. The Nature of a Paradigm. In Lakatos, Imre and Musgrave,
   Alan (eds) 1970. *Criticism and the Growth of Knowledge*. Cambridge: Cambridge Univer-
   sity Press.
Meinecke, Friedrich 1972. *Historism: The Rise of a New Historical Outlook*. Translated by J.E.
   Anderson of F. Meinecke 1936. *Die Entstehung des Historismus*. London: Routledge and
   Kegan Paul.
Melden, A.I. 1961. *Free Action*. London: Routledge and Kegan Paul.
Mele, Alfred R. 1992. *Springs of Action*. Oxford: Oxford University Press.
Merton, Robert K. 1957. *Social Theory and Social Structure*. Glencoe, Illinois: The Free Press.
Mill, John Stuart 1843. *A System of Logic*. London: Longmans.
Miller, David 1972. Back to Aristotle? *British Journal of the Philosophy of Science*, vol. 23, pp.
   69–78.
Millikan, Ruth Garrett 1984. *Language, Thought, and Other Biological Categories*. Cambridge,
   Mass.: MIT Press.

Mink, Louis 1987. *Historical Understanding.* Edited by E. Golob, B. Fay, and R. Vann. Ithaca, New York: Cornell University Press.

Mischel, Theodore (ed.) 1974. *Understanding Other Persons.* Oxford: Blackwell.

——(ed.) 1977. *The Self.* Oxford: Blackwell.

Mitchell, W.J.T. (ed.) 1981. *On Narrative.* Chicago: University of Chicago Press.

Monmonier, Mark 1995. *Drawing the Line.* New York: Henry Holt and Company.

Moon, J. Donald 1975. The Logic of Political Inquiry. In Fred I. Greenstein and Nelson W. Polsby (eds), *The Handbook of Political Science,* vol. 1. Reading, Mass.: Addison-Wesley.

Nagel, Thomas 1979. *Mortal Questions.* Cambridge: Cambridge University Press.

——1986. *The View from Nowhere.* Oxford: Oxford University Press.

Novick, Peter 1988. *That Noble Dream. The "Objectivity Question" and the American Historical Profession.* Cambridge: Cambridge University Press.

Nozick, Robert 1981. *Philosophical Explanations.* Cambridge, Mass.: The Belknap Press of Harvard University.

Obeyesekere, Gananath 1992. *The Apotheosis of Captain Cook. European Mythmaking in the Pacific.* Princeton: Princeton University Press.

Olafson, Frederick 1979. *The Dialectic of Action.* Chicago: University of Chicago Press.

Olson, Mancur 1965. *The Logic of Collective Action.* Cambridge, Mass.: Harvard University Press.

Outhwaite, W. 1975. *Understanding Social Life. The Method Called "Verstehen."* London: Allen and Unwin.

Parfit, Dereck 1984. *Reasons and Persons.* Oxford: Oxford University Press.

Parsons, Talcott 1951. *The Social System.* Glencoe, Ill.: The Free Press.

Pears, David 1984. *Motivated Irrationality.* Oxford: The Clarendon Press.

Petit, Phillip 1977. *The Concept of Structuralism.* Berkeley, Calif.: University of California Press.

Piaget, Jean 1970. *Genetic Epistemology.* New York: W.W. Norton Company.

Pitkin, Hannah Fenichel 1972. *Wittgenstein and Justice.* Berkeley, Calif.: University of California Press.

Pocock, J.G.A. 1971. *Politics, Language, and Time. Essays on Political Thought and History.* New York: Atheneum.

Popper, Karl 1948. *The Open Society and Its Enemies,* fourth edn. London: Routledge and Kegan Paul.

——1957. *The Poverty of Historicism.* London: Routledge and Kegan Paul.

——1959. *The Logic of Scientific Discovery.* New York: Harper and Row.

——1968. *Conjectures and Refutations.* New York: Harper and Row.

Putnam, Hilary 1975. The Meaning of "Meaning." In Keith Gunderson 1975. *Language, Mind and Knowledge.* Minnesota Studies in the Philosophy of Science, vol. 7. Minneapolis: University of Minnesota Press. Reprinted in Hilary Putnam 1975. *Mind, Language, and Reality. Philosophical Papers Volume 2.* Cambridge: Cambridge University Press.

——1978. *Meaning and the Moral Sciences.* London: Routledge and Kegan Paul.

——1981. *Reason, Truth, and History.* Cambridge: Cambridge University Press.

——1992. *Realism with a Human Face.* Cambridge, Mass.: Harvard University Press.

Quine, W. V. O. 1960. *Word and Object.* Cambridge, Mass.: Harvard University Press.

——1973. *The Roots of Reference.* Lasalle, Ill.: Open Court.

Rabinow, Paul and Sullivan, William (eds) 1979. *Interpretive Social Science. A Reader*. Berkeley: University of California Press.

Radcliffe-Browne, A.R. 1952. *Structure and Function in Primitive Societies*. Glencoe, Ill.: The Free Press.

Rawls, John 1955. Two Concepts of Rules. *Philosophical Review*, vol. 64, pp. 3–32.

Reill, Peter 1975. *The German Enlightenment and the Rise of Historicism*. Berkeley, Calif.: University of California Press.

Rich, Adrienne 1979. *On Lies, Secrets, and Silence*. New York and London: W.W. Norton.

Rickman, H.P. (ed.) 1976. *Dilthey, Selected Writings*. Cambridge: Cambridge University Press.

Ricoeur, Paul 1981. *Hermeneutics and the Human Sciences*. Edited and translated by John B. Thompson. Cambridge: Cambridge University Press.

—— 1984. *Time and Narrative*, vol. 1. Translated by K. McLaughlin and D. Pellauer. Chicago: University of Chicago Press.

—— 1992. *Oneself as Another*. Translated by Kathleen Blamey. Chicago: University of Chicago Press.

Rorty, Richard 1979. *Philosophy and the Mirror of Nature*. Princeton: Princeton University Press.

—— 1982. *Consequences of Pragmatism*. Minneapolis: University of Minnesota Press.

—— 1991. *Objectivity, Relativism, and Truth*. Cambridge: Cambridge University Press.

Rosaldo, Renato 1989. *Culture and Truth*. Boston: Beacon Press.

Roscoe, Paul B. 1995. The Perils of "Positivism" in Cultural Arthropology. *American Anthropologist*, vol. 97, no. 3, pp. 492–504.

Rose, Phyllis 1983. *Parallel Lives*. New York: Knopf.

Rosenau, Pauline Marie 1992. *Post-Modernism and the Social Sciences*. Princeton: Princeton University Press.

Rosenberg, Alexander 1980. *Sociobiology and the Preemption of Social Science*. Baltimore, Maryland: The Johns Hopkins University Press.

Roth, Paul 1987. *Meaning and Method in the Social Sciences*. Ithaca, New York: Cornell University Press.

—— 1988. Narrative Explanation: The Case of History. *History and Theory*, vol. 27, no. 1, pp. 1–13.

—— 1989. How Narratives Explain. *Social Research*, vol. 56, pp. 449–78.

—— 1991. Interpretation as Explanation. In David R. Hiley, James F. Bohman, and Richard Shusterman (eds) 1991. *The Interpretive Turn*. Ithaca, New York: Cornell University Press.

Rouse, Joseph 1987. *Knowledge and Power*. Ithaca, New York: Cornell University Press.

—— 1994. Power/Knowledge. In Gary Gutting (ed.) 1994. *The Cambridge Companion to Foucault*. Cambridge: Cambridge University Press.

—— 1996. *Engaging Science. Science Studies after Realism, Rationality, and Social Constructivism*. Ithaca, New York: Cornell University Press.

—— Forthcoming. Feminism and the Social Construction of Scientific Knowledge. In Lynn Hakinson Nelson and Jack Nelson (eds). *A Dialogue between Feminism, Science, and the Philosophy of Science*. Dordrecht, Holland: Reidel.

256

Rousseau, Jean Jacques 1986 (1748). *The First and Second Discourses*. Edited and translated by Victor Gourevitch. New York: Harper and Row.

Rudner, Richard 1966. *Philosophy of Social Science*. Englewood Cliffs, NJ: Prentice Hall.

Runciman, W.G. 1972. *A Critique of Max Weber's Philosophy of Social Science*. Cambridge: Cambridge University Press.

Ruse, Michael 1979. *Sociobiology: Sense or Nonsense?* Dordrecht, Holland: D. Reidel Publishing Company.

Ryle, Gilbert 1949. *The Concept of Mind*. London: Hutchinson.

Sahlins, Marshall, 1985. *Islands of History*. Chicago: University of Chicago Press.

Sahlins, Marshall 1995. *How "Natives" Think. About Captain Cook, For Example*. Chicago: Chicago University Press.

Said, Edward 1978. *Orientalism*. New York: Random House.

—— 1993. *Culture and Imperialism*. London: Chatto and Windus.

Sarbin, Theodore (ed.) 1986. *Narrative Psychology. The Storied Nature of Human Conduct*. New York: Praeger.

Sartre, Jean-Paul 1956. *Being and Nothingness*. New York: The Philosophical Library.

Schafer, Roy 1978. *Language and Insight*. New Haven, Connecticut: Yale University Press.

—— 1981. *Narrative Actions in Psychoanalysis*. Worcester, Mass.: Clark University Press.

Scheffler, Israel 1982. *Science and Subjectivity*. Indianapolis: Hackett Publishing Co.

Schelling, Thomas 1960. *The Strategy of Conflict*. Cambridge, Mass.: Harvard University Press.

Schlesinger, Arthur 1992. *The Disunity of America. Reflections on a Multicultural Society*. New York: W.W. Norton.

Searle, John 1983. *Intentionality*. Cambridge: Cambridge University Press.

Sedgwick, Eve 1991. *The Epistemology of the Closet*. Berkeley: University of California Press.

Seidman, Steven. 1994. *Contested Knowledge. Social Theory in the Postmodern Era*. Oxford: Blackwell.

Sen, Amartya 1992. Objectivity and Position. *The Lindley Lecture*. University of Kansas.

Senge, Peter 1990. *The Fifth Discipline*. New York: Doubleday.

Shapiro, Gary and Sica, Alan 1984. *Hermeneutics: Questions and Prospects*. Amherst, Mass.: University of Massachusetts Press.

Shoemaker, Sydney 1963. *Self-Knowledge and Self-Identity*. Ithaca, New York: Cornell University Press.

Skinner, B.F. 1957. *Verbal Behavior*. New York: Appleton, Century, Crofts.

Skinner, Quentin 1969. Meaning and Understanding in the History of Ideas. *History and Theory*, vol. 8, no. 3, pp, 3–53.

—— 1972. Motives, Intentions, and the Interpretation of Texts. *New Literary History*, vol. 3, pp. 393–408.

Smith, Dorothy 1987. *The Everyday World as Problematic*. Boston: Northeastern University Press.

—— 1990. *Texts, Facts, and Feminism*. London: Routledge.

Soper, Kate 1986. *Humanism and Anti-Humanism*. London: Hutchison.

Spence, Donald 1982. *Narrative Truth and Historical Truth*. New York: Norton.

Stich, Steven 1990. *The Fragmentation of Reason*. Cambridge, Mass.: MIT Press.

Suppe, Frederick 1974. *The Structure of Scientific Theories.* Urbana, Illinois: University of Illinois Press.

Sutherland, Stuart 1994. *Irrationality.* New Brunswick, New Jersey: Rutgers University Press.

Tannen, Deborah 1990. *You Just Don't Understand.* New York: William Morrow.

Taylor, Charles 1964. *The Explanation of Behaviour.* London: Routledge and Kegan Paul.

—— 1971. Interpretation and the Sciences of Man. *Review of Metaphysics,* vol 5. Reprinted in Charles Taylor 1985. *Philosophy and the Human Sciences.* Cambridge: Cambridge University Press.

—— 1975. *Hegel.* Cambridge: Cambridge University Press.

—— 1981. Understanding and Ethnocentricity. Reprinted in Taylor, 1985. *Philosophy and the Human Sciences. Philosophical Papers 2.* Cambridge: Cambridge University Press.

—— 1985a. *Human Agency and Language. Philosophical Papers 1.* Cambridge: Cambridge University Press.

—— 1985b. *Philosophy and the Human Sciences. Philosophical Papers 2.* Cambridge: Cambridge University Press.

—— 1989. *Sources of the Self.* Cambridge, Mass.: Harvard University Press.

—— 1991. The Dialogical Self. In David R. Hiley, James F. Bohman, and Richard Shusterman (eds) 1991. *The Interpretive Turn.* Ithaca, New York: Cornell University Press.

—— 1992. *Multiculturalism and "The Politics of Recognition."* Princeton: Princeton University Press.

Thompson, E.P. 1963. *Making of the English Working Class.* London: Victor Gollancz.

Thompson, Martyn P. 1993. Reception Theory and the Interpretation of Historical Meaning. *History and Theory,* vol. 32, no. 3, pp. 248–72.

Trevor-Roper, H.R. 1951. *The Last Days of Hitler.* London: Macmillan.

—— 1969. *The European Witch-Craze.* New York: Harper & Row.

Trigg, Roger 1973. *Reason and Commitment.* Cambridge: Cambridge University Press.

Troeltsch, Ernest 1957. *Christian Thought, Its History and Application.* Translation by E. von Hugel, Baron of Troeltsch of *Historismus und Seine Uberwindung* (1924). New York: Meridian Books.

Truzzi, Marcello 1974. *Verstehen. Subjective Understanding in the Social Sciences.* Reading, Mass.: Addison-Wesley.

Tully, J. (ed.) 1988. *Meaning and Context. Quentin Skinner and His Critics.* Princeton: Princeton University Press.

Turner, Stephen 1980. *Sociological Explanation as Translation.* Cambridge: Cambridge University Press.

Ulin, Robert C. 1984. *Understanding Cultures.* Austin: University of Texas Press.

Vesey, Godfrey 1991. *Inner and Outer. Essays on a Philosophical Myth.* New York: St. Martin's

Veyne, Paul 1990. *Writing History.* Translated by M. Moore-Rinvolucri. Middletown, Connecticut: Wesleyan University Press.

Villiers, Alan 1967. *Captain James Cook.* New York: Charles Scribner's Sons.

Von Hayek, Frederich 1949. *Individualism and Economic Order.* London: Routledge & Kegan Paul.

Von Neumann, John and Morgenstern, Oskar 1944. *Theory of Games and Economic Behavior.* Princeton: Princeton University Press.

Von Wright, Georg Henrik 1971. *Explanation and Understanding*. Ithaca, New York: Cornell University Press.

Walsh, W.H. 1960. *The Philosophy of History. An Introduction*. New York: HarperCollins.

Walzer, Michael 1992. *What It Means to Be an American*. New York: Marsilio.

—— 1994. Multiculturalism and Individualism. *Dissent*, Spring 1994.

Weber, Max 1949. *The Methodology of the Social Sciences*. Translated and edited by Edward Shils and Henry Finch. New York: Free Press.

Weeks, Jeffrey 1991. *Against Nature: Essays on History, Sexuality, and Identity*. London: Rivers Oram Press.

Weinsheimer, Joel C. 1985. *Gadamer's Hermeneutics. A Reading of Truth and Method*. New Haven, Connecticut: Yale University Press.

Wellmer, Albrecht 1971. *Critical Theory of Society*. New York: Herder and Herder.

West, Cornell 1993. *Keeping Faith. Philosophy and Race in America*. New York: Routledge.

White, Hayden 1973. *Metahistory*. Baltimore, Maryland: The Johns Hopkins University Press.

—— 1987. *The Content of the Form*. Baltimore, Maryland: The Johns Hopkins University Press.

Whorf, Benjamin Lee 1954. *Language, Thought, and Reality*. Cambridge, Mass.: MIT Press.

Williams, Bernard 1973. *Problems of the Self*. Cambridge: Cambridge University Press.

—— 1993. *Shame and Necessity*. Berkeley: University of California Press.

Wilson, Bryan (ed.) 1979. *Rationality*. Oxford: Blackwell.

Wilson, Edward O. 1978. *On Human Nature*. Cambridge, Mass.: Harvard University Press.

Winch, Peter 1958. *The Idea of a Social Science*. London: Routledge and Kegan Paul.

—— 1964. Understanding a Primitive Society. *American Philosophical Quarterly*, vol. 1. Reprinted in Peter Winch 1972. *Ethics and Action*. London: Routlege and Kegan Paul.

—— 1970. Comment on I. C Jarvie, "Understanding and Explanation in Sociology and Social Anthropology," In Robert Borger and Frank Cioffi, *Explanation in the Behavioural Sciences*. Cambridge: Cambridge University Press.

Wittgenstein, Ludwig 1963 (1921). *Tractatus-Logico-Philosophicus*. Translated by D.F. Pears and B.F. McGuiness. London: Routledge and Kegan Paul.

—— 1968 (1953). *Philosophical Investigations*. Translated by G.E.M. Anscombe. Oxford: Blackwell.

—— 1980. *Culture and Value*. Translated by Peter Winch. Chicago: University of Chicago Press.

—— 1992. *Last Writings on the Philosophy of Psychology. Volume 2: The Inner and the Outer, 1949–1951*. Edited by Georg Henrik von Wright and Heikki Nyman. Translated by C.G. Luckhardt and M.A.E. Aue. Oxford: Blackwell.

Wolin, Sheldon 1968. Paradigms and Political Theories. In Preston King and B.C. Perekh (eds) 1968. *Politics and Experience*. Cambridge: Cambridge University Press.

Woolgar, Steve 1988a. *Science, The Very Idea*. London: Tavistock Press.

—— (ed.) 1988b. *Knowledge and Reflexivity. New Frontiers in the Sociology of Knowledge*. Beverly Hills, Calif. and London: Sage.

Wright, Erik Olin 1978. *Class, Crisis, and the State*. London: NLB.

Young, Iris 1990. *Justice and the Politics of Difference*. Princeton: Princeton University Press.

Index

relation to description, 163ff
and understanding, 133–4
see also causality; genetic explanation;
  narrative explanation; nomological
  explanation

Fabian, Johannes, 222
facts, 73–4
  infinite number of, 187–8
  theory-impregnated, 74
fairness (and objectivity), 212, 244
fallibilism, 208–12, 216, 220–1, 227
  and objectivity, 212–15, 216, 220–1
  and realism, 208–10
  and relativism, 215
false consciousness, 128–9
falsificationism, 207
Faulkner, William, 227
feminism, 58, 130
Foucault, Michel, 2, 51–2, 71, 120–1,
  200
Freire, Paulo, 67
Freud, Sigmund, 25, 31–2, 100–3, 128,
  130, 225, 236
Froude, James Anthony, 186–8
fusion of horizons, 143–4

Gadamer, Hans Georg, 142
  see also Gadamerian hermeneutics
Gadamerian hermeneutics, 142–7, 189
  and the hermeneutic circle, 145–6
  relation to intentionalism, 150ff
  role of intentions in, 150–1
  temporal distance and, 145
game theory, 125–6
Gasking, D., 176
Geertz, Clifford, 93, 137
gender, 58–9
  see also sex
genealogy, 120–1
general laws *see* laws, scientific
genetic explanation, 170–2, 174–6, 226
  inadequacy of, 172–4
  as presupposing laws, 172–4
  see also narrative explanation

Giddens, Anthony, 65, 70
Gilligan, Carol, 245
Goffman, Erving, 27
Gramsci, Antonio, 2
Grandy, Roger, 107
Graves, Robert, 182
Grice, Paul, 138
Griffin, John Howard, 13–14

Habermas, Jürgen, 124, 126, 128
Harré, Rom, 177
Hayek, Friedrich von, 31
Hegel, G.W.F., 43, 141, 143–4, 169
hegemony, 226, 232,
Hempel, Carl, 158
Herder, Johann, 156
hermeneutic circle, 145–6, 230
hermeneutics, 142
  see also Gadamerian hermeneutics
heteronomic explanations, 173, 175
historical laws, 168–9, 175
historicism, 155–6, 169–72, 174–6,
  226
  and intentionality, 171
Hitler, Adolf, 23–4, 184
Hobbes, Thomas, 31
holism, 50–3, 69–70, 224–5, 228
  and society, 63
  see also methodological holism
homonomic explanations, 173

identity
  and culture, 55–7, 243
  and difference, 46, 229–33
  and group membership, 50–4
  and meaning-interpretation, 146–7
  processural view of, 37–9, 227, 242
  and society, 67, 243
  substantivist view of, 37–9, 227, 242
  see also personal identity
ideology-critique, 129–30, 132, 133
incommensurability, 80–4
insider epistemology, 9–12, 17, 26–8
intelligibility, 107–10, 188–90, 211
intention, 94–5, 110

model), 158–9
present, the, 191–2, 227, 244
Principle of Charity, 105–7
Principle of Humanity, 107–10
propaganda, 199–200, 215, 220
psychoanalysis, 192–3
Putnam, Hilary, 221

quantity theory of money, 205–7

Rat Man, 100–2
rational choice theory, 123, 125
rationalism, 92–5, 98, 103
rationality, 86–7, 94–5, 103–5, 109–
    10, 225–6
  expressive, 108–9
  instrumental, 108, 125
  see also action
realism, 202–4, 227
  causal, 177
  and fallibilism, 208–10
  narrative, 179–83
reason-explanations, 95–8
  and irrational actions, 98–103
  rationality in, 103–5, 110
reasons, 94–5
  and causes, 95–8
recruitability, 237–41
Redfield, Robert, 116
re-enactment, Collingwood on, 138–41
  difference from interpretation, 141
Reid, Thomas, 176
relativism, 2–3, 7, 77–84, 88–90, 205,
    211, 215, 220, 228
  epistemological relativism, 77–9
  and objectivism, 220, 227
  ontological relativism, 79–84
resistance, 57, 232
respect for difference, 239–41, 244
Robinson, Pastor John, 144
Rose, Phyllis, 183ff
Rosenberg, Alexander, 164
rules, 64–5, 113, 115, 123
  constitutive rules, 64–5, 123
  regulative rules, 64–5

rule-following, 56–7, 65, 66, 123
  essentially normative, 124
Ryle, 93

Sahlins, Marshall, 135, 245–6
Sartre, Jean-Paul, 41–2
scapegoating, 240
Schafer, Roy, 192
Schleiermacher, F., 145
science
  and cartography, 210–11
  explanation in, 52–3, 156–9
  fallibilist construal of, 209–12
  objectivist understanding of, 203–4
  solipsism and, 10–12
  standing of, 2
  uncertainty in, 205–8
scientific law, 156–7
self, the, 32–3, 36–9, 70, 232–5
  and difference, 46
  inherently social, 40–7
  and others, 39–48, 228–32, 233–5,
    241
  processural view of, 38–9, 227–8,
    232, 242
  self-consciousness, 34–6, 41–3
  self-distance, 33–6
  self-ignorance, 21–2
  substantivist view of, 37–8, 227, 242
  unity of, 37–9
self-knowledge
  and experience, 17–24
  and interpretation of meaning, 24–8,
    229
  and knowledge of others, 229, 233–
    5, 236, 241
  and narrative realism, 178
self-understanding, 114ff
  role of in social science, 123, 126–7,
    132–3, 133–4
Sen, Amartya, 221
separatism, 233–5, 242
sex, 58–9
  see also gender
shame, 41, 43–4

265